Springer Proceedings in Business and Economics

Springer Proceedings in Business and Economics brings the most current research presented at conferences and workshops to a global readership. The series features volumes (in electronic and print formats) of selected contributions from conferences in all areas of economics, business, management, and finance. In addition to an overall evaluation by the publisher of the topical interest, scientific quality, and timeliness of each volume, each contribution is refereed to standards comparable to those of leading journals, resulting in authoritative contributions to the respective fields. Springer's production and distribution infrastructure ensures rapid publication and wide circulation of the latest developments in the most compelling and promising areas of research today.

The editorial development of volumes may be managed using Springer's innovative Online Conference Service (OCS), a proven online manuscript management and review system. This system is designed to ensure an efficient timeline for your publication, making Springer Proceedings in Business and Economics the premier series to publish your workshop or conference volume.

More information about this series at http://www.springer.com/series/11960

Francisco J. Martínez-López ·
Steven D'Alessandro
Editors

Advances in Digital Marketing and eCommerce

First International Conference, 2020

Springer

Editors
Francisco J. Martínez-López
Department of Business Administration 1
University of Granada
Granada, Spain

Steven D'Alessandro
School of Management and Marketing
University of Tasmania
Sandy Bay, TAS, Australia

ISSN 2198-7246 ISSN 2198-7254 (electronic)
Springer Proceedings in Business and Economics
ISBN 978-3-030-47594-9 ISBN 978-3-030-47595-6 (eBook)
https://doi.org/10.1007/978-3-030-47595-6

This Springer imprint is published by the registered company Springer Nature Switzerland AG
The registered company address is: Gewerbestrasse 11, 6330 Cham, Switzerland

Preface

The Digital Marketing & eCommerce Conference aims to bring together leading researchers and research scholars to exchange and share their experiences and research results on any aspects of ecommerce and digital marketing. It also offers a platform for academicians and practitioners to present and discuss the most recent breakthroughs, trends, and concerns as well as practical challenges encountered and solutions adopted in the fields of ecommerce and digital marketing.

Each paper submitted to DMeC 2020 has gone through a stringent peer review process by members of the Program Committee, which comprises over 60 researchers from around 30 countries.

This edition has been dedicated to social media and ecommerce as main topics. Social media dominates nowadays people's digital time. With the development of Social Web technology and Internet technology, a novel socialized value co-creation approach has been evolving over time. The social media-enabled value creation approach has engendered new business models for online business such as Facebook commerce and Wechat commerce. It is interesting approaching how companies can extract maximum value from their social media strategy, and how companies leverage unique characteristics of social media, such as social interactions and product recommendations, to improve their marketing performance.

Social commerce, deemed as a combination of social media and ecommerce, has sparked increasing interests among digital marketing and ecommerce researchers, because it refreshes people's perspective on what socialized ecommerce should be, how socialized commercial activities are conducted on social media platforms, and what factors facilitate social media users' transactional behavior, as well as increase social ads' conversion rates. Due to its distinctions from traditional ecommerce contexts, the socialized context can play a role in evolving and refreshing these aspects. For instance, when people are shopping on social media platforms, their product-seeking behavior is less oriented by their shopping goals, which is distinct from traditional ecommerce modes, in which shoppers have clearer shopping goals.

A total of 26 papers have been accepted, and they address diverse areas of application and topics, not necessarily connected with the primary topic of this edition, such as advertising, social media, omni-channel, tourism, blockchain technology, eWOM, influencer marketing, or sales, among others. A wide variety of theoretical and methodological approaches have been used.

We believe that this first edition has achieved the aim set initially: to encourage, promote, and publish high-quality contributions on digital marketing and ecommerce that can aid academics and practitioners in dealing with a wide range of issues.

Finally, we wish to acknowledge the support of our sponsors and publisher: the Business School at the University of Barcelona (Spain), EAE Business School (Spain), and Springer. Last but not least, we would like to thank all the contributing authors, members of the Program Committee, and the rest of the Organizing Committee for their highly valuable work in enabling the success of this first edition of DMeC. It has merit and deserves to be mentioned, considering that the preparation of this conference was in the middle of the coronavirus disease (COVID-19) outbreak.

Francisco J. Martínez-López
Steven D'Alessandro

Contents

Marketing and Advertising: Trends of the Sector

Joan-Francesc Fondevila-Gascón(✉), Josep Rom-Rodríguez, Marc Polo-López, and Javier L. Crespo

Blanquerna-Universitat Ramon Llull, CESINE, EAE Business School, EU Mediterrani, Euncet-UPC, CECABLE, Barcelona, Spain
{joanfrancescfg, joseprr, marcospl}@blanquerna.url.edu, fjlopez@campus.eae.es

Abstract. The marketing and the advertising and public relations sector is immersed in a period of change in various ways, from the structural to the type of insertions to be made in the media. We analyze the reality and the trends of this essential sector for the enterprise communication. Methodologically, to develop this prospective, we use Delphi qualitative technique, the most advisable in prospective approaches to incipient objects of study. It is concluded that the key factors that define the advertising sector are the digital transformation and the business model, and, after three years, personalization, automation and programmatic. As communication channels that will use advertising more, social networks rise, and as knowledge, skills and competencies that the advertising professional of the future must gather, the strategy stands out.

Keywords: Marketing · Advertising · Digitalization · Public relations · Prospective

1 Introduction

Marketing and advertising evolve in both content and form. This allows differentiating between traditional advertising and new advertising media. Despite this distinction, the main objective of advertising remains the same: to publicize a product or service and make the consumer want it (Cano 1994). Fugue increases in new media, a constant stream of ads on many platforms, where each brand struggles to unseat the competition.

Television, radio and paper support are the conventional channels (Above the Line) to publicize a product. The content, frequency and time are agreed by the companies without consumers intervening in this process (Geirinhas 2014). These media have created some saturation: an average of 92 advertising impacts throughout the day per adult, resulting in reduced effectiveness towards the potential consumer (López de Aguileta Clemente 2007).

Technology, in the middle of the Broadband Society (Fondevila-Gascón 2013a), increases the possibilities of engagement with consumers (Mir et al. 2015). Therefore, social networks are becoming the main weapon of companies to reach the maximum number of people with a minimum cost. The consumer gives the message to potential customers, a factor that gives confidence and truthfulness (Brown et al. 2007).

F. J. Martínez-López and S. D'Alessandro (Eds.): *Advances in Digital Marketing and eCommerce*, SPBE, pp. 1–8, 2020.
https://doi.org/10.1007/978-3-030-47595-6_1

The digital transformation extends into marketing, advertising and journalism (Fondevila-Gascón and Del Olmo 2011; Fondevila-Gascón 2013b; Fondevila-Gascón et al. 2016a, b). In fact, the comparison of competencies and professional profiles in advertising and public relations reflects innovative needs to be implemented in the advertising field (Fondevila-Gascón et al. 2017). Consumers themselves present a product through social networks such as Instagram, Twitter, YouTube and Facebook, where brands act to control and improve their e-reputation by creating a partnership with a public character. Brands contact those brand prescribers, influencers or brand ambassadors to sponsor a product or service (Santana et al. 2019). This business strategy achieves maximum visibility with minimal investment (Castelló and Del Pino 2015).

The analyzed phenomenon starts with blogs (Findlay 2015), prior to networks such as Instagram, so they can be considered a first form of social media. Users trust the opinion of these bloggers if they want to buy a product (Kerr et al. 2012). Bloggers often impact on various networks (Instagram, Facebook, Twitter or YouTube).

2 Methodology

The objective of the research is to detect angular motivations and prospective trends in the field of communication and interactive advertising. For this purpose, a qualitative technique is chosen: Delphi, which polls specialists in a subject on a subject of study of a certain complexity, with analytical depth and purpose, in order to agree on the kaleidoscope of collected opinions (Landeta 1999; Hsu and Sandford 2007), although that agreement is not the ultimate goal (Dalkey and Helmer 1963).

After focusing the analysis on the new forms of interactive advertising on television, Internet and digital media, and real applications on HbbTV, the group of experts was selected, a first questionnaire was prepared for a first round of interviews, the questionnaire was tested between Professionals and academics, the contact material was prepared, the questionnaire was sent online and the field work was monitored. The research was carried out between April and July 2019.

The profile of participants in the panel is professional and academic. The selection criteria were the accumulation of more than five years of experience, a solid position (for example, leaders of advertising or media agencies, companies or associations, positions related to the advertising or technological sector, members of academic institutions) and knowledge about discipline and professional reality. Professionals execute tasks related to the object of study, and academics complement the vision thanks to scientific knowledge. The n = 34, high considering the specialization of HbbTV, is broken down into 26 Spanish specialists, 5 from other European countries and 3 from the rest of the world. Of the Delphi members, 6 are academics and 28 professionals. The split of nationalities was (Table 1):

Table 1. Split of nationalities of the Delphi members

Spain	18
France	1
Belgium	1
United Kingdom	1
Germany	2
USA	1
Singapore	1
Australia	1

Source: own elaboration

The online questionnaire was tested among 12 people (6 professionals in advertising and information technology, and 6 academics) analyzing the current advertising model, interactivity and advertising effectiveness, television advertising, technology and advertising and an open section. The second exploratory phase was implemented in two rounds (Okoli and Pawloski 2004).

A content analysis emerged from the first questionnaire (Berelson 1967), a synthesis that led to the second questionnaire, validated among 12 other people with profiles similar to the previous 12. The questionnaire was sent back to the panellists, explaining the findings and requesting that they assess their initial positions on the sample responses. Finally, a statistical analysis of the data was developed.

3 Results

The objective of Delphi was to determine the three key factors that define the state of the art of the advertising sector in 2019, with a view to possible prospective trends.

The group of experts mentioned five items: changes in the business model, changes in digital transformation, and changes in the fragmentation of audiences, importance of analytics and profitability and quality of creativity.

The item mentioned with greater relevance (top two box) in the responses was the digital transformation, with a 63.6% acceptance. The changes in the business model follow, with 54.4%.

In the minor range (bottom two box), the quality of creativity stands out, with 54.5%. In an intermediate position, without being polarized to any extreme, we find the items "Importance of analytics and profitability" and again "the quality of creativity" both with 27%.

The phenomenon of advertising digitalization is more than consolidated. Investment data favors the Internet option to the detriment of other alternatives. That is why from the advertising sector the leadership is granted to this digital change and, by sympathy, for the business model, closely linked to the parallel phenomenon. In the case of digital journalism, the total wall model, the premium or the freemium are examples of adaptation of analog to digital model.

Regarding the changes in the business model, they were evaluated by the group of experts with 54.5% as important or very important, with 4.5% as something important and with 40.9% as unimportant or not important.

The changes in the digital transformation were evaluated by the group of experts with 63.6% as important or very important, with 18.2% as something important and with 18.2% as unimportant or not at all important.

On the changes in the fragmentation of the hearings, they were evaluated by the group of specialists with 31.8% as important or very important, with 27.3% as something important and with 40.9% as unimportant or nothing important.

In fact, the phenomenon of audience fragmentation has been occurring for years, and has affected analog television at the time and other analog media. That is why the members of Delphi probably do not give much prominence to this criterion.

Changes in the importance of analytics and profitability were evaluated by the group of experts with 36.4% as important or very important, with 27.2% as something important and with 36.4% as unimportant or not at all important. Therefore, a balance is observed in these options.

One possible cause is that the search for profitability has been consolidated for years in the advertising environment. As this pragmatic prioritization, materialized in recent times in metrics (Fondevila-Gascón et al. 2016) such as the Cost per Acquisition (CPA) or the digital ROI (Return on Investment digital), is not a novelty for managers.

In reference to the changes in the quality of creativity, they were evaluated by the group of experts with 18.18% as important or very important, with 27.7% as something important and with 54.5% as unimportant or not at all important.

Another focus of issues focused on the most relevant changes that will define advertising in the next three years. The mentioned items were the following: changes in personalization, changes in digitalization, and changes in the standardization of measurement, changes in the co-creation of content between producers and consumers and changes in automation and programmatic. The item mentioned in the top two boxes of the responses was that of changes in personalization, with 52%. It is followed by changes in automation and programmatic, with 46.6%.

In the range of minor importance (bottom two box, from now on) it stands out with 50% the changes in the standardization of the measurement and with the same percentage the changes in the co-creation of contents between producers and consumers.

Changes in personalization were evaluated by the group of experts with 52.4% as important, with 33.4% as something important and with 9.5% as unimportant and 4.7% not at all important. The addressability feature of current advertising messages explains the primacy of personalization as a relevant change. In the AdSense and programmatic dynamics of Search Engine Marketing (SEM), individualized messages and at the right time are the cornerstone of agency strategies.

The changes in digitalization were evaluated by the group of experts with 42.8% as important, with 28.6% as something important and with 28.6% as unimportant. Personalization goes hand in hand with digitalization, since without it the work of CRMs would be impossible. This explains the weight of this criterion.

The changes in the standardization of the measurement were evaluated by the group of experts with 0% as important, with 27.3% on average and with 72.7% as little or nothing important. It is curious this assessment, possibly anchored in the atavistic conservatism of media agencies and, not so much, of advertisers. The GRP mentality still weighs heavily, based on these responses.

The changes in the co-creation of content between producers and consumers were evaluated by the group of experts with 13.6% as important, with 18.2% as something important and with 68.2% as little or nothing important. The dynamic co-creative premium in e-commerce and social networks, although its impact in advertising terms is not easy to make tangible. This would justify that pyrrhic assessment.

Regarding the changes in automation and programmatic, they were considered by the group of experts in 46.6% as important, with 13.4% as something important and with 40% as little and nothing important. There is a certain polarization in the responses, depending on the plausible function of the task developed by the interviewees.

In Delphi, experts were asked which communication channels will be used most by advertising. The following items were mentioned: social networks, sponsorship and sponsorship, television and multimedia media. The item mentioned in the top two boxes of the responses were changes in social networks, with 59%. No other response item stands out above 40%. In the minor range, television stands out with 50% and sponsorship and sponsoring with 40.9%.

Social networks as communication channels that advertising will use most were evaluated by the group of experts with 59% as important, with 32% as something important and with 9% as little or nothing important. The tendency to insert social networks such as Instagram, Facebook, Twitter or LinkedIn is reflected in this response.

The communication channels that advertising will use most were evaluated by the group of experts with 0% as important, with 27.3% as something important and with 72.7% as little or nothing important for sponsorship and sponsorship. In fact, except for cases of much defined thematic sections or websites of major events, sponsorship is giving way to other forms of advertising.

Television as the communication channel that will use advertising the most was evaluated by the group of experts with 13.6% as important, with 18.2% as something important and with 68.2% as little or nothing important. In principle, this would imply a certain condition for HbbTV, although the type of television content source and interactivity were not qualified.

The communication channels that advertising will use most were evaluated by the group of experts with 27.7% as important, with 22.3% as something important and with 50% as little and nothing important for multimedia media.

The group of experts, when asked about what knowledge, skills and competencies the advertising professional of the future should gather, mentioned the four following items: digital competence, data analysis, strategy and creativity.

The item mentioned with greater relevance in the answers was the strategy with 72.72%. No other item exceeds 40%; the closest, with 36.6%, is creativity.

In the minor range, no item exceeds 40% determined as a minimum to highlight the analysis responses. It is noteworthy that the item that most closely matches the marked percentage is also creativity, with 31.8%, therefore the polarized response.

The knowledge, skills and competencies that the professional of the future must gather were evaluated by the group of experts with 45.3% as important, with 22.7% as something important and with 32% as unimportant and nothing important for digital competition.

For the data analysis, the knowledge, skills and competencies that the professional of the future must gather were evaluated by the group of experts with 31.8% as important, with 31.8% as something important and with 36.4% as little or nothing important for data analysis. Therefore, relevance is conferred to an essential activity in the environment of databases and prevailing CRM.

The knowledge, skills and competencies that the professional of the future should gather were evaluated by the group of experts with 72.7% as important, with 22.3% as something important and with 5% as little or nothing important for the strategy.

Finally, the knowledge, skills and competencies that the professional of the future must gather were evaluated by the group of experts with 36.6% as important, with 9% as something important and with 54.4% as little or nothing important for creativity.

4 Conclusions

From the analysis of results, we highlight as conclusions the consonance of the responses between the different profiles that have participated in the Delphi (academics and professionals) and nationalities (Spanish and European). The immediate and three-year prospective view also does not present relevant changes. Yes, it is worth highlighting some answers that differ depending on the question, as is the case of the importance of creativity (scarce in the present and important as a competence of the professionals of the future). There is agreement regarding the relevance of digital transformation, social networks and automation, programming and personalization of impacts, in media that are not expected to be the current investment leader, television:

After tabulating the answers, in terms of the state of the matter, five items are mentioned on which the importance that the participants in the study give to factors such as digital transformation and changes in the business model is highlighted, and the low relevance given to factors such as creativity (in a sector such as advertising) is surprising or the assumption of the dispersion of the audience (which suggests that it is considered an already consolidated phenomenon).

Regarding the most relevant changes that will define advertising in the next three years, four aspects are mentioned (changes in personalization, changes in digitalization, changes in the standardization of measurement, changes in the co-creation of content between producers and consumers and changes in the automation and programmatic) of which the changes in personalization and the changes in automation and programmatic stand out and the changes in the standardization of the measurement and in the co-creation of contents are mentioned as irrelevant between producers and consumers. These responses seem to indicate that the path towards which the advertising sector tends puts its weight on the adaptation and segmentation of the messages that must be adapted in time and content to the public. Similarly, co-creation and standardization of measurement are not valued, both factors difficult to specify in places such as e-commerce or social networks.

Precisely, social networks are the communication channels mentioned par excellence as the one that will most use advertising, well above the others mentioned (sponsorship and sponsorship, television and multimedia media) and especially television, the medium to whom minor importance is given, which contravenes what is indicated annually in the summary made by Infoadex in which it places it around 40% of the investment, which indicates that, if its future it is not good, its present is. From the advertising point of view, the relevance of advertising related to HbbTV and the interactivity in television means to open a wide range of new opportunities to the so called “old media”.

Finally, it should be noted that the strategy is valued as the skill and competence that the advertising professional of the future must gather, over others such as digital competence, data analysis or creativity, the latter mentioned in second place, which differs from the importance attached to this factor at present, as can be seen in the first paragraph of the conclusions.

Acknowledgement. This research is a part of the project “New Formats of Interactive Advertising on the Television, Internet and Digital Media. Applications on HbbTV”, funded by the Ministry of Economy, Industry and Competitiveness (Spain), reference CSO2017-88895-R (MINECO/FEDER).

References

Berelson, B.: Content analysis. In: Handbook of Social Psychology. New York, Lindzey (1967)

Brown, J., Broderick, A.J., Lee, N.: Word of mouth communication within online communities: conceptualizing the online social network. J. Interact. Mark. **21**(3), 2–20 (2007)

Cano, A.: La publicidad que vivimos. Editorial Eresma, Madrid (1994)

Castelló, A., Del Pino, C.: La comunicación publicitaria con influencers. Revista académica de marketing aplicado **14**, 21–50 (2015)

Dalkey, N., Helmer, O.: An experimental application of the Delphi method to the use of experts. Manag. Sci. **9**, 458–467 (1963)

Findlay, R.: The short, passionate, and close-knit history of personal style blogs. Fash. Theory: J. Dress Body Cult. **19**(2), 157–178 (2015)

Fondevila-Gascón, J.F.: Periodismo ciudadano y cloud journalism: un flujo necesario en la Sociedad de la Banda Ancha. Comunicación y Hombre **9**, 25–41 (2013a)

Fondevila-Gascón, J.F.: Características de la publicidad en el ciberperiodismo en España: el caso de El Mundo y El País. Index. comunicación: Revista científica en el ámbito de la Comunicación **3**(1), 41–61 (2013b)

Fondevila-Gascón, J.F., del Olmo, J.L.: La interactividad y el multimedia en la prensa digital internacional: los casos de España y el Reino Unido. III Congreso Internacional de Ciberperiodismo y Web 2.0, Bilbao (2011)

Fondevila-Gascón, J. F., Crespo, J.L., Mir-Bernal, P., Rom-Rodríguez, J., Santana-López, E., Botey-López, J.: Tendencias en métricas en medios sociales. Impacto en la publicidad. In: Zacipa-Infante, I., Tur-Viñes, V., Segarra-Saavedra, J., (eds.) Tendencias publicitarias en Iberoamérica. Diálogo de saberes y experiencias, pp. 155–170, Universidad de Alicante, Alicante (2016a)

Fondevila-Gascón, J.F., Rom-Rodríguez, J., Santana-López, E.: Comparativa internacional del uso de recursos digitales en el periodismo digital deportivo: estudio de caso de España y Francia”. Revista Latina de Comunicación Social **71**, 124–140 (2016b)

Fondevila-Gascón, J.F., Santana-López, E., Rom-Rodríguez, J.: Comparativa sobre las competencias y los perfiles profesionales en publicidad y RRPP en Barcelona. In: Perlado Lamo de Espinosa, M., Cachán Alcolea, C., Ramos Rodríguez, M., (eds.) Competencias y perfiles profesionales en el ámbito de la comunicación, pp. 79–90, Editorial Dykinson, Madrid (2017)

Geirinhas, G.G.A.: Social Media: The New Tool in Firms' Marketing Strategies. NOVA – School of Business and Economics, Lisboa (2014)

Hsu, Ch., Sandford, B.: The Delphi Technique: making sense of consensus. Pract. Assess. Res. Eval. **12**, 10 (2007)

Kerr, G.F., Mortimer, K., Dickinson, S., Waller, D.: Buy, boycott or blog exploring online consumer power to share, discuss and distribute controversial advertising messages. Eur. J. Mark. **46**(3–4), 387–405 (2012)

Landeta, J.: El método Delphi: Una técnica de prevención para la incertidumbre, Ariel, Barcelona (1999)

López de Aguileta Clemente, C.: Medios y Soportes Alternativos Para Una Publicidad Convencional: Publicidad «Off the Line» . Pensar en la Publicidad, I, pp. 117–130 (2007)

Mir, P., Calderón, R., Recalde, M., Fondevila-Gascón, J.F.: Perspectivas Cómo Internet transforma la gestión de la reputación, Telos, pp. 1–8 (2015)

Okoli, C., Pawlowski, S.: The Delphi method as a research tool: an example, design considerations and applications. Inf. Manag. **42**, 15–29 (2004)

Santana, E., Fondevila-Gascón, J.F., Arteaga-Rico, M.-J.: Claves de las estrategias de branded content y marketing experiencial combinadas con la participación de influencers. In: Sierra Sánchez, J., Lavín, J.M., (eds.) Redes sociales, tecnologías digitales y narrativas interactivas en la sociedad de la información, pp. 189–200. MacGraw-Hill, Madrid (2019)

Influence of Social Networks on Responsible Behaviour by Smart Tourists

Marios Sotiriadis(✉), Shiwei Shen, and Qing Zhou

Ningbo University, Ningbo, People's Republic of China
sotermarios@outlook.com, shiwei_shen@163.com,
zhouqing970502@163.com

Abstract. The aim of this paper is to report on a research project that explores the perceptions of Chinese tourists about the influence of Social Networking Sites (SNSs) on responsible and sustainable behaviour by tourists within the context of smart tourism paradigm. To achieve this aim, first a research framework encompassing three hypotheses related to the influence of SNSs at the three main stages of travel cycle was designed. Then, an exploratory quantitative research was carried out (Sample size = 325), using the online survey technique. The study's findings indicate that the influence of SNSs on Chinese consumers on adopting a responsible behaviour as smart tourists is determined by all stages of the travel cycle, the stronger influence being at the first two stages (before and during the consumption experience). This study constitutes the first theoretical/conceptual approach and empirical research into the influence of SNSs on responsible behaviour by smart tourists.

Keywords: Smart tourism · Social networking sites · Smart tourists · Travel/trip cycle · Responsible behaviour · China

1 Introduction

Over the last decades information and communication technologies (ICTs) have been so tightly knitted into the fabric of the tourism experience and management of tourism offerings (Xiang et al. 2015) resulting to what was coined 'smart tourism'. Smart tourism (ST) refers to the application of information and communication technologies (ICTs) for developing innovative tools and approaches to improve tourism (Gretzel et al. 2015a, b). define smart tourism as "a tourism supported by integrated efforts at a destination to collect and aggregate/harness data derived from physical infrastructure, social connections, government sources and human bodies/minds in combination with the use of advanced technologies to transform that data into on-site experiences and business value-propositions with a clear focus on efficiency, sustainability and experience enrichment." (Gretzel et al. 2015a, b, p. 181).

The strategic goal of every Smart Tourism Destination (STD) should be to enhance smart tourist to change their attitude and adopt a more responsible behaviour. Therefore, the smart tourism technologies are a medium for achieving that aim. Nowadays, smart tourists are active; they are creating and sharing information, and attempting to

F. J. Martínez-López and S. D'Alessandro (Eds.): *Advances in Digital Marketing and eCommerce*, SPBE, pp. 9–16, 2020.
https://doi.org/10.1007/978-3-030-47595-6_2

influence and persuade other users. The proliferation of SNSs also increases inspirational messages and the ability of consumers to identify suitable products and services through their virtual communities/networks. In this smart context, digital media have become much more than an information source for tourists and are used for multiple purposes (Morrison 2019).

It is generally recognized that the tourists - a crucial element and key actors of the smart tourism ecosystem – are rather neglected by academic research (Femenia-Serra et al. 2019). Our study constitutes a contribution to addressing this research gap. It is the argument of this paper that the ultimate goal of SDT should be to render smart tourists more responsible to reduce some of the effects of their activities. The paper's aim is twofold, namely (i) to suggest a framework of the influence of SNSs on responsible behaviour by smart tourists; and (ii) to empirically investigate the suggested framework within the Chinese context by exploring the perceptions of Chinese tourist consumers.

2 Literature Review

Tourists themselves are one centrepiece of the Smart tourism (ST) ecosystem, as it has been pointed out by Femenia-Serra et al. (2019). Over the last 15 years, tourist behaviour has undergone a great transformation because of consumers' use of ICTs for tourist purposes. The advances in ICTs have evolved very quickly with the rapid emergence of user-generated online content and social media (SM) (Sigala et al. 2012; Munar 2016), the rise of smartphones, context and location-aware services, and the impact of them on experiences (Choe and Fesenmaier 2017; Sotiriadis 2017). The implications of these changes have been vast and have shaped a digital tourist (Pearce 2018). Cutting-edge technologies have introduced new factors, such as real-time interaction and ubiquitous connectedness, new types of technology-mediated social connections, or superior levels of context-awareness (Buhalis and Foerste 2015; Choe and Fesenmaier 2017). The consumption behaviour of tourists (travel/trip cycle) has several stages; all of them being important in terms of smart technologies.

The paper by Femenia-Serra et al. (2019) defines the smart tourist as: "The tourist who, by being open to sharing his or her data and making use of smart technologies, interacts dynamically with other stakeholders, co-creating in this way an enhanced and personalised smart experience. This tourist is open to innovations, social and pro-active and finds his or her natural environment in the smart tourism ecosystem and the smart destination." (p. 125). Our study adopts and elaborates on this theoretical background to investigate the influence of a specific smart technology (the SNSs) on responsible behaviour by smart tourists. SNSs offer not only social communication, but also an ambience, which is established with contributions and interactions by all online participants. Tourists' attitudes towards SNSs in the information-intensive tourism industry have changed the way they make decisions (Kim et al. 2015; Sotiriadis 2017). They allow users to create, publish, and comment on digitized content worldwide (Munar 2016). They have become 'prosumers', an Internet/digital era business term meaning "production by consumers". Technological breakthrough has fastened the development of prosumption. The development of SM has transformed the role of people, changing from being 'consumers' to 'prosumers' and consumers now have far more influence than ever before. Instead of just consuming products, people are now able to have a voice and register their opinion about products and they can drastically impact the success or failure of brands and products. This is mainly due to their involvement on the Internet through SNSs (Kotler 1986a). Kotler (1986b) considered prosumer as a new challenge for marketers and described forces that would lead to more prosumption activities and to more sustainable lifestyles (Szymusiak 2015).

SNSs have undoubtedly transformed tourists from passive consumers to active co-producers of experiences engaging in online reviews. When using SNSs, tourists become co-producers, co-marketers and co-consumers of tourism experiences (Sigala et al. 2012; Brandt et al. 2017). These changes can be explained in perspective of smart tourism (Gretzel et al. 2015a). Scholars have shown support for the potential and benefit of smart tourists to interact and co-create experiences involving other stakeholders, paying particular attention to SNSs as the preferred channel. The study by Huang et al. (2017) examines the mechanism of how tourists use smart technologies to enhance tourism satisfaction. It was found that the attributes of smart tourism technologies promote both explorative and exploitative use, while user's security and privacy concerns have a negative effect.

There is a close link and pairing between STD and sustainable tourism management in the sense that one of the key goals of every STD is to encourage smart tourists to adopt a more responsible behavior. Sustainable management within the ST paradigm requires and involves smart and responsible tourists who are behaving in an environmentally friendly manner (Gretzel et al. 2015b; Pearce 2018). Therefore, STD should encourage smart tourists to become co-creators of sustainable tourism experiences and co-managers of tourism resources at the destination. The ultimate goal should be to make tourists more responsible to reduce some of the effects of their activities. Within this context, SNSs could have an influence on responsible behaviour by smart tourists, if appropriately used (Pearce 2018; Morrison 2019). Tourists make choices across and use digital media and SNSs at all stages of their travel/trip cycle beginning with dreaming and ending with recollecting (Morrison 2019). Elaborating on the previous discussion, we could formulate the following framework of responsible behaviour by smart tourists in temporal terms/stage of travel cycle: before consumption (BC), during consumption experience (DC), and post-consumption (PC). It is believed that smart tourists, who have at the same time responsible and sustainable behaviour (RSB), have to adopt the appropriate attitude and take a series of actions (Pearce 2018; Gretzel et al. 2015b). The suggested framework of RSB by smart tourists is summarized in Table 1.

By being a responsible tourist and sustainable guest, a smart technology user could contribute to significantly reduce the environmental and social impacts of tourism activities (Pearce 2018). Therefore, our study suggests a framework for RSB by smart tourists with a specific focus on the appropriate use of SNSs.

Table 1. Responsible and sustainable behaviour by smart tourists

Stage of travel/trip cycle (and related actions)	Responsible and sustainable behaviour by tourists
Before consumption (Searching, Planning, Buying, Expectations, Anticipation, Preparation)	- Building an understanding - Self-educating - Getting ready
During consumption on-site (Experiencing, Enjoying, Searching, On-site purchase, On-site evaluation)	Travelling, visiting and enjoying - Learn rather than just seeing - Getting insights of the local culture - Immersing themselves in the new culture - Ensuring a positive experience for themselves and the local populations
Post-consumption (Evaluation, Remembering and Sharing their experiences on SNSs)	- Making suggestions/recommendations - Influence other tourists to behave in responsible way

3 Research Framework and Hypotheses

The behaviour of smart tourists could and should be changed if they are keen to make a contribution in terms of sustainability, by adopting a responsible and sustainable behaviour (***RSB***). A very good tool is the SNSs; therefore, how do tourists should use this smart tourism technology to attaining this aim? Our study advances three research hypotheses. Smart tourists should perform a set of anticipatory activities before they travel; i.e. build an understanding, self-education and getting ready for their trip (Chung et al. 2017; Pearce 2018, UNWTO 2017, 2018). Hence, this study states the following hypothesis. *H1: The SNSs positively influence the* ***before consumption (BC) stage of travel cycle*** *by providing update and reliable information aiming at adopting a responsible and sustainable behaviour.*

Likewise, smart tourists should adopt a RSB with the aim to assisting STDs to achieve their aim. They should use SNSs adequately with the aim of learning and not just seeing; immersing themselves in the new culture, and trying to ensure a mutually beneficial experience, for themselves and the local communities (Pearce 2018, UNWTO 2017). Hence, this study proposes the following *H2: The SNSs positively influence the* ***consumption (on-site) (DC) stage of travel cycle*** *by properly assisting smart tourists in travelling, visiting and enjoying the destination.* Smart tourists should also help other tourists to adopt RSB. It could be argued that SNSs could be influential in assisting smart tourists and STDs to identify and address environmental issues and minimize the impact of their acts (Buffa 2015; Chung et al. 2017; Pearce 2018; UNWTO 2017). Thus, this study posits the following hypothesis: *H3: The SNSs positively influence the* ***post-consumption (PC) stage of travel cycle*** *by providing the adequate tools and services to smart tourists to evaluate their experience and sharing it with their peers and friends, mainly posting reviews and photos and online recommendations on SNSs.*

In order the test the above three hypotheses, an empirical study has been carried out to explore the influence of SNSs on adopting a responsible behaviour.

4 Empirical Study and Methodology

A survey was conducted to empirically test the research framework. This study opted to explore this issue by investigating the perceptions and attitudes of Chinese tourist consumers about the influence of SNSs. Why China? The Chinese tourist market is the biggest in the world, in terms of domestic and outbound tourism flows. Business reports (see, for instance, McKinsey 2018) highlight that Chinese outbound tourism has become the biggest tourist market in the world when measured by trips and expenditures. On the other hand, in contemporary China, smart tourism is used in destination construction and attraction management for several purposes. Digital platforms (mobile apps and SNSs) have also been massively adopted by Chinese tourists at all stages of travel cycle. China has the world's largest and most active SM users, with the most internet users, 634 million (45% internet penetration rate, 50% of the world's online users). Chinese spend 25 h online per week, increasingly connected via their mobile device and 70% of the bookings are made online. (McKinsey 2018). Therefore, for all above mentioned reasons, this study has opted for the China market as the most appropriate setting/context to conduct the empirical study.

A total of 14 items were measured on a 5-point Likert scale by rating from strongly disagree (1) to strongly agree (5), not all important/useful (1) to very important/useful (5). Items used to measure the consumers perceptions were derived from literature review. The study collected data using an online survey research. All respondents were selected by using a random sampling method. Sampling procedures started with posting links to the online questionnaire on popular forums and SNSs among Chinese consumers for two weeks. The SNSs investigated were the most popular among Chinese consumers, namely: Sina Weibo, WeChat, QQ/Qzone, Xiecheng, Douyin, Tieba, and Zhihu. All respondents were informed about the study's general purpose in advance and assured that their answers are voluntary and anonymous. In total we have collected 325 questionnaires from SNSs users in November 2019. The data collection was followed by a statistical analysis on SPSS Version 25.0 (descriptive and regression analysis).

5 Data Analysis and Discussion

It is worth noticing that the results reported below are provisional since the research project is under way (only Phase 1 has been completed). As already highlighted, the aim of research framework was to explore the influence of SNSs on adopting RSB by smart tourists. The dependent variable is the SRB. The independent variables are the influence of SNSs at the three stages of the travel cycle (before-, during- and post-consumption). The Pearson product–moment correlation was conducted to determine the inter-correlation of the constructs (Table 2).

Table 2. Pearson correlation coefficient

	BC	DC	PC	Y
X1: BC	1	.615*	.674*	.695*
X2: DC	.718*	1	.592*	.637*
X3: PC	.635*	.647*	1	.656*
Y: RSB	.695*	.637*	.656*	1

*Correlation is significant at the 0.01 level/Sig. (2-tailed).

The scores between the constructs were significantly positively related. The Pearson product–moment correlation coefficient (*r*) was varying between 0.592 and 0.718, $n = 325$ ($\rho \leq 0.01$), large effect size. As all the relationships between the constructs were significant, positive influence of SNSs on RSB can be explored.

The Durbin–Watson statistic had a value of 1.943, which was within the required range of 1.00–2.00. All three stages of travel cycle were significantly correlated with the influence of SNSs on smart tourists to adopt a RSB ($\rho \leq 0.01$). A simple linear regression was conducted between the degree on which the use of SNSs influence the smart tourists' RSB during the 3 stages. The overall Sig. Value was 0.000, indicating that the overall fitting of the model met the demand. Among them, X1(= 0.173, t = 7.616, p = 0.000), X2 (= 0.160, t = 5.318, p = 0.000), X3 (= 0.272, t = 4.634, p = 0.000), explained the variance of 60.84% of influence.

Table 3. Model and Summary of regression analysis results

	R	R^2	ΔR^2	*P*	*Durbin-Watson*
Model	.748[a]	.568	.568	.000	1.943

	B	SEB (Standard Error of *B*)	*β* (The standard regression coefficient)	T	*p*
X1: BC	.173	.035	.343	7.616	.000
X2: DC	.160	.031	.278	5.318	.000
X3: PC	.272	.034	.248	4.634	.000

Based on the results shown in Table 3, the dependent variable RSB is influenced and determined by the use of SNSs by the smart tourists at all three stages of travel cycle; the stronger influence being at the two first stages, i.e. before and during the consumption experience.

6 Conclusion and Implications

The purpose of this study was to explore the influence of SNSs on tourists to adopt a responsible behaviour within the context of smart tourism. Firstly, this study has suggested a research framework to address the study's aim. Based on the related extant literature, this study postulated three stages of the tourism experience/travel cycle – before consumption (BC), during consumption (DC) and post consumption (PC) - at which smart tourists could be influenced by the use of SNSs to adopt a responsible and sustainable behaviour (RSB). Secondly, the suggested research framework was tested and empirically investigated in the Chinese context, exploring the perceptions of Chinese smart tourists about the determining influence of SNSs. The results support the development of a model of adopting RSB with all three stages influencing the consumers' willingness to do so. Based on the results, the most determining stages are the two first, before and during the experience consumption. The study's findings are valuable in the sense that they: (i) make a theoretical contribution to the field of smart tourism, and (ii) have marketing implications.

Firstly, this study contributes to the body of knowledge from a theoretical perspective. It constitutes the first theoretical/conceptual approach and empirical research into the influence of SNSs (a smart technology) on consumers behaviour within the smart tourism paradigm. The core contribution is to consider the issue in an integrated manner, exploring the influence at all three stages of travel cycle. Therefore, it offers a further theoretical contribution to extant literature by extending the role and the characteristics of smart tourists in achieving sustainable management of tourism resources, which constitutes one of the main aims of smartness. This contribution is the appropriate use of SNSs) in line with the sustainable tourist behaviour (Buffa 2015).

Secondly, it is believed that the study's findings provide marketing implications for industry practitioners. First, from a marketing management perspective, the tourism destinations and providers (principals) should consider the use of SNSs, their efficiency and effectiveness, and select the most appropriate mix to influence accordingly the behaviour of their visitors and guests. These findings are of practical importance to tourism managers and marketers, in the sense that they indicate the consumer-centric strategies to influence the adequate usage of SNSs as a medium to attain sustainable and responsible management of their assets; in other words, render their visitors and guests co-producers, co-managers and co-marketers of their destination and enterprise with the ultimate aim to make a contribution to sustainable management of resources and assets.

It is believed that STDs should manage their resources in a sustainable way and smart technologies should make their contribution. Sustainable management within the smart tourism paradigm requires and involves smart and responsible tourists who are caring and behaving properly/responsibly in a way that enhances a better management of destinations and experience facilitation.

References

Brandt, T., Bendler, J., Neumann, D.: Social media analytics and value creation in urban smart tourism ecosystems. Inf. Manag. **54**(6), 703–713 (2017). https://doi.org/10.1016/j.im.2017.01.004

Buffa, F.: Young tourists and sustainability. Profiles, attitudes, and implications for destination strategies. Sustainability **7**(10), 14042–14062 (2015)

Buhalis, D., Foerste, M.: SoCoMo marketing for travel and tourism: empowering co-creation of value. J. Destin. Mark. Manag. **4**(3), 151–161 (2015)

Choe, Y., Fesenmaier, D.R.: The quantified traveler: Implications for smart tourism development. In: Xiang, Z., Fesenmaier, D.R. (eds.) Analytics in Smart Tourism Design, Tourism on the Verge. Springer, Cham (2017)

Chung, N., Tyan, I., Chung, H.C.: Social support and commitment within social networking site in tourism experience. Sustainability **9**, Article 2102 (2017). https://doi.org/10.3390/su9112102

Femenia-Serra, F., Neuhofer, B., Ivars-Baidal, J.A.: Towards a conceptualization of smart tourists and their role within the smart destination scenario. Serv. Ind. J. **39**(2), 109–133 (2019)

Gretzel, U., Reino, S., Kopera, S., Koo, C.: Smart tourism challenges. J. Tour. Res. **6**(1), 41–47 (2015a)

Gretzel, U., Sigala, M., Xiang, Z., and Koo, C.: Smart tourism: foundations and developments. Electron. Mark. **25**(3), 179–188 (2015b)

Huang, C.D., Goo, J., Nam, K., Yoo, C.W.: Smart tourism technologies in travel planning: the role of exploration and exploitation. Inf. Manag. **54**(6), 757–770 (2017)

Kim, W.G., Lim, H., Brymer, R.A.: The effectiveness of managing social media on hotel performance. Int. J. Hosp. Manag. **44**(1), 165–171 (2015)

McKinsey: Chinese tourists: dispelling the myths. An in-depth look at China's outbound tourist market (2018). www.mckinseychina.com

Kotler, P.: Prosumers: A new type of customer. Futurist (September–October), 24–28 (1986a)

Kotler, P.: The prosumer movement. a new challenge for marketers. Adv. Consum. Res. **13**(3), 510–513 (1986b)

Morrison, A.M.: Marketing and Managing Tourism Destinations, 2nd edn. Routledge, Oxon (2019)

Munar, A.M.: Social media. In: Jafari, J., Xiao, H. (eds.) Encyclopaedia of Tourism, pp. 869–871. Springer, New York (2016)

Pearce, P.L.: Limiting overtourism; the desirable new behaviours of the smart tourist. T-Forum: The Tourism Intelligence Forum, Palma, Spain (2018)

Sigala, M., Christou, E., Gretzel, U. (eds.): Social Media in Travel, Tourism and Hospitality: Theory, Practice and Cases. Ashgate, London (2012)

Sotiriadis, M.: Sharing tourism experiences in social media: a literature review and a set of suggested business strategies. Int. J. Contemp. Hosp. Manag. **29**(1), 179–225 (2017)

Szymusiak, T.: Prosumer – Prosumption – Prosumerism. OmniScriptum, Düsseldorf (2015)

Xiang, Z., Tussyadiah, I., Buhalis, D.: Smart destinations: foundations, analytics, and applications. J.Destin. Mark. Manag. **4**(3), 143–144 (2015)

UNWTO: Tips for a Responsible Traveller. UN World Tourism Organisation, Madrid (2017)

UNWTO: Overtourism - understanding and managing urban tourism growth beyond perceptions, UN World Tourism Organization, Madrid, Spain (2018)

Information Use Under Quality Uncertainties and Its Impact on the Digital Goods Production

Amy Wenxuan Ding(✉)

Artificial Intelligence and Business Analytics, Emlyon Business School, Écully, France
ding@em-lyon.com

Abstract. The wide application of digital technologies has created an enriched digitized environment and changed many people's lifestyles. Such a digitized environment also provides a free and open playing field for average people in the public to pursue innovative digital activities such as digital goods production. However, users face severe uncertainty on both general quality and taste-match quality of digital goods, considering the lack of formal training of average people as producers and standards for producing such goods. So far, little is known about how users deal with the severe dual quality uncertainties issue in a digitized environment, which in turn influences producers' successes in digital goods production in both short and long terms. This paper presents a novel theory-based model to address these issues based on the signaling theory. Empirical testing using real-world data provides strategies to users on quality inference, and offers actionable knowledge to average people as producers and the platform on how to design effective signal devices to build their user bases and earn revenue in the short and long runs. This study thus sheds light on such an IT-enabled production by the public in digital goods markets.

Keywords: Digital goods production · Information use · Quality uncertainty · Digital markets · Signaling

1 Introduction

The prevalence and intensification of the use of mobile devices and digital platforms has created an enriched digitized environment in people's everyday lives. Besides offering information, entertainment, and convenience of shopping services, such a digitized environment also provides a fair and transparent playing field for the public to engage in various innovative/creative activities. One of particular interest is the production of experiential digital goods (e.g., apps, online literature, digital games, or music) by average people. Digital goods refer to any goods that are sold, delivered, and consumed in a digital form, including online music, books, game apps, and videos. Such goods are usually non-rival (consumption of the good does not decrease its availability to others), have near zero marginal cost of production and distribution, low marginal cost of consumer search, and low transaction costs compared to non-digital products (Lambrecht et al. 2014). Moreover, more importantly using a simple information system – a smartphone or computer with internet access, an individual can

F. J. Martínez-López and S. D'Alessandro (Eds.): *Advances in Digital Marketing and eCommerce*, SPBE, pp. 17–24, 2020.
https://doi.org/10.1007/978-3-030-47595-6_3

engage in digital goods creation. Thus, fuelled by digital technologies, this trend grows fast. According to PricewaterhouseCoopers's annual global entertainment and media outlook forecast (PWC US 2017), the digital goods production of U.S. will reach $190 billion in size in 2021, and increase from $110 billion in 2016. Globally, digital goods will be an $855 billion market by 2021.

We are interested in the "success" of digital goods production as a two-step achievement: the short-term accomplishment in terms of attracting user attention, consumption and recommendation given that many competing goods are available, and the long-run performance in terms of business revenue generation. From a producer point of view, the success of digital goods relies on user online engagement and consumption behaviour. That is, when digital goods appear online, its performance depends on whether users like it, rather than how much money the producer has invested in. If a product does not get users' attention, it will not receive clicks and is unlikely to attract wider user or media attention. However, from the user point of view, she faces severe uncertainty on the quality of digital goods, considering the lack of formal training of many people as producers and standards for producing such goods. Therefore, both producers and digital platforms need to help users resolve the quality uncertainty issue.

Previous research has focused on using information such as prices, brand names, editors' featured products, or money back guarantee as quality indicators to assist a user's quality inference. For example, the high price of an item, a money back guarantee, or a well-known brand may suggest high quality of the product. The interface of Apple's Apps Store often displays apps by "editor's featured items" to signal their high qualities by implicitly using the Apple brand. Obviously, these methods may not work well when such goods are free and producers of digital goods are average people rather than famous developers or firms.

Recently, many digital platforms adopt machine learning technologies to generate recommendations to users. These algorithmic recommendation systems with different interfaces all share a common working philosophy: first, users' electronic behaviour traces are collected, and then analysed to see whether certain patterns exist reflecting the user's preference or suggesting how much each digital good in the portfolio would fit the user's quality requirement. Finally, the platform displays the goods that the algorithm believes to have the highest predicted match to the user's requirement. Hence, the degree of the user's satisfaction relies on whether accurate user preference data can be obtained. If user profile data is not available, a recommendation is typically generated using other users with similar actions (Chen et al. 2011; Iacobucci 1998; Trusov et al. 2010). In fact, many studies in economics, finance, information systems, and marketing have found that people may follow others' behaviours (e.g., WOM) in the presence of uncertainty (e.g., Bikhchandani et al. 1992; Lee et al. 2015). However, the fact is that quality of any experiential digital goods can be assessed only after its consumption (Akerlof 1970). Therefore, using predetermined recommendations may not fully help users resolve the quality uncertainty issue. Moreover, past research on customized recommendation did not simultaneously consider how the user behaviour of resolving quality uncertainty (or adopting the recommendation) affects a producer's production of the digital goods. So far, little is known in the literature about how the user behaviour of resolving quality uncertainty in the encountered digitized environment influences her consumption and/or purchase decision, which in turn affects average people's success in digital goods production in short and long runs.

To fill this gap, we propose that users in the digitized environment face dual uncertainties about the quality of the digital goods produced by average people: uncertainty on the general quality of the product and uncertainty on the product match with the user's preference. Producers therefore might signal the quality of their works to assist users. Based on the signalling theory, we develop a theory-based hierarchical Bayes model to addresses the following research questions: (1) how user resolve the dual quality uncertainties with limited information in a digitized environment, and what drives their attention and consumption behaviours in the short run? (2) What determine the reproduction of the digital goods (e.g., as movies, games, TV dramas) to generate business revenue in the long run? and (3) what should the producer do to obtain the two-step achievements and sustain a successful creation?

Answering these questions is important because the current development of artificial intelligent (AI) as a service has become a new type of production force with a heavy and broad impact on human labour markets, and the capability of AI in performing innovative and creative tasks is extremely low comparing to a human brain. Our research provides insights on how average people in the public as producers succeed in producing digital goods, and offers actionable knowledge on designing a better environment helping users deal with quality uncertainty and creating values for both users and producers.

2 Data and Methodology

For illustration, we use online literature as the context because it is ideal for studying experiential digital goods production and consumption. Online literature is a new, rapidly growing digital entertainment and self-publishing market, where individuals write, update, and publish their books, read others' work, and communicate with one another. Traditionally, publication of literature such as novels and poems is strictly controlled by publishers and media outlets; the hurdle that one has to overcome before s/he can publish anything is significant. It is certainly a tough process that would intimidate individuals to the point that publishing was almost impossible for them. However, the Internet and digitized environment have made it possible. Not only does the digitized environment with Internet access makes it incredibly easy to publish one's work, but also it has created markets that can attract publishers' attention to the potentially rich "gold mine" of literature. For example, if a book story is attractive and the content becomes hot, a chain reaction may occur such that media coverage increases, leading the book to become widely popular. The book may be reproduced as a movie, television drama series, or digital game. The 2013 dramatic film *So Young*, which was based on a Chinese online novel, grossed $116 million on a $5 million budget in 2013 (Gu 2014). In 2015 "Tang Jia San Shao" (a pen name) earned 110 million RMB ($15 million USD) in royalties in China (Qin 2016).

Such literature platforms receive high traffic on a daily basis; for example, 297 million users, accounting for 43% of the Internet users in China, visited these markets in 2015 (Li 2016). In Canada, a leading online literature app, Wattpad, had two million writers producing 100,000 pieces of work a day for 20 million readers on an intricate international social network in 2014 (Streitfeld 2014). In the United States, Amazon, Barnes & Noble, Apple and Google all offered self-publishing programs to allow individuals to write, update, publish, and sell their e-books, with the number of e-books reaching 6 million and a 24% market share of overall trade book revenue in 2014. These trends are not specific to China, Canada, and US, there are growing e-book markets in Germany, France, Spain, Italy, Brazil, Russia and India, too (Anthony 2012).

For this study, we randomly collected data from the top Chinese literary platform on a weekly basis between January 2009 and May 2010. The literary platform enjoyed a 43.8% market share in China (www.china.com.cn 2012) and attracted consumers from mainland China, Taiwan, South Korea, Hong Kong, the United States, and Japan, prompting a global traffic rank of 568 in 2012 (alexa.com). The platform publishes, reproduces, and disseminates tens of thousands of Chinese novels contributed by authors, the vast majority of whom are average people. Long-term data about whether each completed book was reproduced as a movie/television drama series, physical book, or digital game was collected between August 2012 and December 2013, or at least three and half years after the book's first appearance on the platform. We collected data about 351 authors, 400 books, and 4,498 observations. We randomly chose three-quarters of the books (300 books) as estimation data, including 259 authors and 3,357 observations. The remaining data constitute the out-of-sample data, with 92 authors, 100 books, and 1,141 observations, which we used for model prediction and comparison.

2.1 Conceptual Framework

Similar to any digital media platform, the digital literature platform displays all types of literary works. Most of them are books with short abstracts and some have a digital cover picture. Two unique features exist. First, not only the quality of those books is uncertain to users, but also is much more diverse than the quality of professional publishing, considering their lack of any formal professional screening and editing. This characteristic means that users face significant uncertainty about the quality of the books. Second, authors often publish and update ongoing works in section, before the entire work is completed. Thus, most literary works listed on the platform are unfinished and on-going, and their statuses are being updated continuously. To completely read a book, users need to frequently revisit the platform and check for new updates. This unfinished and on-going feature leads to an era of perpetual revision and updating. In turn, users may engage in different consumption behaviour than those who visit conventional digital platforms such as Amazon.com and barnesandnoble.com.

Now imagine a new user visits such a platform. What the user can directly observe is information on book category, book cover image, abstract, book status (on-going or completed), author name, update time (the time of the last update on chapters), the number of clicks and recommendations received by each book, and those promoted or top (weekly, monthly, overall) clicked lists. Given these direct observations as inputs in our research, we analyze which of them have a signaling power to effectively help the user infer the quality. Figure 1 displays our proposed model.

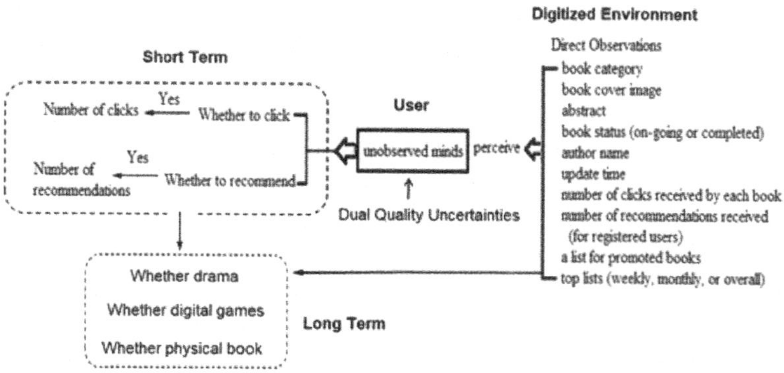

Fig. 1. Conceptual framework

2.1.1 Short-Term Performance

We measure a books' short-term performance in terms of whether it receives any clicks and recommendations from users with the book's perceived qualities, and if yes, how many would be. Prior research in information system and marketing has shown that customer recommendations increase customer lifetime value and firm profits, when managed appropriately (Ding et al. 2015; Kumar et al. 2010). We are interested in whether quality signals can help a book receive any recommendations from registered users and if yes, the number of recommendations received. Thus, we investigate both the whether and how many aspects of consumption (clicks) and recommendation actions that users take during or after their quality inferences.

2.1.2 Long-Term Performance

We measure a book's long term performance in terms of whether it can be reproduced as a movie/television drama, physical book, or digital game three and half years after a book's first appearance on the platform. Books reproduced as movies/TV dramas, physical books, or digital games receive greater recognition and commercial approval, considering the stringent screening process for such productions. Therefore, they provide a good indicator of a book's long-term performance (Sun 2012).

2.1.3 User Side Perception

Information conveys meaning and resolves uncertainty. Information processing can generally be described as an input-output function that takes inputs from observations and transforms them into a meaningful pattern or signal as outputs. According to information theory and cognitive research, such transformation provides a reasonable concept that involves at least two related entities from the input in order to make quantitative sense (Vigo 2011). The two entities are any dimensionally defined category of object O and its representational information about O. In our case, the object is any book on the platform, and a reasonable concept that the user needs to acquire from the observations is the book's two qualities: the general and the taste-match qualities. Let $GenQ_{ijrtl}$ and $MatchQ_{ijrtl}$ denote book j's general quality and taste-match quality of author i, respectively, when the user determines whether ($l = 1$) to make an action

r (1 = click to consume, 2 = recommendations) and if yes, how many (l = 2) at time t (weeks). Then, the information processing function of the two types of perceived quality are:

$$\begin{aligned} GenQ_{ijrtl} &= \gamma_{ijrl}^{G\prime} X_{ijt1} + \varsigma_{ijrl1} \\ MatchQ_{ijrtl} &= \gamma_{ijrl}^{M\prime} X_{ijt2} + \varsigma_{ijrl2} \end{aligned} \tag{1}$$

where l indicates features of the responses, such as whether to act (l = 1) and if yes, how many (l = 2) responses occur. X_{ijt1} and X_{ijt2} denote potential signals of the quality types drawn from the observations. γ_{ijrl}^{G} and γ_{ijrl}^{M} are vectors of author-, book-, and response- specific preferences related to perceived general quality and the book–reader match quality, respectively. The ς_{ijr} term refers to the author-, book-, and response-specific unobserved quality components that are not captured by the various signals from the observations.

What types of information from the observations (inputs) that can generate a quality-signaling power? According to the signalling theory in Spence (1973) and Kirmani and Rao (2000), two conditions must be met before observations represent signaling devices. First, it should be costly for information producer (in our case, book authors) to adopt the signaling device; in the terminology of signaling literature, the device must induce signaling costs. Second, the signaling costs must satisfy the single-crossing property that such costs are higher for "bad" books than for "good" books so that a separating equilibrium occurs. In such an equilibrium, users correctly infer the book's true type based on the different signaling strategies adopted.

We develop a hierarchical Bayes framework to learn and infer (1) whether a book receives user clicks or recommendations, and how many; (2) how they affect business revenue generation such that the book may be reproduced as a movie, TV drama series, a digital game or a physical book in the long run. Moreover, we capture unobserved author and book heterogeneity using a random coefficient approach (Rossi et al. 1996). We also account for endogeneity of authors' book updating behavior and endogeneity of top clicked, strongly recommended, or promoted book list signals.

3 Empirical Test and Findings

Our empirical testing is to check (1) if the limited observations from the platform can serve as quality signals to help users make appropriate consumption or/recommendation decisions, and (2) what factors drive average people's book success in both short and long terms and what insights or actionable knowledge can be drawn. We also conduct a number of robustness checks for the proposed model.

We find that the two quality uncertainties exist simultaneously and strongly affect whether producers' works receive any clicks or recommendations. On the user side, information that exhibits comparison properties can help users infer the general quality. Thus, quality indicators such as the top clicked, strongly recommended, or promoted book lists on the platform can serve as general quality signals. Information that defines a concept/category, or describes producers' characteristics helps the user infer the taste-match quality. General users and registered users rely on different quality signals. For example, book update frequency increases the number of clicks from general readers and the number of recommendations from registered users. On the producer side, we find that selecting a hot topic such as the metropolis or supernatural category may attract users to click. If the author increases her book chapter updating frequency level by 1%, it will increases the book's chance of entering the top weekly, monthly or overall clicked lists by 0.075%, 0.379% or 0.35%, respectively. Entering onto the top overall clicked list will increase the book's probability of getting any clicks (attention) by 87.53% in the short term and being produced as a digital game by 96.21% in the long run.

4 Contribution and Conclusions

Digitalized environments bring an open and fair opportunity for average people in the public to engage in digital goods creation such as self-publishing literature works. This study is the first empirical investigation to jointly consider the general quality and taste-match quality inference decisions in such a digitized environment. We contribute to the literature by presenting a novel theory-based model that examines how dual quality uncertainties affect users' consumption behaviors and understand the drivers of producers' successes in both short and long terms simultaneously. Without knowing the user's profile data, we show that the platform and producers of digital goods may design different quality signals in the absence of price and brand name, and achieve the goal of increasing users' consumption and generating reputation and revenue for the digital goods. The proposed model is general and can be applied to other digital platforms.

References

Akerlof, G.A.: The market for 'lemons': quality uncertainty and the market mechanism. Q. J. Econ. **84**(3), 488–500 (1970)

Anthony, J.: The challenge of E-book growth in international markets. Res. Q. **28**, 273–284 (2012)

Bikhchandani, S., Hirshlleifer, D., Welch, I.: Theory of fads, fashion, custom, and cultural change as information cascades. J. Polit. Econ. **100**(5), 992–1026 (1992)

Chen, Y., Wang, Q., Xie, J.: Online social interactions: a natural experiment on word of mouth versus observational learning. J. Mark. Res. **48**(2), 238–254 (2011)

Ding, A.W., Li, S., Chatterjee, P.: Learning user real-time intent for optimal dynamic web page transformation. Inf. Syst. Res. **26**(2), 339–359 (2015)

Gu, W.: Writers don't need books to make big bucks. The Wall Street Journal, August (2014)

Iacobucci, D.: Interactive marketing and the magnet: network of networks. J. Interact. Mark. **12** (Winter), 5–16 (1998)

Kirmani, A., Rao, A.R.: No pain, no gain: a critical review of the literature on signaling unobservable product quality. J. Mark. **64**(2), 66–79 (2000)

Kumar, V., Petersen, J.A., Leone, R.P.: Driving profitability by encouraging customer referrals: who, when, and how. J. Mark. **74**(September), 1–17 (2010)

Lambrecht, A., Goldfarb, A., Bonatti, A., Ghose, A., et al.: How do firms make money selling digital goods online? Mark. Lett. **25**, 331–341 (2014)
Lee, Y.J., Hosanagar, K., Tan, Y.: Do I follow my friends or the crowd? information cascades in online movie ratings. Manag. Sci. **61**(9), 2241–2258 (2015)
Li, Y.: Online fiction becomes Chinese cultural force. The Wall Street Journal, 20 July 2016
PWC US.: PWC's entertainment & media outlook forecasts U.S. industry spending to reach $759 billion by 2021 (2017). https://www.prnewswire.com/
Qin, A.: Making online literature pay big in China. The New York Times, 31 October 2016
Rossi, P.E., McCulloch, R.E., Allenby, G.M.: The value of purchase history data in target marketing. Mark. Sci. **15**(4), 321–340 (1996)
Spence, M.A.: Job market signaling. Q. J. Econ. **87**(3), 355–374 (1973)
Streitfeld, D.: Web fiction, serialized and social. The New York Times, 23 March (2014)
Sun, M.: How does the variance of product ratings matter? Manag. Sci. **58**(4), 696–707 (2012)
Trusov, M., Bodapati, A.V., Bucklin, R.E.: Determining influential users in internet social networks. J. Mark. Res. **47**(August), 643–658 (2010)
Vigo, R.: Representational information: a new general notion and measure of information. Inf. Sci. **181**, 4847–4859 (2011)

Impacts of Blockchain Technology in Marketing

Debika Sihi(✉)

Southwestern University, Georgetown, USA
sihid@southwestern.edu

Abstract. The use of blockchain for different functions across various industries has become a popular topic in recent years. While commonly referenced for enabling cryptocurrency exchanges like Bitcoin, the secure, distributed ledger of blockchain may be applied for many other purposes. This contribution examines current and potential uses of blockchain for marketing activities. Benefits and challenges in implementation are also discussed.

Keywords: Blockchain · Marketing data · Channel management · Online ad fraud · Referrals

1 Introduction

Marketing is a dynamic field that continues to evolve with changing technology and greater access to consumer data. Marketers have utilized new technologies including crowdsourcing ideas in the new product development process (Lilien et al. 2002), aggregating consumers' digital data for predictive behavior modeling (Trusov et al. 2016), and using virtual reality (VR) and augmented reality (AR) technologies for improved customer experiences (Javornik 2016). Building on this literature which examines the evolution of marketing practices through the integration of new technologies, this research examines the impacts of blockchain technology on marketing.

Blockchain technology allows the creation of a ledger or set of records between parties that is encrypted and secured (Brakeville and Perepa 2016). It is most closely associated with the mining of Bitcoin digital currency. However, blockchain can be used for a variety of purposes. For example, it can be used in tracking distribution channels; Starbucks is using it to track the "bean to cup" journey (Palmer 2019). It has also been suggested as a possible way to mitigate online advertising fraud by verifying each aspect of online advertisement delivery to an individual (Ghose 2018). This contribution examines how blockchain as been utilized in marketing thus far and offers insight on ways it be leveraged in the future.

F. J. Martínez-López and S. D'Alessandro (Eds.): *Advances in Digital Marketing and eCommerce*, SPBE, pp. 25–30, 2020.
https://doi.org/10.1007/978-3-030-47595-6_4

2 Blockchain

Blockchain is essentially a cryptographic ledger in which blocks of data among users belonging to the same network are stored in a protected and verifiable way. The data is saved inside blocks which are connected and comprise what is referenced as the "chain" in a blockchain (Marr 2017). The blocks of data are stored on nodes which are computers or services connected to the Internet. Below are additional details on the key characteristics of blockchain.

Consensus. In order to add a block of data or append any changes to an existing blockchain, the new data must be verified by other nodes in the network. A block will only be added to the chain if its cryptographic hash function produces a certain unique signature (known as the mining process).

Decentralization. Since different actors with access to a blockchain network can add data to a blockchain with consensus approval, there is not one agent or organization administering centralized control. One caveat to this is the distinction between a public and private blockchain. While a public blockchain is truly decentralized a private blockchain, also known as a permissioned blockchain, can restrict who can participate (e.g., if sensitive data is stored on the blockchain).

Resilience. Data in a blockchain exists on the different nodes of a network, rather than one centralized database. Therefore, the data is less susceptible to the loss of information.

The next sections outline the ways organizations are beginning to use blockchain for different marketing functions, describing both the advantages and challenges with implementation.

3 Blockchain in the Marketing Channel

Imagine a consumer purchasing a bottle of wine at the local grocery store. The packaging on the bottle states that the wine was produced in California and the name of the winemaker. However, tracing the contents back to the grapes with which it was produced can be a cumbersome and expensive process. There are so many people and steps involved in the production process starting from picking the grapes.

Solutions. Blockchain provides a tenable way to trace the grapes used to make the wine from vine to bottle. The farmer can provide detail about the grape crops which are used for each batch of wine produced into the blockchain, and this data will only be added to the chain if verified by other members of the supply chain who are part of this blockchain network. Traceability of source product is what motivated Walmart to begin using blockchain technology in their supply chain networks. With significant consumer safety and financial implications of food borne diseases, Walmart collaborated with IBM to begin tracing products like pork, mangos (Kamath 2018), and lettuce (Corkery and Popper 2018) back to suppliers. Blockchain not only improved transparency of the process but also improved the tracking time from seven days to 2.2 s. Starbucks began partnering with Microsoft to use its Azure Blockchain Services to trace their coffee from bean to cup (Palmer 2019). In addition to more transparency about their own supply chain, Starbucks hopes this information will be valuable to farmers growing coffee beans so they have a better idea of where their beans are sold. Blockchain also offers a mechanism for better traceability in cross-border e-commerce, a growing market sector (Wang et al. 2019)

Challenges. Despite time and transparency efficiencies, there are challenges in implementing blockchain to manage a marketing channel. Members of the channels at different levels must participate in the blockchain network for this to work. It also requires an inherent level of trust among parties that may have very little existing contact or knowledge about each other. In addition, the process of mining and appending information to the blockchain requires Internet connectivity and computing power that may not be readily available in all markets (Valache 2019).

4 Blockchain to Reduce Advertising Fraud

In recent years, one of the biggest challenges facing digital marketers is ad fraud. Imagine you are the same wine producer described in the prior section. You would like to run an online ad through an ad network (e.g., Google Network, Facebook Audience Network) to show up on different websites (ad publishers) or to different, targeted users. The wine producer may pay for the ad by clicks (people who click the ad) or impressions (people who are served or shown the ad) and will track the traffic (people who come to their website) from the ad. Ad fraud can take place in a number of ways. Fraudulent or fake clicks and impressions can be generated via bots which mimic actual clicks or impressions. Further, fraudulent publishers may engage in ad stacking, a practice where ads are stacked on top of one another where only the first ad is visible but its click and impression data is connected to the ads upon which it is stacked (these ads are never seen). The World Federation of Advertisers estimates that ad fraud may cost advertisers more than $50 billion by 2025 (Handley 2018).

Solution. Blockchain technology can be used to create a direct link between an advertiser and publisher with smart contracts along each step of the network. A smart contract is essentially an agreement that transacts through computer code. Thus, in the context of an ad network, it would mean that advertisers could see how their ad dollars are being spent through the ad network and each publisher.

Challenges. However, the advertisers, ad networks, and publishers may have separate, private blockchain networks which do not integrate easily. Further, each party in this context would need to utilize blockchain. According to a poll by Advertiser Perceptions (2018), only 11% of the 300 US marketers polled had ever even completed a blockchain transaction. Thus, more adoption of the technology is necessary for it to be effective. In addition, online ad transactions occur in milliseconds while blockchain transactions take seconds (Benes 2018), so the processing capability needed for blockchain to be effective in this context may not be viable yet.

5 Blockchain for Incentivized Referrals

One of the strongest customer acquisition tools is referrals from other customer customers. Referred customers tend to generate higher contribution margins and have higher retention rates (Schmitt et al. 2011). Companies like Airbnb and Dropbox have achieved tremendous growth through formal referral programs (Edwards 2015) where referrers receive incentives (in the case of Dropbox both the referrer and referred clients received incentives). Imagine the same wine producer referenced in earlier sections starting a loyalty program where customers were rewarded not only for purchases but also referring new customers.

Solution. The traceability of blockchain would presumably allow customer referrals to be traced back to the referring source. Smart contracts would allow referrers to be automatically paid when a referred individual/business became a client through the form of digital currency or tokens. This can be used in a variety of referral contexts. Ponder is an online dating platform in which users are incentivized for referred matches. qiibee allows organizations to run their loyalty programs through their blockchain. Operating loyalty programs with a blockchain should also reduce many of the administrative and processing costs associated with the operation of traditional loyalty programs (Deloitte 2016).

Challenges. Adoption is a key challenge as the incentives earned for referrals must be accessible and redeemable by referrers (and referred sources). Unless there is fairly seamless integration between the networks and digital wallets of the different parties involved in the referral network, the network would be unlikely to scale and grow.

6 Going Forward

While blockchain has the potential to improve many business and marketing processes, use of the technology is still in early stages in most industries. Going forward, there are some key factors that must be addressed for blockchain to become truly effective for marketing and other functions.

Widespread Adoption. For blockchain to be effective in providing transparency in a supply chain, related to an ad network, or even a referral network, all parties involved must participate in the blockchain network, otherwise the information will be incomplete. Blockchain has a strong association with cryptocurrencies such as Bitcoin and Facebook's Libra. Given the strong governmental and public scrutiny of these currencies, it is likely implementation of blockchain will be met with some apprehension in many legacy organizations. More proof of concept will be necessary for different industries to invest in this. However, with large organization like Walmart, IBM, and many financial services companies (Tapscott and Tapscott 2017) investing in blockchain, market validation becomes more likely.

Rules of Engagement. Blockchain is inherently built up on trust and understanding among the dispersed nodes in a network which authenticate new blocks of data. As more organizations/individuals begin to use blockchain, both public and permissioned networks, more formal rules of engagement maybe necessary while still balancing the decentralized structure that is valued by users.

Energy Efficiency. Mining, the process through which a blockchain grows requires a lot of processing power and energy consumption. In 2018, Morgan Stanley estimated that the original blockchain would use more energy than the country of Argentina (Zhao 2018). If it to be applied to challenges like ad fraud which require processing at the milliseconds, the process will need to be come more energy efficient. One possible solution is the use of more private blockchains which limit the number of participants to the chain, thereby using less energy. There are also private or permissioned blockchains (e.g., Hyperledger Fabric) which have removed the mining part of the approval process. All of these modifications; however, require some tradeoff between blockchain as a truly public, decentralized technology to one that has some constraints to be feasible for more widespread and continued application.

Strategic Application. While blockchain has been proposed as solution to many organization challenges related to data security, transparency, and transmission, careful assessment of blockchain compared to alternate technologies will need to be conducted to gauge where blockchain truly provides an advantage of existing processes (e.g., electronic data interchange (EDI)).

References

Benes, R.: Advertisers have mixed confidence in blockchain (2018). https://www.emarketer.com/content/advertisers-have-mixed-confidence-in-blockchain

Brakeville, S., Perepa, B.: Blockchain basics: introduction to distributed ledgers. IBM (2016)

Corkery, M., Popper, N.: From farm to blockchain: Walmart tracks its lettuce (2018). https://www.nytimes.com/2018/09/24/business/walmart-blockchain-lettuce.html

Deloitte: Making blockchain real for customer loyalty rewards programs. Deloitte Center for Financial Services (2016)

Edwards, S.: How Airbnb and Dropbox achieved tremendous growth with referral marketing (2015). https://www.entrepreneur.com/article/248867

Ghose, A.: What blockchain could mean for marketing. Harvard Bus. Rev. **5**, 2–5 (2018)

Handley, L.: US and UK join up to tackle ad fraud (2018). https://www.cnbc.com/2018/10/23/us-and-uk-join-up-to-tackle-ad-fraud-a-50-billion-problem.html

Javornik, A.: Augmented reality: research agenda for studying the impact of its media characteristics on consumer behavior. J. Retail. Consum. Serv. **30**(May), 252–261 (2016)

Kamath, R.: Food traceability on blockchain: Walmart's Pork and Mango Pilots with IBM. J. Br. Blockchain Assoc. **1**(1), 3712 (2018)

Lilien, G.L., Morrison, P.D., Searls, K., Sonnack, M., von Hippel, E.: Performance assessment of the lead user idea-generation process for new product development. Manag. Sci. **48**(8), 1042–1059 (2002)

Marr, B.: A complete beginner's guide to blockchain (2017). https://www.forbes.com/sites/bernardmarr/2017/01/24/a-complete-beginners-guide-to-blockchain/#65f09cf16e60

Palmer, D.: Starbucks to track coffee using Microsoft's blockchain service (2019). https://www.coindesk.com/starbucks-to-track-coffee-using-microsofts-blockchain-service

Schmitt, P., Skiera, B., Van den Bulte, C.: Referral programs and customer value. J. Mark. **75**(1), 46–59 (2011)

Tapscott, A., Tapscott, D.: How blockchain is changing finance. Harvard Bus. Rev. **1**(9), 2–5 (2017)

Trusov, M., Ma, L., Jamal, Z.: Crumbs of the cookie: user profiling in customer-base analysis and behavioral targeting. Mark. Sci. **35**(3), 405–426 (2016)

Valache, C.: Blockchain to track your purchases to their origin (2019). https://interestingengineering.com/blockchain-to-track-your-purchases-to-their-origin

Wang, Y., Jia, F., Schoenherr, T., Gong, Y., Chen, L.: Cross-border e-commerce firms as supply chain integrators: the management of three flows. Ind. Mark. Manag. (2019, in press)

Zhao, H.: Bitcoin and blockchain consume an exorbitant amount of energy. These engineers are trying to change that (2018). https://www.cnbc.com/2018/02/23/bitcoin-blockchain-consumes-a-lot-of-energy-engineers-changing-that.html

Brand Anthropomorphism and Brand Voice: The Role of the Name-Brand Voice Assistant

Maria Vernuccio(✉), Michela Patrizi, and Alberto Pastore

Sapienza University of Rome, Rome, Italy
{maria.vernuccio,michela.patrizi,
alberto.pastore}@uniroma1.it

Abstract. The name-brand voice assistant (NBVA), allowing the brand to dialogue directly with consumers by its brand name and its brand voice, could theoretically activate the brand anthropomorphism perception in the consumer's mind. Despite the growing use of NBVAs and the theoretical possibility to recognise important branding implications, the role that companies can assign to NBVAs in the context of brand strategies has not yet been addressed by marketing scholars. Therefore, the objective of our work is to begin to fill this gap by investigating the role that the NBVA might have in the brand anthropomorphisation strategy, adopting the managerial perspective. To this end, we have conducted qualitative research based on a single in-depth case study, the first in-car NBVA to be release in the international market.

Keywords: Brand anthropomorphism · Name-brand voice assistant · Brand voice · Case study

1 Introduction

The voice assistant (VAs) is an artificial intelligence (AI) software that can simulate human intelligence through vocal dialogue (Fivesight Research 2017). In 2018, in the USA alone, VAs had already been used by about 200 million people, mainly in cars (114 million), on smartphones (91 million) and smart speakers (46 million) (Voicebot 2019a). The growing importance of the car as a context of VA application is promoting the diffusion of the so-called name-brand voice assistants (NBVAs) (e.g., Mercedes' Mercedes-Benz User Experience - MBUX, BMW's Intelligent Personal Assistant – IPA). The NBVAs are in-house developed VAs activated by the user by saying the brand name, speaking with a specific brand voice instead of the voice of the technology provider's VA (e.g., Alexa – Amazon, Siri – Apple) (Vernuccio *et al.* 2019). Early academic studies have focused on VAs of technology providers in the fields of conversational commerce (Vassinen 2018; Lahoual and Frejus 2019; Pagani *et al.* 2019) and advertising (Jones 2018; Smith 2018); besides, studies of the possible perception of VA anthropomorphism have started. In this regard, Cho *et al.* (2019) show that voice interaction through a laptop with a utilitarian task enhances the VA perceived human likeness. Considering specifically NBVAs, studies in Marketing and Branding fields are still at an early stage. Braun *et al.* (2019) have studied the BMW in-car NBVA,

F. J. Martínez-López and S. D'Alessandro (Eds.): *Advances in Digital Marketing and eCommerce*, SPBE, pp. 31–39, 2020.
https://doi.org/10.1007/978-3-030-47595-6_5

showing how the NBVA personality, as in human interactions, can dynamically develop as a function of the user's emotions and real traffic conditions. Moreover, Vernuccio *et al.* (2019) conceptually have analysed how NBVAs can help to activate the brand anthropomorphism perception in the consumer's mind, by allowing the brand to acquire for the first time its voice with peculiar characteristics. Despite the growing use of NBVAs as well as the theoretical possibility to recognise significant implications for the NBVA in the brand anthropomorphisation process, no study has empirically investigated the role that companies can assign to the NBVA in brand strategies. For this reason, the objective of our work is to investigate the role that the NBVA might have in the brand anthropomorphisation strategy, by adopting the managerial perspective. In this way, we respond to the calls by Guido and Peluso (2015) and Belk and Kniazeva (2018) for researches on the role of VAs in anthropomorphisation strategies, contributing with a managerial perspective to the literature on brand anthropomorphism that, until now, has only adopted the consumer point of view and ignored the voice as a driver of the brand anthropormorphisation process. Moreover, our study can provide managers with important guidelines for designing NBVA from a branding perspective. To this end, we have analysed a single in-depth case study. Given the importance of the automotive sector as a context of use of NBVAs, the selected case is the first in-car NBVA to be released in the market in 2018 (Voicebot 2019a), which presented the characteristic of uniqueness during the research period (Yin 2017). The paper is structured as follows. In the next section, we illustrate the literature review on the brand anthropomorphism and the role of the voice in the branding field. Then, we outline the methodology and findings. Finally, the discussion of the results, theoretical and practical implications and future research lines are presented.

2 Brand Anthropomorphism and Brand Voice

In marketing literature, anthropomorphism is the consumer perception based on the tendency of imbuing human characteristics, motivations, intentions and emotions to non-human objects and agents (Epley *et al.* 2007). However, the term "anthropomorphisation" refers to the process or the strategy underlying the anthropomorphism perception defined by companies (e.g., Puzakova *et al.* 2009; Kwak *et al.* 2015). Although the concept of anthropomorphism was so far connected mainly to physical attributes (e.g., human body lineaments, human facial physiognomy), some cognitive aspects were also considered, such as the mind (Epley *et al.* 2008a; Waytz *et al.* 2010), free will (Epley *et al.* 2008a; Kim and McGill 2011; Waytz *et al.* 2010), intentions (Epley *et al.* 2008a; Kim and McGill 2011; Waytz *et al.* 2010), emotional states (Puzakova *et al.* 2009) and personality (Epley *et al.* 2008b). Moreover, the anthropomorphism was related to the brand personification concept, defined as imbuing brands "with a human form and/or human attributes, including a generally distinctive physical appearance and personality" (Cohen 2014, p. 3). Amid "the set of human characteristics associated with a brand" (Aaker 1997, p. 347) that constitute brand personality, we find the warmth and competence (W&C) dimensions (Aaker 1997). The first dimension refers to traits such as being amicable, kind and trustworthy, while the latter refers to traits such as capability, intelligence and ability (Malone and Fiske 2013). In the advertising context, several marketing scholars pointed out that the consumer's perception of W&C traits can be enabled by distinctive voice characteristics, i.e. quality, gender, pitch, and timbre (brightness and roughness). Concerning the voice quality, Wiener and Chartrand (2014) identified six types: breathy, creaky, nasal, tense, whispery and harsh voices. Creaky voice is perceived as less warm and less competent, breathy and whispery voices are judged warmer and tense voice is perceived as more competent than the other voice types. Furthermore, experiential context of VAs, also the type of voice that follows an ideal regarding gender, female voices are perceived as warmer and more competent than male voices. Regarding the pitch, low-pitched voice is associated with adjectives such as competent, strong and mature, while high-pitched voice is associated with happy, weak and youth (Zoghaib 2017). Finally, low-pitched, dull (vs. bright) and smooth (vs. rough) voices are perceived as warmer, while high-pitched and smooth voice is judged to be the most competent (Zoghaib 2019). In the continuum between the human voice and the synthetic voice produces significant effects on the VA anthropomorphism perception. In this regard, Chérif & Lemoine (2019), comparing the effect of the human voice versus the synthetic voice, show that consumers have a stronger perception of anthropomorphic characteristics of the VA when it speaks with a human voice. In general, consumers prefer the human voice to the synthetic voice (Voicebot 2019b). NBVA allows the brand to dialogue directly with the consumer using its brand name and its brand voice. The latter can be designed with peculiar characteristics to activate the perception of specific brand personality traits in the consumer, enabling the brand anthropomorphisation process. Then, it is theoretically possible to recognise significant implications for the NBVA in the brand anthropomorphisation process. However, the effective role that companies can assign to the NBVA in the context of brand strategies and, more specifically, in the brand anthropomorphisation strategy, remains unknown. Consequently, we formulate the following RQ: What is the role of the NBVA in the brand anthropomorphisation strategy?

3 Methodology

The lack of previous empirical studies has led us to the use of a "single in-depth case study" (Yin 2017). The choice of context and case study was based on a preliminary analysis of the available literature. In particular, the selected context, given the growing relevance as a context of use of NBVAs, is the automotive sector and the selected case is the first NBVA developed in-house by a global player, henceforth referred to as "Company X"[1]. Inside the car, users can activate the NBVA by pronouncing "Hey, [brand name of the Company X]!". Therefore, consumers call the brand by name and the NBVA responds with its voice, creating a direct dialogue. The study was conducted in 2019, using primary and secondary sources to guarantee the triangulation of data (Flick 2008). In particular, we have conducted six interviews (face-to-face), following the key

[1] For reasons of confidentiality, the Company name cannot be disclosed.

informant technique (Robson and Foster 1989) to identify the interviewees, and collected public online documents (e.g., the corporate website, business reports) and internal documents. Within the Company X, we have interviewed four senior managers in the undermentioned organisational areas: marketing, external relations and research and development (R&D). Moreover, to understand how the NBVA voice was designed and created, we have interviewed two text-to-speech (TTS) providers in the R&D organisational area, who were involved in the speech software development and who served as a supplier of the voice command data. The respondents requested full anonymity; therefore, they have been classified as Interviewee 1 to 6. The interviews, which lasted about 90 min on average, were based on an interview guide adapted according to the interviewee's reference area. The interview guide was designed following the reflexive pragmatic approach (Alvesson 2003), formulating open-ended questions to elicit spontaneous answers on the design aspects (what?), the design methods (how?) and the objectives pursued by the Company X (why?). The interviews were recorded, transcribed and finally analysed separately by two coders within the research team, through the thematic content analysis technique (King and Horrocks 2010). After careful and repeated reading, the so-called "descriptive codes" have been defined, i.e., very punctual codes, descriptive of specific portions of text. Based on these descriptive codes, we defined more general interpretative codes, which were identified by clustering the former and interpreting the meanings of clusters. This procedure has allowed us to define the key themes about the role of the NBVA in the brand anthropomorphisation strategy. At the end of this phase, the results of the thematic analysis processes have been compared, discussed and harmonized by the two coders. Finally, following the "*code-confirming*" approach (King and Horrocks 2010), the reliability of the results has been verified by an independent coder, a marketing expert and specifically methodologically trained. The interjudge reliability, calculated through the so-called "agreement ratio", amounted to 88%, above the minimum expected level (Powell 2007).

4 Findings

The content analysis led to the identification of two key themes concerning the crucial role of the NBVA in the brand anthropomorphisation strategy: 1) developing the human-like brand voice; 2) developing the human-like consumer-brand dialogue. Then, the two macro-themes were articulated into more specific sub-themes.

4.1 Developing the Human-Like Brand Voice

There is a widespread consensus among interviewees about the fundamental contribution of NBVA to the brand anthropomorphisation strategy in terms of developing a brand voice that could be perceived by consumers as "human". The meaning associated with the concept of the humanity of voice is linked to three sub-themes emerging from the interviews: *1) brand voice quality; 2) brand voice pitch; 3) brand voice prosody.*

1) *Brand voice quality.* In the NBVA development, firstly the Company X has focused on the voice quality, which is based on the concatenation through algorithms of whole sentences recorded by human speakers with short speech pieces

that are stored in a database. In specific, the Company X has improved the sentences recorded by the human speaker as well as the concatenation algorithms to raise the quality and to make in this way the brand voice as similar as possible to the human voice.

"They [Company X managers] always think in terms of voice quality and they want a quality that is as human as possible. So, we try to get the highest quality of the voice by trying to make it as human as possible" [...] "The quality of the voice is very clear and in the optimized part I have no problems that make me perceive that it is a synthesis" (Interviewee 6, R&D, TTS provider).

2) *Brand voice pitch.* The second characteristic on which the Company X has focused is the pitch, which is the melodic height with which a syllable is pronounced. Although artificial aspects remain, the objective of the Company X is to make the brand voice pitch as similar as possible to the human pitch, creating variations (up and down) during a speech.

"The brand voice pitch should be very close to human pitch" [...] "For me, you still feel that it [the brand voice] is artificial, you feel that it does not have the tone of voice that we can have, but surely you feel that it has made great strides compared to previous technologies" (Interviewee 1, Marketing, Company X).

3) *Brand voice prosody.* Finally, to favour the perception of the brand voice as human, the Company X has worked on prosody, i.e., intonation, rhythm and accent, to obtain the right melodic movement for each type of sentence (affirmative, interrogative, exclamation and imperative).

"We had to work a lot on prosody to create a human voice. For example, in an interrogative sentence, the intonation must rise. In this case, we have some correction tools that we have used to correct all prosody defects" (Interviewee 6, R&D, TTS provider).

According to interviewees, quality, pitch and prosody were designed to make the voice enabled by the NBVA an identifying element of the brand personality, favouring the perception of specific personality related to both the warmth dimension (e.g., "informal") and the competence dimension (e.g., "intelligent").

"Vocal characteristics have been chosen to enable the perception of specific brand personality traits in the consumer's mind, such as informal, intelligent, brilliant, solution-oriented..." (Interviewee 1, Marketing, Company X).

4.2 Developing the Human-Like Consumer-Brand Dialogue

The second role of the NBVA in the brand anthropomorphisation strategy is to contribute to the development of a human-like consumer-brand dialogue, to allow the users to interact with the brand through the NBVA as if they were interacting with a human being. The meaning associated with the concept of the humanity of dialogue is linked to two sub-themes emerging from the interviews: *1) naturalness in the dialogue; 2) speed in the dialogue.*

1) *Naturalness in the dialogue.* To make the consumer-brand dialogue as similar as possible to human interaction, the Company X has worked on naturalness trying to make the dialogue as simple, fluid and intuitive as possible. Thanks to the Natural Language Understanding technology, the NBVA becomes a human interlocutor able to understand any type of sentence. Besides, the naturalness of the dialogue is also considered a fundamental requirement to reduce driving distractions and therefore to ensure driving safety.

"The Company X wanted an intuitive vocal interaction that did not require reading manuals to use it. For this reason, they have used the Natural Language Understanding, that, unlike grammar recognition, allows the VA to understand any type of sentence even if it is indirectly formulated" (Interviewee 6, R&D, TTS provider).

"Voice interaction has been designed to be very 'fluid' and simple, in a word as natural as possible, to engage the driver only for what is strictly necessary and not distract him from the main task of the guide" (Interviewee 3, External Relations, Company X).

2) *Speed in the dialogue.* The second sub-theme linked to the concept of human-like consumer-brand dialogue is speed, which, like naturalness, is considered a fundamental requirement to ensure driving safety. In particular, the content analysis led to the identification of two types of speed: the NBVA fast response time and the brevity of the dialogue. Concerning the former, to simulate the pauses in human interactions, the reaction time of the NBVA was reduced, to ensure that the user, after vocally formulating his request, does not have to wait longer than he would expect by talking to a person.

"The Company X wanted an interface that was responsive, very responsive, fast with a maximum of two seconds of delays in any type of interaction, which minimised distractions and this is a general criterion for everything you do in the car. [...] They wanted to minimise latency times. So, we had to work to optimise the algorithms and make sure that the user does not have to wait any longer than he would expect by talking to a human" (Interviewee 6, R&D, TTS provider).

Finally, concerning the brevity, the dialogue has been designed to be essential and concise.

"The system is designed to provide essential information and it has to give the essential information in the fastest and most comprehensible way. So, both in the case of input and in the case of output, the speed linked to essentiality is one of the key requirements of the project" (Interviewee 4, R&D, Company X).

According to interviewees, the human-like consumer-brand dialogue was designed to develop a stronger, more intimate and friendly consumer-brand relationship.

"The consumer-brand relationship thanks to the interaction through the VA changes because it becomes closer, more familiar and more intimate" (Interviewee 1, Marketing, Company X).

5 Conclusion

Our findings allow us to conceptualise the role of the NBVA in the brand anthropomorphisation strategy, i.e., developing the human-like brand voice and the human-like consumer-brand dialogue. In particular, the human-like brand voice is developed through the manipulation of particular vocal characteristics - i.e., quality, pitch and prosody – to favour the perception of specific human-like brand personality traits linked to both the warmth dimension (e.g., "informal") and the competence dimension (e.g., "intelligent", "brilliant"). The human-like consumer-brand dialogue is designed following the criteria of naturalness and speed, to create a stronger and more intimate consumer-brand relationship. Therefore, the contribution to the marketing literature of our study is fourfold. First, it contributes to the line of research on the marketing implications of VAs (Braun *et al.* 2019; Pagani *et al.* 2019) by shifting, for the first time, the focus from consumers to managers. Second, our study is the first contribution that empirically supports the key role of the NBVA in the brand anthropomorphisation strategy (Guido and Peluso 2015; Belk and Kniazeva 2018). In this way, we contribute to the literature on anthropomorphism by conceptualising the "human-like brand voice" and the "human-like consumer-brand dialogue" enabled by the NBVA. Third, our study enriches the sonic branding literature (e.g., Wiener and Chartrand 2014; Zoghaib 2017; Zoghaib 2019), by showing how, voice quality, pitch and prosody could be oriented by the Company X towards W&C brand personality traits development. Finally, our findings contribute to the consumer-brand relationship literature (e.g., Chang 2006) highlighting how the consumer-brand dialogue enabled by the NBVA could be oriented to the creation of a stronger and more familiar consumer-brand relationship. Furthermore, in terms of managerial implications, our study can represent a useful conceptual reference for the design of the brand voice (quality, pitch and prosody) and the design of the consumer-brand dialogue (naturalness and speed), for practitioners engaged in branding anthropomorphisation strategy, also outside from the automotive sector. In particular, our study offers to managers two complementary strategic lines: developing the human-like brand voice to favour the perception of W&C brand personality traits and developing the human-like consumer-brand dialogue to strengthen the consumer-brand relationship. Considering the innovativeness of the managerial challenges opened by the NBVA experience, this study could be extended to other brands, industries and product categories. Moreover, by shifting the focus from managers to consumers, it would be interesting to further elaborate, through experimental research design, the effects exerted by different brand voice characteristics on consumers' anthropomorphic brand perception. Finally, since the measurement scale of brand anthropomorphism empirically validated refers to physical design elements (Guido and Peluso 2015), it would be of great worth to develop a new scale based on brand voice characteristics.

References

Aaker, J.L.: Dimensions of brand personality. J. Mark. Res. **34**(3), 347–356 (1997)

Alvesson, M.: Beyond neopositivists, romantics, and localists: a reflexive approach to interviews in organizational research. Acad. Manag. Rev. **28**(1), 13–33 (2003)

Belk, R., Kniazeva, M.: Morphing anthropomorphism: an update. J. Glob. Scholars Mark. Sci. **28**(3), 239–247 (2018)

Braun, M., Mainz, A., Chadowitz, R., Pfleging, B, Alt, F.: At your service: designing voice assistant personalities to improve automotive user interfaces. In: Proceedings of theCHI Conference on Human Factors in Computing Systems Extended Abstracts, Scottish Event Campus, Glasgow, Scotland, UK, 4–9 May 2019, pp. 40–50. ACM, New York (2019)

Chang, P.L., Chieng, M.H.: Building consumer–brand relationship: a cross-cultural experiential view. Psycho. Mark. **23**(11), 927–959 (2006)

Chérif, E., Lemoine, J.F.: Anthropomorphic virtual assistants and the reactions of Internet users: an experiment on the assistant's voice. Rech. et Appl. en Mark. (Engl. Ed.) **34**(1), 28–47 (2019)

Cho, E., Molina, M.D., Wang, J.: The effects of modality, device, and task differences on perceived human likeness of voice-activated virtual assistants. Cyberpsychol. Behav. Soc. Netw. **22**(8), 515–520 (2019)

Cohen, R.J.: Brand personification: introduction and overview. Psychol. Mark. **31**(1), 1–30 (2014)

Epley, N., Waytz, A., Akalis, S., Cacioppo, J.T.: On seeing human: a three-factor theory of anthropomorphism. Psychol. Rev. **114**(4), 864–886 (2007)

Epley, N., Akalis, S., Waytz, A., Cacioppo, J.T.: Creating social connection through inferential reproduction: loneliness and perceived agency in gadgets, gods, and greyhounds. Psychol. Sci. **19**(2), 114–120 (2008a)

Epley, N., Waytz, A., Akalis, S., Cacioppo, J.T.: When we need a human: motivational determinants of anthropomorphism. Soc. Cogn. **26**(2), 143–155 (2008b)

Fivesights Research: Echoes from Audrey. voice assistants: the sound of machine intelli gence (2017). https://www.fivesightresearch.com/wp-content/uploads/2017/12/Echoes-From-Audrey.pdf

Flick, U.: Managing Quality in Qualitative Research. Sage, London (2008)

Guido, G., Peluso, A.M.: Brand anthropomorphism: conceptualization, measurement, and impact on brand personality and loyalty. J. Brand Manag. **22**(1), 1–19 (2015)

Jones, V.K.: Voice-activated change: marketing in the age of artificial intelligence and virtual assistants. J. Brand Strategy **7**(3), 233–245 (2018)

Kim, S., McGill, A.L.: Gaming with Mr. Slot or gaming the slot machine? Power, anthropomorphism, and risk perception. J. Consum. Res. **38**(1), 94–107 (2011)

King, N., Horrocks, C.: Interviews in Qualitative Research. Sage, London (2010)

Kwak, H., Puzakova, M., Rocereto, J.F.: Better not smile at the price: the differential role of brand anthropomorphization on perceived price fairness. J. Mark. **79**(4), 56–76 (2015)

Lahoual, D., Frejus, M.: When users assist the voice assistants_from supervision to failure resolution. In: Proceedings of the CHI Conference on Human Factors in Computing Systems Extended Abstracts, Scottish Event Campus, Glasgow, Scotland, UK, 4–9 May 2019, pp. 1–8. ACM, New York (2019)

Malone, C., Fiske, S.T.: The human brand: how we relate to people, products, and companies. Wiley, New York (2013)

Pagani, M., Racat, M., Hofacker, C.F.: Adding voice to the omnichannel and how that affects brand trust. J. Interact. Mark. **48**, 89–105 (2019). [Preprint]

Powell, S.: Organisational marketing, identity and the creative brand. J. Brand Manag. **15**(1), 41–56 (2007)

Puzakova, M., Kwak, H., Rocereto, J.F.: Pushing the envelope of brand and personality: antecedents and moderators of anthropomorphized brands. Adv. Consum. Res. **36**, 413–420 (2009)

Robson, S., Foster, A.: Qualitative Research in Action. Edward Arnold, London (1989)

Smith, K.T.: Marketing via smart speakers: what should Alexa say? J. Strateg. Mark. 1–16 (2018, in press)

Vassinen, R.: The rise of conversational commerce: what brands need to know. J. Brand Strategy **7**(1), 13–22 (2018)

Vernuccio, M., Patrizi, M., Pastore, A.: Artificial intelligence and brand anthropomorphisation: the role of voice assistants. In: Proceedings of the 48th Annual Conference for the European Marketing Academy (EMAC), 28–31 May 2018, University of Hamburg, Hamburg, Germany, EMAC, Bruxelles, pp. 1–8 (2019)

Voicebot: In-car voice assistant consumer adoption report (2019a). https://voicebot.ai/in-car-voice-assistant-consumer-adoption-report-2019/

Voicebot: What consumers want in voice app design (2019b). https://voicebot.ai/what-consumers-want-in-voice-app-design-2019/

Waytz, A., Morewedge, C.K., Epley, N., Monteleone, G., Gao, J.H., Cacioppo, J.T.: Making sense by making sentient: effectance motivation increases anthropomorphism. J. Pers. Soc. Psychol. **99**(3), 410–435 (2010)

Wiener, H.J.D., Chartrand, T.L.: The Effect of Voice Quality on Ad efficacy. Psychol. Mark. **31**(7), 509–517 (2014)

Yin, R.K.: Case Study Research and Applications: Design and Methods. Sage Publications, Thousand Oaks (2017)

Zoghaib, A.: The contribution of a brand spokesperson's voice to consumer-based brand equity. J. Prod. Brand Manag. **26**(5), 492–502 (2017)

Zoghaib, A.: Persuasion of voices: the effects of a speaker's voice characteristics and gender on consumers' responses. Rech. et Appl. en Mark. (Engl. Ed.) **34**(3), 83–110 (2019)

Consumers' Online Institutional Privacy Literacy

Eathar Abdul-Ghani(✉)

Business School, Auckland University of Technology, Auckland, New Zealand
eabdulgh@aut.ac.nz

Abstract. Most people, in their daily lives, have a need for privacy – the need at times to left alone. Yet in the Internet age consumer readily reveal aspects of their private lives to a wide circle of contacts, most often via social media apps. Concurrently, big digital businesses such as Google and Facebook operate business models based upon lucrative income streams from the use and sharing of consumer's personal data, a practice referred to as surveillance capitalism. This paper contrasts these two very different aspects of online privacy, social privacy and institutional privacy. The gathering of personal data on consumers is often portrayed by digital marketers and marketing academics as a commercial exchange between a consumer and firm, that is, the exchange of personal data for services or improved service. This exchange relationship has been portraying theoretically with reference to social contract theory and social exchange theory. However, this paper argues that to the extent consumers are not aware (a) what personal information is being taken from them, (b) what that information is used for, and (c) who that information is being shared with, then a social contract or social exchange does not exist. This issue of consumer's online institutional privacy literary is a critical ethical question for the future practice of digital marketing. If consumers' institutional privacy literacy is low, one can question if the gathering of personal data by digital business is accurately represented as a social contract, or if it is more accurately portrayed as an imbalanced exchange operating under conditions of information asymmetry.

Keywords: Online privacy · Personal data · Institutional privacy · Surveillance capitalism · Consumer literacy

1 Introduction – the Issue of Consumer Privacy

Most human beings have a need for privacy. They have a need for some conversations to be private, private information, private thoughts. These intimate, personal details will only be revealed to those in the closest relationships, and kept from the public eye (or ear). The need for privacy appears to be universal to all cultures, though what needs to remain private (e.g. personal finances, medical details, sexual matters) varies from one culture to another (Acquisti et al. 2015).

Smith et al. (2011) provide three views on just what privacy is: (1) privacy is a right, such as the right to be left alone (Warren and Brandeis 1890); (2) privacy is a state, such as the state of limited access to a person and their information; and

F. J. Martínez-López and S. D'Alessandro (Eds.): *Advances in Digital Marketing and eCommerce*, SPBE, pp. 40–46, 2020.
https://doi.org/10.1007/978-3-030-47595-6_6

(3) privacy as control, such as the ability to control what information specific to the individual is shared with other persons and/or businesses (Altman 1975).

Individuals set boundaries between their private lives and private information, and public lives and public information. Just as people have a need to socialise and interact with each other, they also at times, have a need to withdraw from the social sphere, to recharge their batteries, to recoup and realign. To be free to think and feel and act without intrusion and influence from the social group (Acquisti et al. 2015; Schwartz 1968).

The internet age presents many challenges to the maintenance of consumer privacy. Through social media, consumers reveal details of their private lives such as photographs or partners, children and friends. Through their use of online search engines such as Google, consumers reveal their interests, desires and online web search behaviour. While the news media regularly features stories about online hacking and theft of private information, the more ubiquitous issues are issues of social privacy and institutional privacy. Social privacy refers to the revealing or sequestering of personal information from social display. Research suggests consumers, in general, are well aware of the issue of social privacy and frequently adopt measures to protect their social privacy, such as adjusting the privacy settings on the social media apps they (Alkire et al. 2019; Bartsch and Dienlin 2016). Institutional privacy, on the other hand, is the issue of what private data on individual consumers is being collected online, stored and shared by commercial organisations such as Google and Facebook. Research is required to establish the level of awareness amongst consumers of institutional privacy issues and the measures they can take to protect their personal information from institutional intrusion.

A quarter-century ago, writing about ethical marketing practice and consumer privacy in the internet age, Bloom et al. (1994) posed two questions to marketers:

- Should a company be allowed to acquire and store information about individuals without their knowledge and consent?
- Should a company be allowed to disclose information about individuals to other parties without their knowledge or consent?

In the intervening 25 years, the practice of digital marketers reveals that each of these questions has been answered in the affirmative. Modern digital marketing practice assumes that it is legitimate to acquire, store and share information gathered online about individual consumers, without those individuals being well informed about (a) what data has been gathered on them, and (b) who that data has been shared with.

A "privacy paradox" is often demonstrated by consumers (Martin and Murphy 2017), which is the tendency for consumers to report high concerns about online privacy and yet at the same time divulge personal information online. One potential explanation for the privacy paradox is that consumers are not aware of the extent to which they are disclosing personal information online to digital marketers.

This paper addresses the issue of how well-informed consumers are about the data gathered online on them by commercial organisations, and shared with other commercial organisations. This is the issue of consumer online institutional privacy literacy. The paper considers the implications of low levels of consumer institutional privacy literacy for contemporary digital marketing practice.

2 Surveillance Capitalism

The business models of a number of the world's leading digital businesses, including Google and Facebook, are based on an approach to commerce that may be termed "surveillance capitalism".

In these business models, Google and Facebook provide free-of-charge services to consumers. Revenues are not obtained from consumers but from advertisers. Google and Facebook provide consumers with free-of-charge access to valued services (e.g. online information search, and access to social media platforms) in exchange for access to personal information; they then use that personal information to drive effective advertising on behalf of advertisers. The information that can be accessed, stored and shared about individual consumers by "big digital" includes, but is not restricted to: name, date of birth, residential address, location 24/7, email addresses, IP address, devices used, online posts, personal photographs, contact lists, web browsing records, expressed interests and opinions, and online purchases (Fowler 2019). This personal information is gathered by digital businesses tracking a substantial portion of a consumer's online activities, including the consumer's activities on mobile phones, a process sometimes referred to as "data harvesting". Personal data on individual consumers is thus a highly valued asset for digital businesses, worth billions of dollars, information can be on-sold to other online businesses for purposes such as finely targeted communication of advertising messages.

The Cambridge Analytica scandal of 2017 reveals aspects of a commercial ecosystem for harvesting and sharing consumer personal data amongst multiple parties. The basis of the scandal commenced with a small business called Psychological Associates, who wrote a personality test app that was made available through Facebook. Hundreds of thousands of Facebook users filled in the online personality test, and in so doing agreed that the results of the test – their personality profiles - and other personal details could be stored and shared by Psychological Associates. At the time, Facebook approved such behaviour, that app developers could gather personal information on app users and use that information as they saw fit (Lewis 2018). The Facebook users who participated in Psychological Associates' personality test, unknowingly also provided access to their personal contact lists, and in so doing, facilitated access to personal information on some 40 million Facebook users on their contact lists without those users having agreed to their personal data being accessed. This data was on-sold to Cambridge Analytica a political communication firm. It is said the data was used to profile USA and influence the 2016 presidential election. Media interviews with Facebook employees suggest that the Cambridge Analytica case may not be an exception, and that the gathering and sharing of personal information on Facebook users may be commonplace (Lewis 2018).

Kurtz et al. (2018) provide a case study of the commercial ecosystems that developed around Facebook that involved the sharing of consumer personal data, which enabled the Cambridge Analytica scandal to occur. The players in such ecosystems built around the sharing of personal consumer data, include consumers, big digital businesses such as Google and Facebook, app developers, advertisers and advertising agencies, and "third party" data brokers such as DoubleClick (Fig. 1).

One crucial mechanism that enables the comprehensive collection on personal information on individual consumers is the process of aggregation of data on that individual sourced from multiple sites, multiple apps and platforms, and across multiple devices (Brookman et al. 2017). By aggregating such data, a comprehensive profile of each consumer – their identity, demographics, location, attitudes and interests – can be constructed.

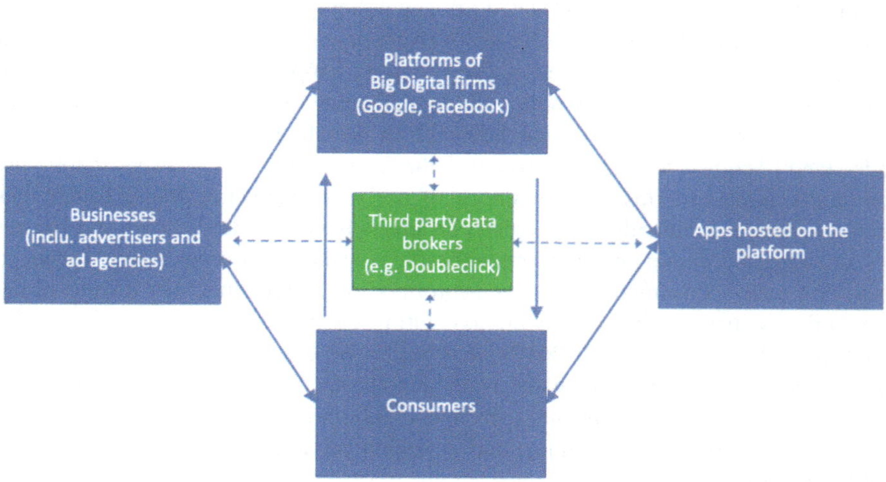

Fig. 1. Commercial ecosystem developed around consumer data sharing (adapted from Kurtz et al. 2018)

3 Absence of a Social Contract

The gathering of personal data on consumers is often portrayed, by digital marketers and marketing academics, as a commercial exchange between a consumer and firm, that is, the exchange of personal data for services or improved service. For example, by knowing a consumer's Internet search history, history of downloads and purchases, the digital service provider can make targeted suggestions for appropriate future purchases that are more targeted to the needs, interests and desires of the consumer.

Commentators who argue in support of the harvesting of consumer data, argue that a legitimate exchange process has occurred, with the consumer knowingly and willingly exchanging access to personal information for access to free-of-charges services (Martin and Murphy 2017). This exchange relationship has been portraying theoretically with reference to social contract theory and social exchange theory (Martin and Murphy 2017).

However, to the extent consumers are not aware (a) what personal information is being taken from them, (b) what that information is used for, and (c) who that information is being shared with, then a social contract or social exchange does not exist. This then becomes a critical ethical issue for the future practice of digital marketing.

If consumers are illiterate regarding online institutional privacy matters, then a situation of information asymmetry and imbalance of power exists between the parties to the exchange, the commercial organisation and the consumer.

4 Consumer's Online Institutional Privacy Literacy

On the face of it, the mechanism that appears designed to protect individual privacy from institutional intrusion is the stated privacy policy published on website and apps. To enable use of the full functionality of a website or app, consumers are invited to read and agree to the privacy policies of the provider. Empirical research indicates that consumers seldom read privacy policies before agreeing to them, and even if they were to read them may find the formal language in which they are written difficult to understand (Acquisti et al. 2015). To enjoy the functionality of a website or app, most consumers agree to terms and conditions of use without reading them. Under these circumstances, it is difficult to argue that consumers have exercised choice and consent.

As suggested earlier, mechanisms exist for consumers to protect their social privacy, and many consumers appear well-informed on actions they can take to protect social privacy such as adjusting the privacy settings on their social media accounts (Fox and Royne 2018; Kelly et al. 2017). It is yet to be established how well-informed consumers are about the mechanisms available to protect their private information from institutional intrusion, mechanisms such as encryption, use of virtual private networks, incognito mode on search engines, and adjusting privacy settings on web browsers mobile phones.

It is likely that some national populations are more aware and concerned about online institutional privacy issues than other national populations. European citizens appear acutely concerned about institutional privacy; in response, the European Union has enacted powerful and far-reaching legislation to protect its consumers from data harvesting by digital firms, the General Data Protection Regulation (European Union 2016). By contrast, the USA which is home to most of the world's largest digital businesses, is very pro-business and reluctant to curtail the powers of digital business to access private data on individual citizens. The exception is the recent enactment of the California Consumer Privacy Act (2019) (Korolov 2019). The cases of nations such as Canada and Australia may lie somewhere between those of Europe and the USA.

A measure of online privacy literacy have been constructed by Masur and colleagues (Masur 2019; Masur, Teutsch and Trepte 2017a, 2017b) though the measure is most specific to German consumers. It would be very valuable for future research to develop other measures on online institutional privacy literacy, and compare literacy level between consumers in various nations and age groups (Hoofnagle et al. 2010).

5 A Question of Ethics

Privacy is often portrayed as a human right – the right to be left alone, the right for private matters to remain private (Smith et al. 2011). Many citizens would be concerned if there was widespread state surveillance, and yet, as consumers we live in time of institutional surveillance, where large digital businesses and marketers are recording many aspects of our private lives. Is the practice of surveillance capitalism right or wrong? This is a question of ethics.

Some companies and brands have sought to distance themselves from the harvesting of consumer data for profit. For example, the business model followed by Apple is a more traditional business model, with income largely derived from the sale of hardware. Apple positions itself in the market as the company that does not compromise user privacy. (And yet, in the contra view, Apple's app store still distributes a multitude of apps from third parties that collect, store and distribute personally identifiable information).

Palmatier and Martin (2019) suggest a number of ways in which the modern corporation may act in an ethical manner regarding the collection, storage, use and dissemination of personally identifiable consumer data. For example, companies can adopt an in-house consumer data privacy policy; minimize unnecessary data collection; empower consumers through practices of data transparency and control; protect stored data from potential data breaches; and regularly audit privacy practices.

6 Conclusion

Online institutional privacy literacy refers to the extent to which consumers are aware of the mechanisms commercial organisations are using to gather personal information on them online, and aware of the tools available to protect personal information from institutional intrusion. This paper questions the extent to which consumers are aware of the personal data being gathered online by digital marketers. If consumers' institutional privacy literacy is low, one can question if the gathering of personal data by digital marketers is accurately represented as a social contract, or if it is more accurately portrayed as an imbalanced exchange under conditions of information asymmetry. This is an important ethical issue that impacts modern digital marketing practice. Future research is required to develop measures of consumers' online institutional privacy literacy to help address this issue.

References

Acquisti, A., Brandimarte, L., Loewenstein, G.: Privacy and human behavior in the age of information. Science **347**(6221), 509–514 (2015)

Alkire, L., Pohlmann, J., Barnett, W.: Triggers and motivators of privacy protection behavior on Facebook. J. Serv. Mark. **33**(1), 57–72 (2019)

Altman, I.: The Environment and Social Behavior: Privacy, Personal Space, Territory and Crowding. Brooks/Cole Publishing, Monterey (1975)

Bartsch, M., Dienlin, T.: Control your Facebook: an analysis of online privacy literacy. Comput. Hum. Behav. **56**, 147–154 (2016)

Bloom, P.N., Milne, G.R., Adler, R.: Avoiding misuse of new information technologies: legal and societal considerations. J. Mark. **58**(1), 98–110 (1994)

Brookman, J., Rouge, P., Alva, A., Yeung, C.: Cross-device tracking: measurement and disclosures. Proc. Priv. Enhanc. Technol. **2017**(2), 133–148 (2017)

European Union: General data protection regulation (GDPR) (2016). https://gdpr-info.eu/
Fowler, G.A.: It's the middle of the night. Do you know who your iPhone is talking to? Washington Post. https://www.washingtonpost.com/technology/2019/05/28/its-middle-night-do-you-know-who-your-iphone-is-talking/. Accessed 29 May 2019
Fox, A.K., Royne, M.B.: Private information in a social world: assessing consumers' fear and understanding of social media privacy. J. Mark. Theory Pract. **26**(1–2), 72–89 (2018)
Hoofnagle, C.J., King, J., Li, S., Turow, J.: How different are young adults from older adults when it comes to information privacy attitudes and policies? (2010). http://ssm.com/abstract=1589864
Kelly, L., Kerr, G., Drennan, J.: Privacy concerns on social networking sites: a longitudinal study. J. Mark. Manag. **33**(17–18), 1465–1489 (2017)
Korolov, M.: California Consumer Privacy Act (CCPA): What you need to know to be compliant. CSO. https://www.csoonline.com/article/3292578/california-consumer-privacy-act-what-you-need-to-know-to-be-compliant.html. Accessed 4 Oct 2019
Kurtz, C., Seemann, M., Schulz, W.: Towards a framework for information privacy in complex service ecosystems. Paper Presented at the Thirty Ninth International Conference on Information Systems, San Francisco (2018)
Lewis, P.: 'Utterly horrifying': ex-Facebook insider says covert data harvesting was routine. The Guardian. https://www.theguardian.com/news/2018/mar/20/facebook-data-cambridge-analytica-sandy-parakilas. Accessed 20 Mar 2018
Martin, K.D., Murphy, P.E.: The role of data privacy in marketing. J. Acad. Mark. Sci. **45**, 135–155 (2017)
Masur, P.K.: Reconceptualizing online privacy literacy. http://philippmasur.de/blog/2019/03/28/reconceptualizing-online-privacy-literacy/. Accessed 28 Mar 2019
Masur, P.K., Teutsch, D., Trepte, S.: Development and validation of the online privacy literacy scale. Diagnostica **63**, 256–263 (2017a). 10.1026/0012-1924/a000179
Masur, P.K., Teutsch, D., Trepte, S.: OPLIS: online privacy literacy scale (2017b). http://www.oplis.de/index_eng.html
Palmatier, R.W., Martin, K.D.: The Intelligent Marketer's Guide to Data Privacy: The Impact of Big Data on Customer Trust. Springer, Cham (2019)
Schwartz, B.: The social psychology of privacy. Am. J. Sociol. **73**(6), 741–752 (1968)
Smith, H.J., Dinev, T., Xu, H.: Information privacy research: an interdisciplinary review. MIS Q. **35**(4), 989–1016 (2011)
Warren, S., Brandeis, L.: The right to privacy. Harv. Law Rev. **4**(5), 193–220 (1890)

Social Media and Omni-Channel Strategies in the Tourism Industry: An Analysis of Club Med

Lala Hu[1(✉)] and Mirko Olivieri[2]

[1] Catholic University of the Sacred Heart, Milan, Italy
lala.hu@unicatt.it
[2] IULM University, Milan, Italy
mirko.olivieri4@studenti.iulm.it

Abstract. In tourism, digital media represent a primary channel to interact with consumers directly or by means of social media and travel-related platforms (e.g., TripAdvisor, Booking.com etc.). Over the past few years, travel companies have increased the usage of social media as tools to communicate and engage with existing and potential consumers. The purpose of this paper is to investigate the role of social media within the omni-channel marketing strategies of tourism companies. We conducted a case study of the company Club Med by collecting semi-structured interviews with key-informants. Findings provide insights regarding the use of social media as main touchpoints for tourism companies' strategies and the type of engagement activated with consumers. Furthermore, this research suggests some practical implications for the management of the social media marketing activities.

Keywords: Digital marketing · Omni-channel · Social media · Touchpoints · Tourism

1 Introduction

Over the past few decades, digital media have strongly impacted the tourism sector. First, Internet distribution systems (IDSs) such as Expedia and Priceline and online travel agencies (OTAs) have emerged as major players in e-commerce hospitality (Runfola et al. 2013). Among the different attributes that impact travelers' choice in online booking, convenience has been found to be the most important factor as on the web consumers search for cheaper alternatives (Kim et al. 2007). Second, the use of social media as platforms for marketing purposes has significantly increased as they allow companies to reach customers with brand-related content and engage them in several phases of the customer journey (Hanna et al. 2011; Iankova et al. 2019; Lemon and Verhoef 2016; Schivinski and Dabrowski 2016). Indeed, social media are used by consumers to search information, compare products, share opinions and experiences (Mangold and Faulds 2009), for instance on review sites like TripAdvisor. According to previous scholars, marketing strategies should explore and exploit social media for two main reasons: (1) there is a growing interest in the use of social media platforms by

F. J. Martínez-López and S. D'Alessandro (Eds.): *Advances in Digital Marketing and eCommerce*, SPBE, pp. 47–55, 2020.
https://doi.org/10.1007/978-3-030-47595-6_7

consumers, and (2) users consider shared information on social media more reliable than information developed by companies (Alves et al. 2016; Castronovo and Huang 2012). Thanks to new technologies, various channels are used interchangeably during the search and purchase phases, making it increasingly difficult for companies to monitor all touchpoints of the customer experience (Verhoef et al. 2015). Therefore, firms should take into account all the different touchpoints by adopting an omni-channel strategy that would permit to achieve a competitive advantage both improving customer experience and increasing performances (Capriello and Riboldazzi 2020).

While there is a broad research on the effects of electronic word-of-mouth (hereafter, e-WOM) and online reviews (Filieri and McLeay 2014; Sotiriadis and Van Zyl 2013) on consumers' perceptions and decisions in tourism, how firms from this industry manage social media marketing (hereafter, SMM) activities in their omni-channel marketing strategies is little explored. Therefore, with the present research we investigate the role of social media in the omni-channel marketing strategies of travel companies. We carried out a qualitative study based on the case study method to analyze Club Med, a leading tourism company, collecting interviews with key informants responsible for the marketing and SMM strategies. Findings provide insights on an underdeveloped area of research and also managerial implications for firms that operate in the tourism industry. The remaining of this chapter is structured as follows: Sect. 2 reviews previous research on the omni-channel evolution and social media as touchpoints. Section 3 presents the research question and methodology. Results of the study follow in Sect. 4. Finally, Sect. 5 discusses the research findings and draws the conclusions.

2 Literature Review

According to Chen and Lamberti (2016), multi-channel marketing research falls into two streams. First, new channels and touchpoints introduce new marketing management logics within companies, therefore research investigates challenges of these dynamics from the firm perspective (Sharma and Mehrotra 2007). Second, consumer behavior is affected by the multi-channel marketing approach and, consequently, scholars study the consequences from the consumer's point of view (Dholakia et al. 2010).

Recently, there has been a move from multi-channel retailing, where channels are developed and managed separately within firms, to omni-channel retailing, where customer experience is modeled across different touchpoints and channels (Neslin et al. 2014; Verhoef et al. 2015). In the omni-channel model, the total integration of various platforms shapes the service interface and creates a seamless experience for the consumers (Yurova et al. 2017).

During the customer journey, several touchpoints are involved. "Touchpoints" consist of individual contacts between the firm and the customer at distinct points in the experience (Homburg et al. 2017; Schmitt 2003). Lemon and Verhoef (2016) classify them in four types: brand-owned touchpoints, which are under the control of the firm (e.g., traditional advertising), partner-owned touchpoints (e.g., a product offering from a distributor), customer-owned touchpoints (e.g., the Instagram account of a consumer), and social/external touchpoints (e.g., a hotel review on TripAdvisor or Google Maps).

In the tourism sector, partner-owned touchpoints and social/external touchpoints are particularly challenging. Among partner-owned touchpoints, IDSs and OTAs are often used by consumers to directly book holidays, changing the distribution channel system in the tourism industry (Dieck et al. 2018). After the experience, consumers also share reviews about their booking on the same platform or on social media. The latter represent social/external touchpoints controlled by third parties (e.g., Facebook, TripAdvisor), which they allow the creation of user-generated content (Kaplan and Haenlein 2010)—reviews, comments, mentions, tags, etc. Social media have become important tools for companies that want to create engagement with consumers (Alves et al. 2016) since they permit to establish a direct dialogue (Constantinides 2014) enhancing word of mouth (Yu et al. 2013), as well as generating additional sales (Kumar and Mirchandani 2012).

The advent of social media has allowed travelers to share their travel experiences (Schmidt-Rauch and Schwabe 2014; Zeng and Gerritsen 2014), Furthermore, content shared on social networking sites is recognized as an important source of information and travel recommendation that can help tourists plan trips or possibly influence their decision-making process (Cheng and Edwards 2015; Hudson and Thal 2013; King et al. 2014).

In the area of reputation, social media strongly influence final traveler's decisions during holidays plans (Fotis et al. 2012). On the one hand, social media decrease uncertainty and increase useful information exchanges; on the other hand, they provide users with a sense of belonging to a virtual travel community (Gretzel et al. 2006). According to Verma et al. (2012), different types of tourists have different behaviors in the use of social media as tools for managing their travels. More and more often, travelers use search engines or OTAs to find out more about the available hotels' offerings. For leisure travelers, however, the suggestions of friends and colleagues are considered the most important ones, followed by travel websites and search engines (Zeng and Gerritsen 2014). Social media offer the opportunity to tourism professionals to provide personalized services to individual tourist in destination marketing (Matloka and Buhalis 2010). Furthermore, social media can help to establish a profitable relationship between companies and users, which can also generate customer loyalty (Senders et al. 2013). If social media are coupled with more traditional forms of online marketing, they can contribute to a better management of tourists' experiences (Tham 2013). Through these platforms, tourists can access new innovative solutions and affordable prices (Ružić and Biloš 2010). Therefore, also companies in the tourism industry have understood the importance of adopting marketing strategies involving social media (Moro and Rita 2018) and have increased their investments to create engagement on these platforms (Su et al. 2015).

3 Research Question and Methodology

This research aims at exploring the management of social media communications from the firm perspective. Hence, this study seeks to answer the following questions:

RQ. What is the role of social media within the omni-channel marketing strategies of tourism companies?

To achieve this explorative research objective, we opted for the case study method (Yin 2009) analyzing the SMM strategy of Club Med, a French company specialized in tourism services. A series of semi-structured interviews was conducted with five key-informants at Club Med that could provide relevant information on the marketing and SMM strategies of the company (i.e. Marketing director of Italy and Southern Europe, Global social media marketing manager, Trade marketing and project manager, Global media manager, and Global brand content and product junior manager). The interviews took place in person in Italy or by phone call between July and September 2019 and lasted about one hour each. Upon informants' consent, all interviewed were recorded and transcribed. Transcripts were analyzed and discussed by the researchers. Moreover, primary data was triangulated with secondary data including sector reports and newspaper articles on Club Med and the overall tourism sector.

4 Results

4.1 Overview of Club Med

Club Med is a French tour operator with direct-owned resorts founded in 1950. In 2015, it was acquired by Fosun International Limited, a Chinese group operating in three business lines (Health, Happiness, and Wealth). Founded in 1992, Fosun has been listed on the main board of the Hong Kong Stock Exchange since 2007. Club Med is the inventor of the "All Inclusive" formula, which indicates a tourism package with travel, hospitality, catering, and transfers. "All Inclusive" holidays are offered in 70 destinations worldwide, organizing all the phases of the tourist journey: from the sale of plane tickets to the resort booking. With regard to the Club Med business model, as stated by one of the key informants, almost the totality of the resorts (99%) are managed with long-term leasing contracts in partnership with investment companies. In 2005, Club Med changed its approach moving from adventurous villages to luxury hotels for families. In 2018, Club Med turnover was 1.6 billion, growing by eight percent from the previous year.[1]

4.2 Omni-Channel Strategies in Tourism

As discussed by the recent literature, companies operating in the tourism field have strengthened the adoption of social media activities within their marketing and communications strategies (Alves et al. 2016). Moreover, physical channels should be integrated with digital ones under an omni-channel perspective. Nowadays, customers communicate with companies through several touchpoints, which should interact as much as possible with each other in the customer journey as it is a dynamic process

[1] https://travelnostop.com/news/senza-categoria/club-med-boom-clienti-aumento-fatturato-record_455694 (accessed 5 January 2020).

(Lemon and Verhoef 2016; Verhoef et al. 2015). The Club Med marketing strategy wants to try to integrate all the channels in order to provide a consistent consumer journey.

> *Marketing has a 360° strategy, which consists of putting experiences at the center, that is, the human component of the Club Med holiday. The touchpoints must be joined and connected. For example, the site must be enriched with content that tells about destinations and experiences, social networks perform the task of directing traffic to such content. You must aim for a total integration between the marketing levers if you want to actually see any result.* (Club Med Marketing director Italy and Southern Europe)

The channels' integration involves both direct and indirect channels: the first ones includes the website, the e-commerce system, call center, social media, the PR system, etc. As regards to indirect channels, travel agencies are still relevant. The indirect channel has proven to be important for a company belonging to the tourism field. According to an interviewed manager, 31% of digital tourists rely on agencies in order to organize a holiday of over three nights and 23% of tourists declare to book travels through agencies. Therefore, the management of the relationship with agencies remains necessary in the digital age: as emerged from the interview to the trade marketing and project manager, Club Med Italia actively collaborates with about 300 agencies. These agencies have been classified by status, which considers the agency's performance with reference to several factors, such as the potential of the agency or the passion and commitment shown towards the brand. Each category corresponds to commission schemes and different benefits for agencies.

Digital media are becoming increasingly important for managing the relationship between tourism companies and agencies. For this reason, Club Med uses different tools to maintain this relationship: dedicated website for agencies, webinars, CRM (Customer Relationship Marketing) and e-mail marketing systems, Facebook group, etc. The integration of physical and digital channels has become essential in order to allow consumers to live a positive experience both during the purchase process and during consumption. Therefore, within the Club Med villages, customers have the opportunity to interact with a wide range of tools, both physical and digital. Among these, digital tools include TV screens inside hotel rooms, digital bracelets or the App, which allows the retrieval of all information regarding activities, schedules or the evening dress code.

4.3 Social Media as Touchpoint

Social media represent a primary touchpoint as they can influence the behavior of their consumers (Fotis et al. 2012; Hudson and Thal 2013) in their travel decisions. Club Med recognizes the importance of these platforms:

> *Travel posts are the main content that people share on social media, so there is a large part of UGC that companies, especially Club Med, must take advantage from. Peer-to-Peer communication, WOM, or at least a communication with someone you can identify with, help tourists in choosing a holiday.* (Club Med Marketing director Italy and Southern Europe)

Regarding Club Med's social media presence, the company uses nine platforms: Facebook, Instagram, Pinterest, YouTube, Twitter, LinkedIn, TripAdvisor, and two Chinese platforms (Weibo and WeChat). Globally, since social media are a key tool for

Club Med, they have created a dedicated team of 80 professionals. The management of social networks is carried out at global level by a team that coordinates the content strategy, platforms' campaigns, and tone of voice. The accounts of each single resort are managed by one person responsible for the entire digital experience that works in that particular resort so they can "record the live experience from the customer's point of view."

Within the aforementioned social platforms, there manage more than 110 pages:

- on Facebook, Club Med has developed a global page and 34 pages for each country where Club Med operates, with a global reach of about 2.5 million users, and 41 pages dedicated to each resort.
- on Instagram there is a global account and 41 accounts managed by each individual resort.
- on YouTube, Club Med opened a global account mainly used as a basic platform to broadcast videos on the properties but can be also activated by single countries through the geolocation of posts and language.
- Club Med also has a brand account on Pinterest and one on LinkedIn, both for internal customers and for all B2B activities.

Through social media, brands can increase customer engagement and brand awareness as these platforms create direct communications channels with consumers and help to promote the brand through e-WOM. Furthermore, from the interviews with Club Med practitioners, it has emerged that these tools are involved in all phases of the customer journey: in the pre-purchase phase to get inspiration or suggestions in order to book travels; during the travel experience, social media are used to share content in real time; and in the post-experience phase, consumers continue to share content and they also evaluate their trips spreading e-WOM. Among the platforms used to share content, as emerged from the literature review (Dieck et al. 2018), TripAdvisor plays a central role.

> *At the beginning of the client path, people check social media to be inspired, to find their next destination, then they will probably check the website in order to have more information. Afterwards they will book and they will receive some emails in order to prepare the stay...* (Club Med Global social media marketing manager)
> *Based on how high your resort is rated, you reach a certain visibility. Regarding reviews' management, you should answer all of them. TripAdvisor is a worldwide platform, so the power in terms of visibility is pretty huge.* (Club Med Global brand content and product manager)

Thus, the company's objective is to ensure that consumers are actively involved in the brand social media communications in order increase awareness and consideration. For example, the Instagram account focuses on branding and mainly targets people that do not know the Club Med brand yet. By means of high-quality content (e.g., beautiful images), Club Med tries to reach prospects. On the contrary, Club Med's Facebook page is more focused on engagement. Through Facebook, the objective of the company's strategy is to create brand communities, therefore human relationships are central on this social media platform by encouraging comments, shares, and interactions.

5 Discussion and Conclusion

In answering our *RQ*, social media hold a primary role in tourism companies' omni-channel marketing strategies as they represent communications tools that allow companies to create a direct dialogue with consumers (Costantinides 2014). On social networks, companies can increase brand awareness and stimulate consumer engagement. Indeed, a primary aspect is the relationship that consumers establish with the brand. Furthermore, findings from the interviews with Club Med key informants suggest that social media channels should be used to tell the experience from client's point of view, so that they can act as brand ambassadors. By doing so, content on social media can represent updates from a different point of view than the travel company's one, adopting a "beyond the scenes" perspective more similar among human relationships. Companies should develop relevant content for the audience with whom they interact, and leverage on social media analytics in order to provide customers with personalized experiences. Confirming previous literature (Juaneda-Ayensa et al. 2016; Verhoef et al. 2015), it is also necessary for tourism companies that all the touchpoints (both digital and traditional ones) interact with each other within an omni-channel perspective. Indeed, in the case of Club Med the various channels developed by the marketing strategy include social media but also traditional touchpoints like travel agencies, which remain relevant channels in the tourism industry (Capriello and Riboldazzi 2020).

In conclusion, the findings of this case study suggest that social media should be managed as main touchpoint of all the customer journey phases within an omni-channel strategy. Moreover, social media should highlight the "human" aspect in order for consumers to perceive them as more authentic and effectively relate to the content published. As this study analyzed a single case, it suffers from the limitations of generalizability, therefore these findings should be compared to other companies in the future research. Moreover, the effects of tourism companies' omni-channel strategies on consumers should be measured in order to understand their effectiveness in terms of sales and engagement.

References

Alves, H., Fernandes, C., Raposo, M.: Social media marketing: a literature review and implications. Psychol. Market. **33**(12), 1029–1038 (2016)

Capriello, A., Riboldazzi, S.: How can a travel agency network survive in the wake of digitalization? Evidence from the Robintur case study. Curr. Issues Tour. **23**(9), 1049–1052 (2020)

Castronovo, C., Huang, L.: Social media in an alternative marketing communication model. J. Market. Dev. Compet. **6**(1), 117–134 (2012)

Chen, S., Lamberti, L.: Multichannel marketing: the operational construct and firms' motivation to adopt. J. Strateg. Market. **24**(7), 594–616 (2016)

Cheng, M., Edwards, D.: Social media in tourism: a visual analytic approach. Curr. Issues Tour. **18**(11), 1080–1087 (2015)

Constantinides, E.: Foundations of social media marketing. Procedia-Soc. Behav. Sci. **148**, 40–57 (2014)
Dholakia, U.M., Kahn, B.E., Reeves, R., Rindfleisch, A., Stewart, D., Taylor, E.: Consumer behavior in a multichannel, multimedia retailing environment. J. Interact. Market. **24**, 86–95 (2010)
Dieck, M.C.T., Fountoulaki, P., Jung, H.: Tourism distribution channels in European island destinations. Int. J. Contemp. Hosp. Manag. **30**(1), 326–342 (2018)
Filieri, R., McLeay, F.: E-WOM and accommodation: an analysis of the factors that influence travelers' adoption of information from online reviews. J. Travel Res. **53**(1), 44–57 (2014)
Fotis, J., Buhalis, D., Rossides, N.: Social media use and impact during the holiday travel planning process. In: Fuchs, M., Ricci, F., Cantoni, L. (eds.) Information and Communication Technologies in Tourism 2012, pp. 13–24. Springer, Vienna (2012)
Gretzel, U., Fesenmaier, D., O'Leary, J.: The transformation of consumer behaviour. In: Buhalis, D., Costa, C., Ford, F. (eds.) Tourism Business Frontiers, pp. 31–40. Routledge, London (2006)
Hanna, R., Rohm, A., Crittenden, V.L.: We're all connected: the power of the social media ecosystem. Bus. Horiz. **54**(3), 265–273 (2011)
Homburg, C., Jozi′c, D., Kuehnl, C.: Customer experience management, toward implementing an evolving marketing concept. J. Acad. Market. Sci. **45**(3), 377–401 (2017)
Hudson, S., Thal, K.: The impact of social media on the consumer decision process: implications for tourism marketing. J. Travel Tour. Market. **30**(1–2), 156–160 (2013)
Iankova, S., Davies, I., Archer-Brown, C., Marder, B., Yau, A.: A comparison of social media marketing between B2B, B2C and mixed business models. Ind. Market. Manag. **81**, 169–179 (2019)
Juaneda-Ayensa, E., Mosquera, A., Sierra Murillo, Y.: Omnichannel customer behavior: key drivers of technology acceptance and use and their effects on purchase intention. Front. Psychol. **7**, 1–11 (2016)
Kaplan, A.M., Haenlein, M.: Users of the world, unite! The challenges and opportunities of Social Media. Bus. Horiz. **53**(1), 59–68 (2010)
Kim, D.J., Kim, W.G., Han, J.S.: A perceptual mapping of online travel agencies and preference attributes. Tour. Manag. **28**(2), 591–603 (2007)
King, R.A., Racherla, P., Bush, V.D.: What we know and don't know about online word-of-mouth: a review and synthesis of the literature. J. Interact. Market. **28**(3), 167–183 (2014)
Kumar, V., Mirchandani, R.: Increasing the ROI of social media marketing. MIT Sloan Manag. Rev. **54**, 55–61 (2012)
Lemon, K.N., Verhoef, P.C.: Understanding customer experience throughout the customer journey. J. Market. **80**(6), 69–96 (2016)
Mangold, W.G., Faulds, D.J.: Social media: the new hybrid element of the promotion mix. Bus. Horiz. **52**(4), 357–365 (2009)
Matloka, J., Buhalis, D.: Destination marketing through user personalised content (UPC). In: Gretzel, U. (ed.) Information and Communication Technologies in Tourism 2010, pp. 519–530. Springer, Vienna (2010)
Moro, S., Rita, P.: Brand strategies in social media in hospitality and tourism. Int. J. Contemp. Hosp. Manag. **30**(1), 343–364 (2018)
Neslin, S.A., Jerath, K., Bodapati, A., Bradlow, E.T., Deighton, J., Gensler, S., Verhoef, P.C.: The interrelationships between brand and channel choice. Market. Lett. **25**(3), 319–330 (2014)
Runfola, A., Rosati, M., Guercini, S.: New business models in online hotel distribution: emerging private sales versus leading IDS. Serv. Bus. **7**(2), 183–205 (2013)

Ružić, D., Biloš, A.: Social media in destination marketing organisations (DMOs). Tour. Hosp. Manag., 178–190 (2010)

Schivinski, B., Dabrowski, D.: The effect of social media communication on consumer perceptions of brands. J. Market. Commun. **22**(2), 189–214 (2016)

Schmidt-Rauch, S., Schwabe, G.: Designing for mobile value co-creation – the case of travel counselling. Electron. Market. **24**(1), 5–17 (2014)

Schmitt, B.H.: Customer Experience Management: A Revolutionary Approach to Connecting with Your Customers. Wiley, New York (2003)

Senders, A., Govers, R., Neuts, B.: Social media affecting tour operators' customer loyalty. J. Travel Tour. Market. **30**(1–2), 41–57 (2013)

Sharma, A., Mehrotra, A.: Choosing an optimal channel mix in multichannel environments. Ind. Market. Manag. **36**, 21–28 (2007)

Sotiriadis, M.D., Van Zyl, C.: Electronic word-of-mouth and online reviews in tourism services: the use of twitter by tourists. Electron. Commer. Res. **13**(1), 103–124 (2013)

Su, N., Reynolds, D., Sun, B.: How to make your Facebook posts attractive: a case study. Int. J. Contemp. Hosp. Manag. **27**(8), 1772–1790 (2015)

Tham, A.G.J.: Social media in destination choice: distinctive electronic word-of- mouth dimensions. J. Travel Tour. Market. **30**(1–2), 144 (2013)

Verhoef, P.C., Kannan, P.K., Inman, J.: From multi-channel retailing to omni-channel retailing: introduction to the special issue on multi-channel retailing. J. Retail. **91**(2), 174–181 (2015)

Verma, R., Stock, D., McCarthy, L.: Customer preferences for online, social media, and mobile innovations in the hospitality industry. Cornell Hosp. Q. **53**(3), 183–186 (2012)

Yin, R.K.: Case Study Research, Design and Methods. Sage, London (2009)

Yu, Y., Duan, W., Cao, Q.: The impact of social and conventional media on firm equity value: a sentiment analysis approach. Decis. Support Syst. **55**, 919–926 (2013)

Yurova, Y., Rippé, C.B., Weisfeld-Spolter, S., Sussan, F., Arndt, A.: Not all adaptive selling to omni-consumers is influential: the moderating effect of product type. J. Retail. Consum. Serv. **34**, 271–277 (2017)

Zeng, B., Gerritsen, R.: What do we know about social media in tourism? A review. Tour. Manag. Perspect. **10**, 27–36 (2014)

Business Is Business: The Difference in Perception of Influencer's Morality Between Generation Y and Z

Nina Grgurić Čop(✉) and Barbara Culiberg

School of Economics and Business, University of Ljubljana, Ljubljana, Slovenia
nina.grguric.cop@efri.hr,
barbara.culiberg@ef.uni-lj.si

Abstract. Parallel to increased usage of influencer marketing among practitioners this type of advertising gained increased attention of the scientific community. Existing literature on the topic provides various findings on consumer responses to influencer marketing and this research adds to it by examining the potential moral issues from the followers' perspective. The results of four focus groups among members of Generations Y and Z showed there are four types of unethical conduct noticed, and they vary depending on the respondent's age. This research provides a starting point for examining potential consequences of different immoral actions that can be found in influencer marketing and gives practitioners more insight on the follower's responses toward influencer's online behavior, depending on their age.

Keywords: Influencer marketing · Native advertising · Deceptive behavior · Disclosure

1 Introduction

Social media influencers (SMIs) can advise thousands or millions of people at once (Thomas 2019) as they represent 'a new type of independent third-party endorser who shape audience attitudes through blogs, tweets, and the use of other social media' (Freberg et al. 2011). Although the research arena of social media influencers has grown immensely in the past few years, several literature gaps can be found that offer researchers the opportunity to push the field forward. As Woods (2016) noticed, there are some serious ethical issues arising from advertising through SMIs, because SMIs can take advantage of their position. In addition, Appel et al. (2019) recognized influencer marketing as a topic that needs immediate attention, especially when it comes to the type of content being posted, influencer's characteristics and sponsorship. The purpose of this paper is to shed light on the problematic behaviors of SMIs from the perspective of consumers from different generations since it was shown members of generations Z and Y respond differently to influencer marketing efforts (Kadekova and Holienčinová 2018). Existing studies on influencer marketing can generally be divided into the stream dealing with network theory research (e.g. Borrego et al. 2019) and the stream in business research with marketing and advertising journals

F. J. Martínez-López and S. D'Alessandro (Eds.): *Advances in Digital Marketing and eCommerce*, SPBE, pp. 56–61, 2020.
https://doi.org/10.1007/978-3-030-47595-6_8

predominating. In business research authors mainly explore relationships formed between influencers and their followers (Cooley Parks-Yancy 2019; Lou and Yuan 2019; De Veirman et al. 2017) or the interplay between brands and SMIs (e.g. Jimenez-Castillo and Sanchez-Fernandez 2019). Some researchers have taken the agency's perspective (Stoldt et al. 2019) while some focused on the comparison between platforms used (Arora et al. 2019) and metrics of SMI influence in general (Grave 2019). In understanding the issues associated with SMI, we also need to turn to literature on native advertising, which is a type of advertising where a brand "borrows from the credibility of another publisher by paying to distribute content on the publisher's platform that resembles the publisher's own content in format and substance" (Sweetser et al. 2016). The concept itself embraces the idea that some advertising is purposely embedded in the communicator's content what seems to fit the existing notion of influencer marketing. This brings about various ethical issues, the most common sort being non-disclosure where the question is whether informants disclosed the collaboration with brands to their audience. Stubb et al. (2019) note the importance of disclosure in native advertising showing justification for compensation generates most positive outcomes. Boerman et al. (2017) examined disclosure issue in the context of celebrities as SMIs and showed the negative effects of add recognition are diminished by the fact third-party (not a celebrity) is promoting the brand. And although disclosure was found to increase credibility of influencer marketing (Chapple and Cownie 2017) when the quality of presented content was high (Hwang and Jeong 2019) and increasing of positive attitudes towards the promoted brand (Evans et al. 2017) recent study by Dhanesh and Duthler (2019) indicates followers do not need disclosure since they are aware this kind of collaboration is payed. Compared to existing studies on the disclosure issue (e.g. van Reijmersdal et al. 2016) we undertake an exploratory approach, which provides a more granulated insight into how unethical behavior can be operationalized besides the disclosure issue that had been researched so far and thus the main contribution is expected to be broadening the possible pool of unethical behavior adopted by SMIs, beyond the disclosure itself. Besides that, previous research found it was experience with social media ads, and not the disclosure that leads to ad recognition (Jung and Heo 2019) which makes defining other potential moral issues necessary. In addition, we will provide a comparison of the attitudes of different generational cohorts in terms of different identified problematic activities of SMIs.

In sum, while studies on SMIs have focused on the issue of disclosure, other deceptive practices could be associated with influencer marketing as well. Based on this outline, we propose the following research question which will guide us in the empirical study: Which problematic activities do consumers associate with SMIs?

2 Sample and Methodology

In deciding what kind of research would be appropriate authors decided on using focus groups. The condition to be a suitable respondent was that they have followed or still follow at least one influencer on social media. In total, four focus groups were conducted. In the first two groups, there were 16 respondents belonging to Generation Z (one had 7 respondents, of which 7 were women, the other had 9 respondents, 5 of them were women). The other two focus groups were conducted among respondents of the Generation Y, aged 26 to 32 years. There were 25 respondents in total, 5 of which were male. Focus groups lasted from 40 to 60 min. A semi-structured approach was applied and questions on perception of influencers and potential moral issues in influencer marketing (perceived by respondents as followers) were posed. Transcripts were then analyzed without using a specific software, applying Corbin and Strauss's (2015) analyzing strategies - making comparisons, thinking about various meaning of a word, looking at language used. Then, on a printed version of transcripts different parts of text were detected and afterwards highlighted in digital version of transcripts.

3 Results

The main interest of this exploratory study was in examining the (un)ethical practices of SMIs. In the following, the main themes that emerged are presented and contrasted by comparing the younger (Generation Z) and older (Generation Y) followers.

Generation Y were the ones questioning who SMIs really are and expressed their **skepticism** about 'becoming' an influencer while respondents from Generation Z did not question it at all. All of the respondents were well aware that influencer marketing is just a novel type of advertising, considering brands that use them are '*currently the smartest ones*', '*keeping up with the times*' explaining they would '*do the same*' and those brands '*obviously do their job right*'.

Not surprisingly, the most often recognized immoral behavior of influencers was related to the **lack of disclosure**. In addition, the most obvious difference was noticed on the disclosure effect which was the breaking point (i.e. reason to unfollow) for older respondents but did not come up as such for younger respondents. Especially, Generation Y respondents found non-disclosing the link between influencers and brands a serious issue, calling such behavior "*horrible*" or a "*catastrophe!*". These respondents often mentioned morality of influencers as an important component for maintaining influencer-follower relationship, although they also expect the regulatory system to set the ground for those who deceive followers to be properly penalized. However, the younger respondents (20–25 years) showed surprisingly low interest in sponsorship disclosure which is in line with existing research (van Dam and van Reijmersdal 2019; Youn and Shin 2019). They appreciated it but did not think it was necessary: *"Not important, I will watch it either way.", "I don't see the need for disclosing"*. However, respondents of Generation Z were more inclined to stop following influencers because their 'perfect lives' made them feel bad about their everyday life. The paper by de Vierman et al. (2017) indicated brand's perceived uniqueness might be at risk when hiring an influencer with large number of followers to promote divergent products and Torres et al. (2019) found the importance of brand-influencer congruence. Indeed, the biggest concern for younger respondents was the fact some influencers **change 'expertise'** as the number of followers, and consequently brands to collaborate with, grows *"I consider that most of those influencers entered that world so to say – normal. I mean they gave good recommendations and so on, but as soon as they reached a certain number of followers and getting paid they shift and see only the money, not only* *to give a good recommendation."* Generation Y respondents considered it rather frivolous to act as an expert in one field and then, for example, give birth and suddenly become expert in babies. All respondents agreed that authenticity needs to be preserved to be taken seriously and perceived as an expert. In all focus groups the **distortion of reality** was mentioned as a negative aspect since their deception (in the form of photoshopped pictures, unreal testimonials, showing spoiled way of life) makes them feel bad, about what they do and how they live as the respondents' life is far from perfect and they can't even imagine living such a glamorous and careless life: *"...I think with young people it evokes jealousy and envy that someone can get big money so easily and then you think to yourself 'why would I bother? Why would I study and go to college why would I, I don't know do some hard-physical work when it can be that easy?'"*. As Byrne et al. (2017) noticed, SMIs often "*share false or misleading nutritional information with no scientific evidence*" and Coates et al. (2019) examined SMI's influence on changing children eating habit, both of which can lead to negative outcomes. Younger respondents in this research, obviously not so concerned with disclosure issues, did show serious concerns about potentially **problematic promotion of some product categories** has on the follower's life: "*...one product can be harmful and the other not, for example proteins (food supplement) can cause harm as oppose to make-up or clothes."*. This is especially problematic for non-convenience products or services which are not used every day, are of high value and have a great effect on people's lives. In all groups respondents expected some kind of **protection** against influencer and brand immoral actions, the only difference is some believe that it is the platform that has to make sure the followers were protected and in some cases it was the state law: *"As for the regulation - if in real life someone can't sell medicine around and has to have pharmaceutical degree on Instagram it should be someone with a degree."*, *"...I think it is important that the platform, i.e. Facebook (sets rules)."*, *"Social network has to set rules on what can be advertised and disclosed..."*.

4 Conclusion

Despite research on native advertising concentrated on the issue of disclosure as the most common deceptive behavior, the results of this study imply that Generation Y might be the last generation receptive to this issue. Future generations of followers (i.e. Generation Z) that grew up with social media will look at emerging advertising tools through a different lens. This might be due to the fact on social media Generation X trust mainly other users but Generation Y trusts company-generated information which would explain they accept SMIs as an extension of brands and see nothing disputable there. Our study provided a deeper understanding on both generational differences related to social media, and deceptive practices in SMI advertising that are worth addressing in future research. Thus, the main theoretical contribution is operationalization of immoral behavior employed in influencer marketing. As for practical implications, marketers should provide their audiences with enough evidence of SMI expertise and be careful when hiring SMI, especially when targeting consumers from different generational cohorts.

Acknowledgements. This paper has been financially supported by the University of Rijeka, for the project ZP UNIRI 1/19.

References

Appel, G., Grewal, L., Hadi, R., Stephen, A.T.: The future of social media in marketing. J. Acad. Market. Sci. **48**, 79–95 (2019)

Arora, A., Bansal, S., Kandpal, C., Aswani, R., Dwivedi, Y.: Measuring social media influencer index-insights from Facebook, Twitter and Instagram. J. Retail. Consum. Serv. **49**, 86–101 (2019)

Boerman, S.C., Willemsen, L.M., Van Der Aa, E.P.: ScienceDirect "This Post Is Sponsored" effects of sponsorship disclosure on persuasion knowledge and electronic word of mouth in the context of Facebook. J. Interact. Market. **38**, 82–92 (2017)

Borrego, C., Borrell, J., Robles, S.: Hey, influencer! Message delivery to social central nodes in social opportunistic networks. Comput. Commun. **137**, 81–91 (2019)

Byrne, E., Kearney, J., MacEvilly, C.: The role of influencer marketing and social influencers in public health. Proc. Nutr. Soc. **76**(OCE3) (2017)

Chapple, C., Cownie, F.: An investigation into viewers' trust in and response towards disclosed paid-for-endorsements by YouTube lifestyle vloggers. J. Promotional Commun. **5**(2) (2017)

Cooley, D., Parks-Yancy, R.: The effect of social media on perceived information credibility and decision making. J. Internet Commer. **18**(3), 249–269 (2019)

Corbin, J., Strauss, A.: Basics of Qualitative Research: Techniques and Procedures for Developing Grounded Theory. Sage, London (2015)

Coates, A.E., Hardman, C.A., Halford, J.C.G., Christiansen, P., Boyland, E.J.: The effect of influencer marketing of food and a "protective" advertising disclosure on children's food intake. Pediatr. Obes. **14**(10) (2019). e12540

Dhanesh, G.S., Duthler, G.: Relationship management through social media influencers: effects of followers' awareness of paid endorsement. Pub. Relat. Rev. **45**(3), 101765 (2019)

De Veirman, M., Cauberghe, V., Hudders, L.: Marketing through Instagram influencers: the impact of number of followers and product divergence on brand attitude. Int. J. Advert. **36**(5), 798–828 (2017)

Evans, N.J., Phua, J., Lim, J., Jun, H.: Disclosing Instagram influencer advertising: the effects of disclosure language on advertising recognition, attitudes, and behavioral intent. J. Interact. Advert. **17**(2), 138–149 (2017)

Freberg, K., Graham, K., McGaughey, K., Freberg, L.A.: Who are the social media influencers? A study of public perceptions of personality. Pub. Relat. Rev. **37**(1), 90–92 (2011)

Gräve, J.F.: What KPIs are key? Evaluating performance metrics for social media influencers. Soc. Media + Soc. **5**(3) (2019)

Hwang, Y., Jeong, S.H.: Editorial content in native advertising: how do brand placement and content quality affect native-advertising effectiveness? J. Advert. Res. **59**(2), 208–218 (2019)

Jiménez-Castillo, D., Sánchez-Fernández, R.: The role of digital influencers in brand recommendation: examining their impact on engagement, expected value and purchase intention. Int. J. Inf. Manag. **49**, 366–376 (2019)

Jung, A.R., Heo, J.: Ad disclosure vs. ad recognition: how persuasion knowledge influences native advertising evaluation. J. Interact. Advert. **19**(1), 1–14 (2019)

Kadekova, Z., Holienčinová, M.: Influencer marketing as a modern phenomenon creating a new frontier of virtual opportunities. Commun. Today **9**(2), 90–105 (2018)

Lou, C., Yuan, S.: Influencer marketing: how message value and credibility affect consumer trust of branded content on social media. J. Interact. Advert. **19**(1), 58–73 (2019)

Van Reijmersdal, E.A., Fransen, M.L., Van Noort, G., Opree, S.J., Vandeberg, L., Reusch, S., Van Lieshout, F.: Effects of disclosing sponsored content in blogs: how the use of resistance strategies mediates effects on persuasion. Am. Behav. Sci. **60**, 1458–1474 (2016)

Stoldt, R., Wellman, M., Ekdale, B., Tully, M.: Professionalizing and profiting: the rise of intermediaries in the social media influencer industry. Soc. Media + Soc. **5**(1) (2019)

Stubb, C., Nyström, A.G., Colliander, J.: Influencer marketing: The impact of disclosing sponsorship compensation justification on sponsored content effectiveness. J. Commun. Manag. **23**(2), 109–122 (2019)

Sweetser, K.D., Joo, S., Ahn, G., Golan, G.J., Hochman, A.: Native advertising as a new public relations tactic (2016). https://doi.org/10.1177/0002764216660138

Thomas, K.: Key opinion leaders supercharged by the Internet: paid doctor and patient influencers on social media. BMJ **2336**(5), 3–5 (2019)

Torres, P., Augusto, M., Matos, M.: Antecedents and outcomes of digital influencer endorsement: an exploratory study. Psychol. Market. **36**(12), 1267–1276 (2019)

Woods, S.: #Sponsored: the emergence of influencer marketing (2016)

van Dam, S., van Reijmersdal, E.: Insights in adolescents' advertising literacy, perceptions and responses regarding sponsored influencer videos and disclosures. Cyberpsychol.: J. Psychosoc. Res. Cyberspace **13**(2) (2019)

Youn, S., Shin, W.: Adolescents' responses to social media newsfeed advertising: the interplay of persuasion knowledge, benefit-risk assessment, and ad scepticism in explaining information disclosure. Int. J. Advert. **39**, 213–231 (2019)

Types of Electronic Word-of-Mouth and Their Impact on Consumer Attitudes

Robert Zniva[1(✉)], Wolfgang J. Weitzl[2], Julian M. Müller[1], and Andrea Schneider[1]

[1] Salzburg University of Applied Sciences, Salzburg, Austria
robert.zniva@fh-salzburg.ac.at
[2] Seeburg Castle University, Salzburg, Austria

Abstract. Numerous eWOM platforms have made it easy for consumers to share product-related information. The aim of the study is to investigate the influence of three commonly used eWOM types on consumer brand attitude. By manipulating the valence of the communicated messages, we shed light on the interaction of different eWOM types and provide insights on the relationship of social tie and valence and its role in attitude formation. Conducting two experiments we confirm three hypothesized relationships: First, by manipulating valence and eWOM type our results confirm that involved consumers are more influenced by conventional eWOM offering comprehensive information about the product from acquaintances or strangers (i.e., weak social ties) than by overall product ratings with their conveyed superficial normative cues (i.e., no social ties). Second, by introducing a third eWOM type in the experiment, so called social media eWOM, our findings confirm that this form of interpersonal communication (i.e., strong social ties) becomes so dominant that any other type of subsequently consulted eWOM – whether it be consistent or inconsistent with SeWOM in valence – becomes neglectable. Based on our results we propose to foster the capacity of review sites to signal social ties.

Keywords: Electronic word-of-mouth · Online reviews · Social media · Social tie · Trustworthiness

1 Introduction

Word-of-mouth (WOM) can be regarded as the most 'old-fashioned' – but often most effective – way for conveying information (Dellarocas 2003). Arndt (1967) defines WOM as a direct, person-to-person communication instrument involving a communicator who shares his/her opinions, feelings, etc. and a receiver who regards this information as independent of commercial influence. The independent influence on consumer behavior by means of interpersonal communication was further extended by the advance of the internet, which extended WOM to various additional virtual Web 2.0 settings. So called electronic word-of-mouth (eWOM), can be defined as any positive or negative statement made by potential, actual, or former customers about a product or company which is made available to a multitude of people and institutions

F. J. Martínez-López and S. D'Alessandro (Eds.): *Advances in Digital Marketing and eCommerce*, SPBE, pp. 62–69, 2020.
https://doi.org/10.1007/978-3-030-47595-6_9

via the internet (Hennig-Thurau et al. 2004). Today, consumers post their opinions, comments and reviews on products in various eWOM forms on different channels. Consumers usually trust other consumers more than sellers (Nieto et al. 2014), which makes eWOM a valuable source of new, relevant product knowledge. Mostly, it is the receiver's perception of truthful communication that makes eWOM one of the most influential factors determining consumer behavior. This perception is strongly dominated by content and source of eWOM messages (e.g. Cheng and Ho 2015). Different virtual channels of communication foster different aspects in terms of content and source of eWOM. Only a few marketing scholars have paid closer attention to the multifaceted appearances of different eWOM types, their characteristics, and their impact on consumer behavior (e.g. Yan et al. 2016). The study at hand identifies three commonly used eWOM types based on interactivity, scope of communication and representation of social tie. Furthermore, it investigates their respective impact on consumer brand perception by manipulating the valence of the communicated messages. By doing so, we shed light on the interaction of different eWOM types in a realistic and holistic scenario and provide more insights on the relationship of social tie and valence and their role in attitude formation.

2 Literature Review and Hypotheses

Litvin et al. (2008) classify different eWOM types according to two basic dimensions: (1) the level of interactivity and (2) the scope of communication. Concerning eWOM's interactivity they acknowledge that information sharing can – similar to traditional WOM – happen synchronously (e.g. instant messaging by WhatsApp) or asynchronously when not all communicators and receivers are required to be present at the same time (e.g. product review websites). The second dimension involves the complexity of consumer participation or – in other words – whether the communication links one consumer with another (i.e., 'one-to-one communication' by email, etc.), it connects a single consumer with many others (i.e., 'one-to-many communication' by product review sites), or eWOM links many consumers with many others (e.g. virtual communities).

Given the multifold appearances and the likelihood that consumers regularly consult various eWOM sources before making (important) purchasing decisions, this research focuses on consumer reactions to sequentially consulted popular eWOM types. More specifically, we investigate the effects on consumers' brand attitude of three discrete eWOM types, which vary in their basic characteristics: First, *social media electronic word-of-mouth* (SeWOM) which are positive or negative full-text reviews on a product or service send by one consumer to a single other consumer (i.e., a dedicated person). This eWOM type exerts informational influences on the receiver given his/her judgment of the relevant content of a message such as its argument quality (Filieri et al. 2018). We assume that this (synchronous) one-to-one-communication is influenced by a high level of interpersonal relationship strength. In literature, tie strength is defined as the degree to which a person is willing to maintain some relationship with peers through social interactions (Wang et al. 2012). SeWOM typically originates from product reviewers who are known by the receiver and with whom the receiver hence has a very close relationship or strong ties. Second, full-text reviews can also come from consumers with whom the receiver has no or only a very causal relationship such as strangers or acquaintances. We define these positive or negative statements about a product or service as *conventional electronic word-of-mouth* (CeWOM). CeWOM is a form of (asynchronous) one-to-many communication which exerts informational influence by means of – often comprehensive – reviews discussing a product's pros and cons. The third form is *rating-based electronic word-of-mouth* (ReWOM). Here, social influence is exerted with normative cues which indicate the social pressure on individuals to conform to the opinions and expectations of a group (Deutsch and Gerard 1955). One typical appearance of ReWOM are product ratings which are any signals that are presented on a website (e.g. overall rating) in an effort to guide consumers towards some products that are recommended based on some criteria (e.g. product attributes). Aggregated ratings represent abstract, superficial, and asynchronous information with little social traces emanating from other consumers, unknown to the receiver.

Literature indicates that *eWOM's valence* (i.e., the positive or negative evaluation of a product or service by the reviewer) can exert strong influences on consumer behaviors (e.g. Mayzlin et al. 2012), demonstrating that positive (negative) eWOM can stimulate (hinder) consumers' approach behaviors (e.g. purchasing likelihood) and increase favorable (unfavorable) thoughts towards the discussed product. This effect seems to originate from eWOM's trustworthiness perceived by the receiver (e.g. Reimer and Benkenstein 2016; Sussman and Siegal 2003). When eWOM is trustworthy, the valence of the review or recommendation leads to the (favorable/unfavorable) direction of the receivers' attitudes intended by the sender.

We assume that in the 'classic situation' – when eWOM receivers are not influenced by prior SeWOM communication – CeWOM is more influential than ReWOM in purchasing situations which are regarded as being relevant for the consumer (e.g. high-cost purchases). According to the dual-process models heuristic-systematic model (HSM; Chaiken 1980) and elaboration likelihood model (ELM; Petty and Cacioppo 1986) individuals typically apply two different modes of information processing to form their product judgments: When their motivation (i.e., involvement) and ability to process information are both sufficiently high, consumers engage in systematic processing (HSM) or follow the central route (ELM). This basically means that they use considerable mental effort to scrutinize the content of a message and to form their personal attitudes towards the discussed product or service based on informational social influences. In case, however, their motivation or cognitive capacity are low, individuals adopt heuristics and simple decision rules for making purchasing decisions (e.g. the recommendation of the masses should be followed). Following this rationale, we argue that for important purchasing decisions involved consumers are more influenced by CeWOM offering comprehensive information about the product from acquaintances or strangers (i.e., weak social ties) than by overall product ratings with their conveyed superficial normative cues (no social tie).

H1: In SeWOM's absence, [positive/negative] CeWOM has a stronger influence on consumers' brand attitude than [positive/negative] ReWOM.

We further assume that in case consumers consult SeWOM in the course of their purchasing process, this form of interpersonal communication becomes so dominant that any other type of subsequently consulted eWOM – whether it be consistent or inconsistent with SeWOM – becomes neglectable. SeWOM is very similar to traditional WOM such that it typically originates from strong ties. Receivers regard SeWOM as conveying useful and relevant knowledge (Levin and Cross 2004) which makes it more influential than eWOM from weak ties (Wang et al. 2018; Choi et al. 2017; De Bruyn and Lilien 2008; Smith et al. 2005). We assume that this effect is so strong that neither information influences (i.e., CeWOM – full-text reviews by unknown others) nor normative influences (i.e., ReWOM – overall product rating by unknown others) that are either supportive or unsupportive to the original SeWOM message (i.e., pro-claiming the same or a different stance towards the discussed product) can affect (involved) consumers' attitudes. Therefore, we hypothesize:

H2: Positive SeWOM leads to a more positive consumers' brand attitude than negative SeWOM.
H3: Neither (a) CeWOM's nor (b) ReWOM's valence moderate the effect of SeWOM's valence on brand attitude.

3 Methodology

In order to test the hypotheses developed, an experiment was conducted. Representing an important field for eWOM, hotel reviews were chosen. Two independent variables are examined. Factor 1 includes the valence of rating, and factor 2 the eWOM type. Using computer assisted personal interviews, a convenience sample of 343 students from a mid-sized German-speaking university were surveyed. These were randomly divided into four subgroups of almost equal size. 57,1% of responses are from females and 42,9% from males, ranging from 18 to 50 years. Both groups showed similar distribution of age, marital status and gender. Regarding the eWOM channels, Booking.com was perceived as a suitable online retailer website to represent examples of ReWOM and SeWOM. Guests who have booked their stay via Booking.com can leave a review. As readers cannot identify the author of the review, there is a weak relationship between the sender and receiver of eWOM and thus a suitable channel for the weak social tie in CeWOM. In addition to the individual reviews, Booking.com offers an overall ranking. where reviewers can assign a rating of one to ten to eight characteristics. This overall rating served as example of ReWOM. Further, WhatsApp was selected as social media channel for exchange with strong social ties. Group conversations can also take place, but the focus is on the private conversation between two people. WhatsApp is thus a closed social media platform and serves as an example of SeWOM.

The first experiment was to investigate H1. It focused on the following scenario: The subjects were instructed that they are searching for a hotel to stay at on Lake Garda and come across reviews of a specific hotel brand. First, the subject was shown the overall ranking on Booking.com. On the next page the latest three personal ratings on Booking.com of the hotel were presented, which contradicted in valence the previously seen overall ranking. After seeing both reviews respondent's attitudes towards the hotel brand were evaluated assessing the valence of the eight in the reviews described attributes rated on a five-point-scale from "I totally agree" to "I totally disagree". The second experiment investigated H2 and H3. It focused on the following scenario: Like in the first setting the participants were instructed that they are looking out for a hotel at Lake Garda. Then test persons received a recommendation for a hotel from a person via WhatsApp (SeWOM), who they defined a priori to have a strong social tie with. Subsequently, the subjects got information about the hotel on Booking.com in form of an overall rating (ReWOM) or a personal review (CeWOM). Evaluations on Booking.com always contradicted the previously seen WhatsApp evaluation. Again, similar to the first experiment, attitudes were measured after exposing participants to both reviews.

The positive and negative content of ReWOM, CeWOM and SeWOM reviews were held constant and evaluated the hotel on Booking.com's eight characteristics (staff, cleanliness, location, value for money, facilities, comfort, WiFi and breakfast) and differed only in the presented format. The investigated hotel brands differed between the first and the second scenario, were invented by the authors, and did not exist as an actual brand at the site. A pretest with 10 participants were conducted before the actual experiment and led to minor changes in wording of the scenarios. Table 1 summarizes the design and test group sizes of the two experiments.

Table 1. Overview of manipulations in valence for both experiments

	Experiment 1		Experiment 2		
	ReWOM	CeWOM	SeWOM	ReWOM	CeWOM
Group 1 (n = 85)	Positive	Negative	Positive	Negative	–
Group 2 (n = 85)			Negative	Positive	–
Group 3 (n = 84)	Negative	Positive	Positive	–	Negative
Group 4 (n = 89)			Negative	–	Positive

4 Results

Before further evaluation, a reliability analysis was conducted. It resulted in a Cronbach Alpha of $\alpha = 0.962$, thus confirming that the attitude items are internally consistent. In the following, the three hypotheses are evaluated.

In order to test H1, the first experiment is examined. Table 2 summarizes the means and standard deviations for both investigated experimental situations. To test differences in attitude between the two groups we conducted a t-test. With a t-value of $t(334.796) = -13.776$ ($p < 0.05$), those test subjects who received a positive overall ranking and negative current evaluations have a rather negative to neutral attitude towards the hotel ($M = 2.6294$, $SD = 0.79812$, $n = 170$), and those subjects who saw a negative overall ranking and positive current ratings have a rather positive attitude towards the hotel ($M = 3.7514$, $SD = 0.70839$, $n = 173$). The effect size according to

Cohen (1992) is $d = -1.4922$, resembling a large effect. Based on the results H1 is accepted and it can be concluded that CeWOM has a greater impact on consumer attitudes than the ReWOM.

Table 2. Results of experiment 1

	Experiment 1		Results
	ReWOM	CeWOM	Overall attitude
Group 1 + 2 (n = 170)	Positive	Negative	M = 2.62; SD = 0.79
Group 3 + 4 (n = 173)	Negative	Positive	M = 3.75; SD = 0.70

In order to test H2 and H3, the second experiment is examined. Table 3 summarizes the means and standard deviations for all investigated experimental situations. To test differences in attitude between the groups an ANOVA was conducted. A value of $F\,(3{,}339) = 51{,}602$ ($p < 0{,}001$) is determined and the overall model is significant. That is, there is a significant difference between the four groups.

Table 3. Results of experiment 2

	Experiment 2			Results
	SeWOM	ReWOM	CeWOM	Overall attitude
Group 1 (n = 85)	Positive	Negative	–	M = 3.61; SD = 0.90
Group 2 (n = 85)	Negative	Positive	–	M = 2.35; SD = 0.93
Group 3 (n = 84)	Positive	–	Negative	M = 3.64; SD = 0.77
Group 4 (n = 89)	Negative	–	Positive	M = 2.60; SD = 0.83

To find out exactly where the difference lies, pair comparisons are carried out, using a Bonferroni post hoc test. Test groups 1 and 3 and test groups 2 and 4 do not differ significantly in their setting ($p > 0.05$). Trial groups 1 and 2 and trial groups 3 and 4 differ significantly ($p > 0.000$). The effect size is $f^2 = 0.675$ and thus one speaks of a strong effect ($f^2 > 0.35$). In summary, it can be said that two groups can be formed (all $p < 0.05$). Groups 1 ($M = 3.612$, $SD = 0.9010$) and 3 ($M = 3.643$, $SD = 0.7706$) form a group, as do group 2 ($M = 2.353$, $SD = 0.9349$) and group 4 ($M = 2.607$, $SD = 0.8342$), $f^2 = 0.675$. In sum, the SeWOM had a significantly greater influence on the attitudes of the subjects compared to ReWOM and CeWOM, regardless of the valence communicated. Based on our results we can accept H2 and H3.

5 Conclusion

The aim of the study at hand is to investigate the influence of three commonly used eWOM types on consumer brand perception. Using two experiments we confirm all three hypothesized relationships. First, by manipulating valence (positive/negative) and eWOM type (ReWOM/CeWOM) our results confirm that involved consumers are more influenced by CeWOM offering comprehensive information about the product from acquaintances or strangers than by overall product ratings with their conveyed superficial normative cues. Second, by introducing the SeWOM type in the experiment, our findings confirm that this form of interpersonal communication becomes so dominant that any other type of subsequently consulted eWOM – whether it be consistent or inconsistent in valence – becomes neglectable. The theoretical contribution of the study lies within the combination of valence and social tie represented by the nature of communication on the investigated platforms. All used eWOM types can be considered as trustworthy information sources. However, while findings of the first experiment are in line with theories like the ELM or the HSM, the inclusion of the third type of SeWOM disrupts these typical relationships. Especially the relationship between CeWOM and SeWOM is noteworthy. These two eWOM types contain, according to our design, the same informational comprehensiveness. Therefore, we argue based on our findings that social tie (a typical heuristic or simple decision rule) plays a more dominant role than informational comprehensiveness in attitude formation and can be triggered by the nature of review type. According to our preliminary results practitioners are well advised to use eWOM platforms which can signal strong social ties. This can be done by introducing typical features of social network sites into one-to-many review sites (e.g. personal messages). Also the communication of reviews on existing social media platforms should be improved. Overall ratings of products and services should be enriched with information of friends and relatives who already participated in the rating or ranked according to social tie strength. Finally, companies are well advised to motivate customers to share their experiences with strong social ties on e.g. messenger platforms. Similar to all studies this research is not exempt from limitations. First the sample is a convenience sample, was composed of students and limited in sample size. Second, the experimental stimulus was limited to a specific industry (travel). Third, manipulation of eWOM type was restricted to a certain hierarchical sequence. Fourth, manipulation of valence did not include congruent scenarios (e.g. positive/positive). Fifth, other source- and content-related aspects (e.g. social identity) can lead to additional insights. We encourage future research to account for these limitations.

References

Arndt, J.: Role of product-related conversations in the diffusion of a new product. J. Market. Res. **4**(3), 291–295 (1967)

Chaiken, S.: Heuristic versus systematic information processing and the use of source versus message cues in persuasion. J. Pers. Soc. Psychol. **39**(5), 752 (1980)

Cheng, Y.H., Ho, H.Y.: Social influence's impact on reader perceptions of online reviews. J. Bus. Res. **68**(4), 883–887 (2015)

Choi, Y., Seo, Y., Yoon, S.: E-WOM messaging on social media: social ties, temporal distance, and message concreteness. Internet Res. **27**(3), 495–505 (2017)

Cohen, J.: A power primer. Psychol. Bull. **112**(1), 155–159 (1992)

De Bruyn, A., Lilien, G.-L.: A multi-stage model of word-of-mouth influence through viral marketing. Int. J. Res. Market. **25**(3), 151–163 (2008)

Dellarocas, C.: The digitization of word of mouth: promise and challenges of online feedback mechanisms. Manag. Sci. **49**(10), 1407–1424 (2003)

Deutsch, M., Gerard, H.B.: A study of normative and informational social influences upon individual judgment. J. Abnorm. Soc. Psychol. **51**(3), 629 (1955)

Filieri, R., Raguseo, E., Vitari, C.: When are extreme ratings more helpful? Empirical evidence on the moderating effects of review characteristics and product type. Comput. Hum. Behav. **88**, 134–142 (2018)

Hennig-Thurau, T., Gwinner, K.P., Walsh, G., Gremler, D.D.: Electronic word-of-mouth via consumer-opinion platforms: what motivates consumers to articulate themselves on the internet? J. Interact. Market. **18**(1), 38–52 (2004)

Levin, D.Z., Cross, R.: The strength of weak ties you can trust: the mediating role of trust in effective knowledge transfer. Manag. Sci. **50**(11), 1477–1490 (2004)

Litvin, S.W., Goldsmith, R.E., Pan, B.: Electronic word-of-mouth in hospitality and tourism management. Tour. Manag. **29**(3), 458–468 (2008)

Mayzlin, D., Dover, Y., Chevalier, J.: Promotional reviews: an empirical investigation of online review manipulation promotional reviews. Yale Working Paper (2012)

Nieto, J., Hernández-Maestro, R.M., Muñoz-Gallego, P.A.: Marketing decisions, customer reviews, and business performance: the use of the Toprural website by Spanish rural lodging establishments. Tour. Manag. **45**, 115–123 (2014)

Petty, R.E., Cacioppo, J.T.: The elaboration likelihood model of persuasion. In: Communication and Persuasion, pp. 1–24. Springer, New York (1986)

Reimer, T., Benkenstein, M.: Altruistic eWOM marketing: more than an alternative to monetary incentives. J. Retail. Consum. Serv. **31**, 323–333 (2016)

Smith, D., Menon, S., Sivakumar, K.: Online peer and editorial recommendations, trust, and choice in virtual markets. J. Interact. Market. **19**(3), 15–37 (2005)

Sussman, S.W., Siegal, W.S.: Informational influence in organizations: an integrated approach to knowledge adoption. Inf. Syst. Res. **14**(1), 47–65 (2003)

Wang, J.J., Wang, L.Y., Wang, M.M.: Understanding the effects of eWOM social ties on purchase intentions: a moderated mediation investigation. Electron. Commer. Res. Appl. **28**, 54–62 (2018)

Wang, X., Yu, C., Wei, Y.: Social media peer communication and impacts on purchase intentions: a consumer socialization framework. J. Interact. Market. **26**(4), 198–208 (2012)

Yan, Q., Wu, S., Wang, L., Wu, P., Chen, H., Wei, G.: E-WOM from e-commerce websites and social media: which will consumers adopt? Electron. Commer. Res. Appl. **17**, 62–73 (2016)

The Drivers of Video Popularity on YouTube: An Empirical Investigation

Ana Cristina Munaro[1](✉), Renato Hübner Barcelos[2], Eliane Cristine Francisco Maffezzolli[1], João Pedro Santos Rodrigues[3], and Emerson Cabrera Paraiso[3]

[1] PPAD, Pontifical Catholic University of Parana (PUCPR), Curitiba, Brazil
ana.munaro@pucpr.edu.br
[2] École des Sciences de la Gestion, UQÀM, Montréal, Canada
[3] PPGIa, PUCPR, Curitiba, Brazil

Abstract. In this article, we present and test a model of drivers for video post popularity on YouTube. In this conceptual model, video characteristics such as linguistics style, subjectivity, emotion polarity and video category influence online video popularity on YouTube (i.e. the number of likes, dislikes, and comments). The results of the analysis of more than 11,000 videos from 150 digital influencers show that not all factors that help to boost the number of likes have a similar effect on the number of comments - or the number of dislikes. In summary, medium-length and long videos posted during non-business hours, using analytical/informative content and subjective language style, are more likely to receive likes and comments. Moreover, the use of negative or moderate emotion helps to promote a general interest in the video.

Keywords: Video popularity · Linguistic style · Emotional polarity · Engagement · YouTube

1 Introduction

Social media has become an essential part of digital marketing strategies (Arora et al. 2019). Among social media platforms, YouTube has emerged as a leader in video sharing (Aggrawal et al. 2018). Worldwide, 1.9 billion users watch more than one billion hours of video every day, and advertisers are predicted to invest 11.76 billion U.S. dollars in the platform in 2020 (Statista 2019).

Given the amounts invested on YouTube, digital marketers are interested in knowing what kind of video content drives customers' online engagement. So far, previous literature has focused mostly on the contents of posts on Facebook pages (e.g., Banerjee and Chua 2019; Hughes et al. 2019; Sabate et al. 2014) and Twitter pages (Francalanci and Hussain 2017). However, engagement in video-sharing platforms may have different characteristics from other social media. Moreover, while YouTube shares some engagement measures with other platforms, such as likes and comments, it also includes dislikes, which have not been considered in those studies.

Hence, in this study, we aim to investigate which features of a video drive its popularity on YouTube. We present and test a conceptual model empirically to determine how elements such as the video's linguistics style, its category and length

F. J. Martínez-López and S. D'Alessandro (Eds.): *Advances in Digital Marketing and eCommerce*, SPBE, pp. 70–79, 2020.
https://doi.org/10.1007/978-3-030-47595-6_10

impact on video popularity. For this purpose, we analyze the transcriptions of the content of more than 11,000 videos from 150 digital influencers across different categories, as well and their number of likes, dislikes, and comments.

The findings of this study contribute to the knowledge about social influencer marketing and online advertising by providing managers with concrete insights on how to develop videos able to attract customer attention and promote online engagement. Moreover, the findings also provide information on how to choose the most appropriate channels for sponsorship/advertisements.

2 Factors Impacting Online Video Popularity

The online video popularity of YouTube videos can be evaluated by the number of views, likes, dislikes, comments and shares (Aggrawal et al. 2018; Banerjee and Chua 2019; Sabate et al. 2014). These measures show the viewers' satisfaction with its content and can indicate whether the product/service featured is going to be a hit in the market or not (Aggrawal et al. 2018). However, not all measures of popularity are influenced in the same way. For instance, some studies show that not some factors responsible for increasing the number of likes of a post do not increase the number of comments (De Vries et al. 2012; Sabate et al. 2014). Overall, it is easier to convince users to like a publication than to share it (Banerjee and Chua 2019). Moreover, a popular video can receive a high number of likes and dislikes at the same time, reflecting mixed feelings towards it. In this study, we focus mainly on the video's linguistics style and its category as determinants of popularity, while considering factors such as its duration and time of publication as control variables.

2.1 Linguistics Style

Language is the most common and reliable way for people to translate their internal thoughts and emotions into a form that others can understand. In this sense, we consider the influencer's analytical thinking, externally focused style, emotional polarity, and subjectivity as the linguistics style of YouTube videos.

Analytical thinking reflects the degree to which texts contain a narrative versus analytical style (Pennebaker et al. 2015). An analytical style is argumentative and presents logical or associative ideas and facts. On the other hand, a narrative style serves as a cognitive vehicle for constructing a sense of self by structuring events in time and space (Escalas and Bettman 2000).

The *external focus* represents a speech that addresses its audience directly with the intent of making them feel as if they are part of the event (Ferchaud et al. 2018). This style usually suggests that the author is speaking from a perspective of high expertise and confidence (Pennebaker et al. 2015), which favours the consumer's engagement (Aleti et al. 2019; Xu and Zhang 2018). People using an externally focused style usually have higher status and exert more influence in social interactions (Jordan et al. 2019).

Emotional polarity represents the degree to which people express emotion and the valence of that emotion (Tausczik and Pennebaker 2010). People usually feel more inclined toward socializing with those individuals who make them feel good (Aleti et al. 2019); thus, positive emotional polarity is associated with more sharing (Xu and Zhang 2018).

Subjectivity expresses a person's feelings, views, or beliefs, as opposed to objectivity, which reveals factual information about the world (Liu and Bing 2012). The followers of trustworthy influencers who show expertise on the subject are more likely to purchase the featured products (Sokolova and Kefi 2020). In this sense, informative videos with more objective sentences than subjective ones can be better evaluated by consumers.

2.2 Video Category

How a video is interacted with and commented is often a result of its content's nature. For instance, the type of comments for a music video will be quite different from those for a comedy video (Yew and Shamma 2011). Hence, different video categories should be associated with different patterns and interactions. By identifying these patterns in the social metadata, it is possible to predict a video's specific category based on particular responses of social activity (Yew and Shamma 2011).

2.3 Control Variables

The *time and date of posting* have a significant influence on post popularity (Sabate et al. 2014). For instance, since YouTube is a platform based on audiovisual content, we assume that consumers will prefer to watch videos at non-business hours. Moreover, we expect consumers to visit brand fan pages more often on weekends than on weekdays, which can result in higher popularity for posts placed during weekends (De Vries et al. 2012; Hughes et al. 2019).

The *video length* can also influence its popularity. Even though the consequences of video length on YouTube have not yet been explored in literature, we expect long and medium-length videos to be more popular than short videos with the audience. On Facebook, Banerjee and Chua (2019) have shown that the length of a post is negatively correlated to its likelihood of sharing. However, consumers' motivations on YouTube are different and they might use it mainly to relax and learn new things.

2.4 Study Model

Based on the previous discussion, we developed a conceptual model about the influence of video characteristics on video popularity (see Fig. 1).

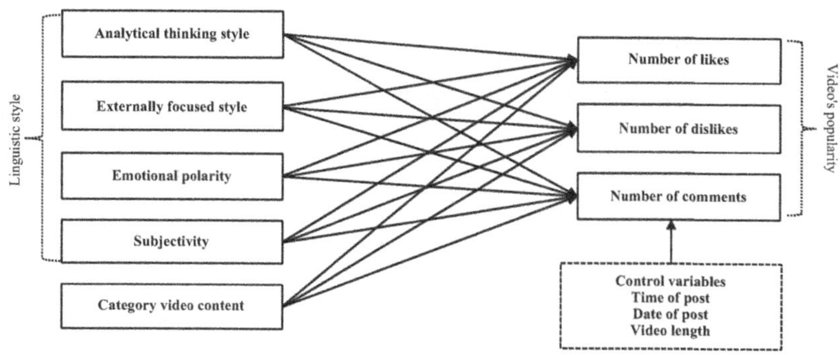

Fig. 1. Conceptual framework.

3 Methodology

Data included the number of likes, dislikes, and comments, among other video post characteristics, from a total of 11,177 published videos. Also, we used an open-source tool to extract all available auto-generated captions for the videos, which converts audio to textual data. Then, these texts were processed through a machine-learning model and the Linguistic Inquiry and Word Count software (LIWC) from Pennebaker et al. (2015) to generate variables of linguistic and emotional style.

Operationalization of Main Variables. We summarize the information and descriptive statistics for all variables in Table 1. The dependent variables of *video popularity* were evaluated by the number of likes, dislikes, and comments, as in similar studies (Aggrawal et al. 2018; De Vries et al. 2012; Arora et al. 2019; Hughes et al. 2019).

The first two elements of linguistic style were calculated through automated text analysis using the software Linguistic Inquiry and Word Count (LIWC) from Pennebaker et al. (2015). Their outcomes were standardized converted to percentiles (0 to 100) and represent the ratio of words corresponding to that specific style. The first element, *analytical thinking*, shows how analytical/argumentative video content is versus a more narrative style. A high number reflects formal, logical, and hierarchical thinking, while a lower number reflects more informal, personal, and narrative thinking (Pennebaker et al. 2015). The second element, the *external focus*, correspond to the 'clout' category in LIWC. A high number suggests that the author is using more we-words and social words and fewer I-words, while a low number indicates a more tentative, humble, even anxious style (Pennebaker et al. 2015; Xu and Zhang 2018). The next two elements, *emotional polarity* and *subjectivity*, were obtained through a machine learning model trained to classify the polarity and subjectivity of an input text. The model used for this classification used a Naive Bayes algorithm with the open-source TextBlob tool. The output values for polarity range from −1 to +1, with +1 being an extremely positive text, −1 extremely negative. For the analysis model, however, these values were normalized to a scale from 0 to +1 using the MinMaxScaler formula. The output values for subjectivity values vary from 0 to +1, +1 being a very subjective text and 0 a very objective one.

The *video's category* is the YouTube classification of a video based on its contents. Similar to Ferchaud et al. (2018), our study sorted videos into one of eleven genres: beauty, entertainment, fashion, fitness, food, gaming, home, kids, parenting, tech & business, and travel.

Table 1. Variable information and descriptive statistics

Continuous variables	Notation	Minimum	Maximum	Mean	Std. dev.
Number of likes	y_{1j}	0.000	8,242,848	71,670.92	193350.98
N. of dislikes	y_{2j}	0.000	591,233	1,900.13	9502.193
N. of comments	y_{3j}	0.000	815,963	6,697.04	23146.8
Analytical thinking	$analytic_j$	0.000	99.00	31.9724	19.61932
External focus	$clout_j$	0.000	99.00	66.4849	20.12769
Emotional polarity	$emotion_j$	0.000	1.000	0.458171	0.061071
Subjectivity	$subjectivity_j$	0.000	1.000	0.514227	0.067938
Categorical variables	**Notation**	**Categories**		**N**	**Percent**
Time of video posting	$post\_hour_j$	1 (Business hour)		3033	27.10%
		0 (Non-business hour)		8144	72.90%
Date of video posting	$post\_weekd_j$	1 (Weekend)		3854	34.50%
		0 (Weekday)		7323	65.50%
Video length	$length_j$	Long length (>20 min)		1415	12.70%
		Medium length (10–19 min)		4274	38.20%
		Short length (<10 min)		5488	49.10%
Video category	$category_j$	Travel		755	6.80%
		Tech & Business		914	8.20%
		Parenting		874	7.80%
		Kids		730	6.50%
		Home		906	8.10%
		Gaming		1293	11.60%
		Food		817	7.30%
		Fitness		1129	10.10%
		Fashion		1142	10.20%
		Entertainment		1265	11.30%
		Beauty		1352	12.10%

Control Variables: Similar to Sabate et al. (2014), we categorized the time of posting between business hours (8 am to 6 pm on Monday to Thursday; 8 am to 3 pm on Friday) and non-business hours (any other time). We also categorized the date of video posting between weekdays and weekends (Sabate et al. 2014; Hughes et al. 2019). Video length was operationalized by the creation of dummy variables representing three total video durations: short videos (from 0 to 9:59 min long), medium-length videos (from 10:00 to 19:59 min long), and long-term videos (more than 20:00 min long).

Analysis Model. As much of the data are overdispersed, we choose a negative binomial distribution (Hughes et al. 2019; van Laer et al. 2018) with maximum likelihood estimates (MLE). This distribution allows better goodness of fit of the model according to the Akaike and the Bayesian information criteria (AIC and BIC) than the Poisson-gamma mixture distribution (NB2). The three dependent variables for video post popularity are the number of likes, the number of dislikes, and the number of comments per video post *j*. The model can be expressed as:

$$\begin{aligned}(log_{\lambda ij})\gamma_{ij} = \beta_0 + \beta_1(category_j) + \beta_2(length_j) + \beta_3(post\_hour_j) \\ + \beta_4(post\_weekday_j) + \beta_5(analytic_j) + \beta_6(clout_j) \\ + \beta_7(subjectivity_j) + \beta_8(emotion_j) + \in_{ij} .\end{aligned}$$

where $log_{\lambda ij}$ is the rate of the negative binomial distribution process and $\in_{ij}$ is the distributed error terms for dependent variables y_{1j}, y_{2j} and y_{3j}.

4 Results

Table 2 reports the results of the model with video likes, dislikes and comments as the dependent variables (N = 11,177). To determine the effect sizes, we used the incidence rate ratio (IRR) or the factor by which positive scores (>1) would be expected to increase the predictor variable by one standard deviation, ceteris paribus.

Number of Likes. The effect of the video's analytic thinking on the number of likes was significant and positive (β = 0.002, p = 0.019, IRR = 1.002), which shows that a more formal and logical style, with hierarchical thinking, promotes a higher number of likes. External focus had a significant and negative effect (β = −0.003, p = 0.003, IRR = 0.997), which suggests that a more tentative, humble, even anxious language style seems to be more appreciated. Emotional polarity also had a negative effect (β = −5,422, p = 0.000, IRR = 0.004), which suggests that a very positive language style is not as effective as one expressing more negative emotions. Subjectivity, on the other hand, influenced the number of likes positively (β = 3.214, p = 0.000, IRR = 24.869), which means that consumers enjoy when influencers express their opinions, beliefs and feelings.

For the effect of the video category, we compared the ten categories with 'beauty' (base variable). The only category positively associated with a higher number of likes was 'entertainment' (β = 0.149, p = 0.023, IRR = 1.161), which means that entertainment videos tend to receive more likes than any others. The categories 'travel' (β = −0.197, p = 0.011, IRR = 0.821), 'kids' (β = −0.153, p = 0.047, IRR = 0.858), 'home' (β = −0.132, p = 0.067, IRR = 0.877), 'fitness' (β = −0.219, p = 0.002, IRR = 0.803) and 'fashion' (β = −0.206, p = 0.002, IRR = 0.814) were negatively associated with the number of likes when compared to the base content, meaning that on YouTube, videos in these categories do not get as many likes than the other ones.

Regarding the posting time, videos posted during business hours receive significantly fewer likes than those posted on non-business hours (β = −0,842, p = 0.000, IRR = 0.431). Moreover, videos posted on weekends receive significantly fewer likes than those posted on weekdays (β = −0.167, p = 0.000, IRR = 0.847). Finally, medium-length videos are associated with a higher number of likes than short ones (β = 0.105, p = 0.003, IRR = 1.111), and long videos receive even more likes than medium and short ones (β = 0.44, p = 0.000, IRR = 1.553). This result shows that YouTube favours long-content videos over short ones.

Table 2. Model Results

Variable	Log post likes	Log post dislikes	Log post comments
Intercept	12.239*** (0.1456)	9.545*** (0.1282)	9.187*** (0.1899)
Date post *(dummy)*	−0.167*** (0.0367)	−0.057 (0.04)	0.083* (0.043)
Time post *(dummy)*	−0.842*** (0.0396)	−0.761*** (0.0426)	−0.845*** (0.0466)
Video length longer *(dummy)*	0.44*** (0.0499)	0.27*** (0.0541)	0.93*** (0.0589)
Video length medium *(dummy)*	0.105** (0.0348)	−0.119** (0.0371)	0.274*** (0.0406)
Video category travel	−0.197** (0.0773)	−0.031 (0.0838)	−0.038 (0.0912)
Category tech & business	−0.088 (0.0718)	−0.027 (0.0777)	−0.035 (0.0843)
Category parenting	0.055 (0.0736)	−0.036 (0.0797)	0.068 (0.0864)
Category kids	−0.153** (0.0772)	0.161* (0.085)	−0.111 (0.0908)
Category home	−0.132* (0.072)	−0.274*** (0.078)	−0.034 (0.0843)
Category gaming	−0.083 (0.0643)	0.05 (0.0696)	0.121 (0.0756)
Category food	0.08 (0.0784)	0.039 (0.0827)	0.316** (0.0926)
Category fitness	−0.219** (0.0696)	−0.114 (0.0752)	−0.165** (0.0817)
Category fashion	−0.206** (0.0667)	−0.207** (0.0718)	−0.14* (0.0783)
Category entertainment	0.149** (0.0658)	0.178** (0.0711)	0.233** (0.0769)
Analytic thinking	0.002** (0.0009)	0.003** (0.0009)	0.001 (0.001)
External focus (clout)	−0.003** (0.0009)	−0.001 (0.001)	−0.001 (0.001)
Emotional polarity	−5.422*** (0.2517)	−3.786*** (0.2198)	−6.674*** (0.299)
Subjectivity	3.214*** (0.205)	−0.281* (0.1597)	4.737*** (0.2867)
Overdispersion (α)	2.691 (0.029)	3.131 (0.0338)	3.717 (0.0415)
AIC	257800.881	172562.24	193313.802
BIC	257947.313	172708.672	193460.234

Notes: For dummy's variables, the results were compared with the baseline variables, not reported in the table. Number of betas (*β*), standard errors are in parentheses. AIC = Akaike information criterion; BIC = Bayesian information criterion. * p < 0.10; ** p < 0.05; *** p < 0.001.

Number of Dislikes. The effect of analytical thinking on the number of dislikes was significant and positive (β = 0.003, p = 0.003, IRR = 1.003), i.e., a more formal and logical style, with hierarchical thinking, promotes a higher number of dislikes. Both positive emotional polarity ($\beta = -3.786$, $p = 0.000$, IRR = 0.023) and subjectivity ($\beta = -0.281$, $p = 0.079$, IRR = 0.755) were significantly associated with fewer dislikes. On the other hand, the external focus did not have a significant effect on the number of dislikes.

Regarding video content category, 'entertainment' videos ($\beta = 0.178$, $p = 0.013$, IRR = 1.194) and videos for 'kids' ($\beta = 0.161$, $p = 0.057$, IRR = 1.175) were positively associated with a higher number of dislikes, which means they receive more dislikes than other categories. At the same time, 'home' videos ($\beta = -0.274$, $p = 0.000$, IRR = 0.761) and 'fashion' videos ($\beta = -0.207$, $p = 0.004$, IRR = 0.813) were negatively associated with a higher number of dislikes. Regarding the post time, videos posted during business hours receive fewer dislikes than those posted during non-business hours ($\beta = -0.761$, $p = 0.000$, IRR = 0.467). Medium-length videos receive fewer dislikes than short ones($\beta = -0.119$, $p = 0.001$, IRR = 0.888), however long videos receive more dislikes ($\beta = 0.27$, $p = 0.000$, IRR = 1.31), perhaps because a long time spent watching the video may induce consumers to manifest more discontent.

Number of Comments. Analytical thinking and external focus were not significantly associated with the number of comments. Positive emotional polarity was significantly associated with fewer comments ($\beta = -6.674$, $p = 0.000$, IRR = 0.001), while subjectivity was significantly associated with more comments ($\beta = 4.737$, $p = 0.000$, IRR = 114.055). Regarding the video category, 'entertainment' videos ($\beta = 0.233$, $p = 0.002$, IRR = 1.262) and 'food' videos ($\beta = 0.316$, $p = 0.001$, IRR = 1.371) received more comments, while 'fitness' ($\beta = -0.165$, $p = 0.044$, IRR = 0.848) and 'fashion' videos ($\beta = -0.14$, $p = 0.074$, IRR = 0.869) received fewer comments. Videos posted on business hours receive fewer comments than those posted on non-business hours ($\beta = -0.845$, $p = 0.000$, IRR = 0.43), while videos posts on weekends receive more comments ($\beta = 0.083$, $p = 0.054$, IRR = 1.086) than those posted on weekdays. Finally, both medium-length videos ($\beta = 0.274$, $p = 0.000$, IRR = 1.315) and long videos ($\beta = 0.93$, $p = 0.000$, IRR = 2.534) receive more comments than short ones.

5 Discussion

The results of our study show that not all factors that help to boost the number of likes have a similar effect on the number of comments - or the number of dislikes. Thus, the choice of a digital influencer or channel on YouTube should not only be related to the number of views and subscribers but also to how they communicate and engage users.

Regarding the video's linguistic style, a more argumentative/informative content receives more likes and seems to be more appreciated by the consumers, somehow contradicting the literature on the effectiveness of narrative content on social media (Aleti et al. 2019; van Laer et al. 2018). It is possible that, on YouTube, consumers are more likely to seek information to solve a problem than in other platforms like Facebook and Instagram.

Our results also show that videos using an externally focused style, or, in other words, posted by digital influencers who demonstrate higher confidence and expertise are less likely to be liked, contradicting previous studies (Aleti et al. 2019; Xu and Zhang 2018; Pennebaker et al. 2015). Perhaps consumers on YouTube experience more closeness and identification with influencers who show their weaknesses and uncertainties (Jordan et al. 2019). This possibility is supported by the findings on the effects of subjectivity, and suggest that self-disclosure may be a strategy to encourage post popularity.

As for the polarity results, consumers prefer videos with moderate emotion, closer to the usual in their lives. It is possible that extreme positive emotions are considered unrealistic or associated with dishonest behaviour.

Moreover, our analysis shows that videos posted on non-business hours during weekdays receive a higher number of likes (and dislikes). This may be a characteristic of online user behaviour on YouTube, as consumers need more time to watch a video than to read a post on Facebook, Instagram or Twitter. Finally, consumers also seem to enjoy medium-length and long videos (i.e. ten minute-long or more) than short ones. Essentially, it means that if a person is willing to watch more than a few minutes to the content of a video, the propensity of liking and commenting on the video is higher.

Managerial Implications. The results suggest that managers wanting to boost the number of likes and comments should focus on medium and long videos, with informative and objective content. Also, they should not focus on videos with extremely positive emotion, probably because negative content enhances a general interest in the video, which leads to more comments (De Vries et al. 2012). Posting on non-business hours helps to increase the number of likes and comments. However, the increased engagement on these videos may also bring a higher number of dislikes, except for medium-length videos posted on weekends. If the main objective is to avoid dislikes, managers may want to avoid sponsoring or associating their ads with some controversial categories like Kids and Entertainment and opt for categories such as Home and Fashion. Finally, content with positive valence emotions, more subjective language, and narrative tend to generate fewer dislikes.

Limitations and Further Research. This research is subject to some limitations. First, our computerized technique extracted all available autogenerated captions from the videos in our sample as textual data. Relying on these captions is not ideal, as they result from an automatic conversion of audio into text, and the quality of this process is dependent on several factors. Second, the current version of LIWC's word dictionary is not fully able to capture the diversity of internet slangs and codes. Third, the unit level of analysis for this study was the video rather than the content creator, which leaves room for further investigation of the influence of the characteristics of digital influencers on video popularity. Finally, the conceptual model focused on the aspects of videos and not on the audience profile. Hence, future research may explore if different audience profiles react differently to distinct language styles.

References

Aggrawal, N., Arora, A., Anand, A., Irshad, M.S.: View-count based modeling for YouTube videos and weighted criteria–based ranking. In: Advanced Mathematical Techniques in Engineering Sciences, pp. 149–160. CRC Press (2018)

Aleti, T., Pallant, J.I., Tuan, A., van Laer, T.: Tweeting with the stars: automated text analysis of the effect of celebrity social media communications on consumer word of mouth. J. Interact. Mark. **48**, 17–32 (2019)

Arora, A., Bansal, S., Kandpal, C., Aswani, R., Dwivedi, Y.: Measuring social media influencer index-insights from Facebook, Twitter and Instagram. J. Retail. Consum. Serv. **49**, 86–101 (2019)

Banerjee, S., Chua, A.Y.: Identifying the antecedents of posts' popularity on Facebook Fan Pages. J. Brand Manag. **26**, 1–13 (2019)

De Vries, L., Gensler, S., Leeflang, P.S.: Popularity of brand posts on brand fan pages: an investigation of the effects of social media marketing. J. Interact. Mark. **26**, 83–91 (2012)

Escalas, J.E., Bettman, J.R.: Using narratives and autobiographical memories to discern motives. The Why of Consumption: Perspectives on Consumer Motives, Goals, and Desires, pp. 237–258 (2000)

Ferchaud, A., Grzeslo, J., Orme, S., LaGroue, J.: Parasocial attributes and YouTube personalities: exploring content trends across the most subscribed YouTube channels. Comput. Hum. Behav. **80**, 88–96 (2018)

Francalanci, C., Hussain, A.: Influence-based Twitter browsing with NavigTweet. Inf. Syst. **64**, 119–131 (2017)

Hughes, C., Swaminathan, V., Brooks, G.: Driving brand engagement through online social influencers: an empirical investigation of sponsored blogging campaigns. J. Mark. **83**(5), 78–96 (2019)

Jordan, K.N., Sterling, J., Pennebaker, J.W., Boyd, R.L.: Examining long-term trends in politics and culture through language of political leaders and cultural institutions. Proc. Natl. Acad. Sci. **116**(9), 3476–3481 (2019)

Liu, B.: Sentiment analysis and opinion mining. Synth. Lect. Hum. Lang. Technol. **5**(1), 1–167 (2012)

Pennebaker, J.W., Boyd, R.L., Jordan, K., Blackburn, K.: The development and psychometric properties of LIWC 2015. University of Texas at Austin, Austin (2015)

Sabate, F., Berbegal-Mirabent, J., Cañabate, A., Lebherz, P.R.: Factors influencing popularity of branded content in Facebook fan pages. Eur. Manag. J. **32**(6), 1001–1011 (2014)

Sokolova, K., Kefi, H.: Instagram and YouTube bloggers promote it, why should I buy? How credibility and parasocial interaction influence purchase intentions. J. Retail. Consum. Serv. **53**(March) (2020)

Statista: Hours of video uploaded to YouTube every minute 2007–2019 (2019). http://www.statista.com/statistics/259477/hours-of-video-uploaded-to-youtube-every-minute/

Tausczik, Y.R., Pennebaker, J.W.: The psychological meaning of words: LIWC and computerized text analysis methods. J. Lang. Soc. Psychol. **29**(1), 24–54 (2010)

Van Laer, T., Edson Escalas, J., Ludwig, S., van den Hende, E.: What happens in Vegas stays on TripAdvisor? A theory and technique to understand narrativity in consumer reviews. J. Consum. Res. **46**, 267–285 (2018)

Xu, W.W., Zhang, C.: Sentiment, richness, authority, and relevance model of information sharing during social Crises. Comput. Hum. Behav. **89**, 199–206 (2018)

Yew, J., Shamma, D.A.: Know your data: understanding implicit usage versus explicit action in video content classification. In: Multimedia on Mobile Devices 2011; and Multimedia Content Access: Algorithms and Systems, vol. 7881, p. 78811A, February 2011

A Tale of Two Social Influencers: A New Method for the Evaluation of Social Marketing

María Teresa Ballestar[1(✉)] and Jorge Sainz[2,3]

[1] ESIC Business and Marketing School, Barcelona, Spain
mariateresa.ballestar@esic.edu
[2] Institute of Policy Research, University of Bath, Bath, UK
[3] Universidad Rey Juan Carlos, Móstoles, Spain
jorge.sainz@urjc.es

Abstract. Political marketing strategies based on social network influencers are becoming increasingly relevant to set political agendas. We develop one of the first methods that will help us to understand the mechanism of transmission of information. We analyze the sentiment of the messages, then find and study how these messages spread over the social network of social influencers. We apply the method to one of the currently hottest topics, climate change, and to two of the most powerful social influencers, Greta Thunberg and Bill Gates, analyzing how they apply their communication strategies to reach their goals.

Keywords: Social influencer · Sentiment analysis · Twitter · Natural Language Processing

1 Introduction

In a recent article in Wired, Emma Ellis (2019) calls Greta Thunberg the "…the evidence of a changing culture of digital activism, one that's skewing younger and younger every time adult-run institutions get stuck in political gridlock." The issue of digital activism marketing has been long neglected in the scientific marketing literature. For a long time, it has been considered the universe of political scientists, who focus on its political implications but not on how the message transcends their technological issues and how their objectives are consumers of the proposals of different policies (Newman 2002; Joyce 2010). There is no doubt that the emergence of certain political ideas, populisms, different forms of resistance against injustices would not have happened without the emergence of social networks, their diffusion and the responses to them.

Relationship networks are not new. Uzzi and Dunlap (2005) carefully describe how another social influencer, philanthropist and entrepreneur; Bill Gates, constructed his network and the effects it had on the development, not only of Microsoft, but also the Bill & Melinda Gates Foundation and its efforts. Among them, being a recipient of its financing represents a signaling of quality social endeavor in different social networks (Van Noorden 2014).

Clearly both are examples of the social movements that are using the new technologies in a successful attempt to get their personal message across to reshape political

F. J. Martínez-López and S. D'Alessandro (Eds.): *Advances in Digital Marketing and eCommerce*, SPBE, pp. 80–90, 2020.
https://doi.org/10.1007/978-3-030-47595-6_11

priorities, hierarchies and political processes (Castells 1996). Both are marketing their ideas to get to a society which is easier to mobilize than probably any time since the 60's, and that is looking for references to follow and trust. Social groups that traditionally are not in related areas now, thanks to digitally networked activism (DNA) are engaging in defending the same positions, shaping the political agenda and driving the consumer agenda in aspects such as plastics use, vegetarianism etc. in a more effective way than any traditional campaign (Shah *et al.* 2012).

In this research, we will present a preliminary analysis of a method for the evaluation of how social influencers manage their messages to their followers across one of the major Social Networks, Twitter, and who responds to them and how. We will apply it by analyzing the tweets of Bill Gates and Greta Thunberg and those that mention them and disentangle both their main content and the reactions and sentiments that they produce in the social audience. Our goal is to show the patterns and the structure of individuals responding to the recommendations of any social influencer that affects, in a similar manner, the marketing of a political idea. We will make a deep analysis of our findings and extract insights for social behavior influencers marketing, trying to bridge the gap existing in the literature.

2 Method

We define influencers as those "...individuals who disproportionately impact the spread of information or some related behavior of interest" and "seed content", that is, they create a large part of their own content (Bakshy *et al.* 2011). We choose Greta Thunberg and Bill Gates because they are two of the more representative social influencers, with more than 52 million followers, providing a rich setting for testing our method and understanding the social dynamics behind current social discussions. This framework allows us to perform a thorough data analysis of opinion mining and sentiment analysis on Twitter to produce relevant insights into the underlying processes and dynamics of the spreading of the messages as well as the positive or negative responses to their messages.

These goals are not trivial. As Giachanou and Crestani (2016) note "...mining opinions and sentiment from social media is very challenging due to the vast amount of data generated". Researchers have to look into the treasures hidden within millions of words. Different approaches of Machine Learning analysis can automatically detect specific text and can effectively mine opinion and sentiment within googols of information.

Yue *et al.* (2019) survey the different techniques and their evolution over time and note the growing number of methods that are used in the analysis of sentiment and how they are rapidly becoming more sophisticated. We use the following waterfall process in this research (Fig. 1).

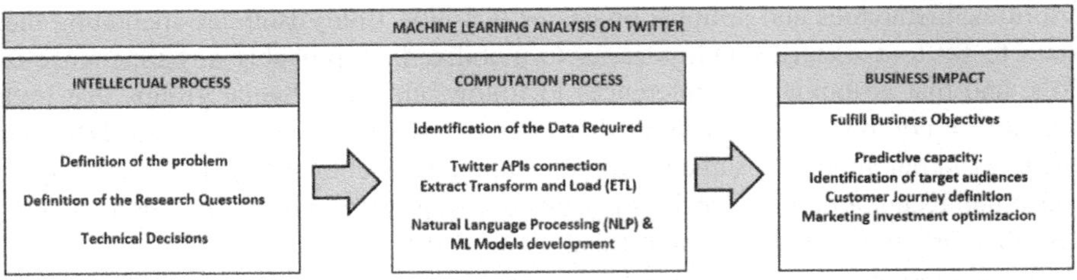

Fig. 1. Waterfall process of Twitter data Analysis using Machine Learning methods

2.1 Data Collection

The analysis performed in this research has two main objectives. The first consists of the analysis of Bill Gates' and Greta Thunberg's messages and who mentions them on Twitter, and disentangles their main content and the reactions and sentiments that they produce in their social audience. With this aim a sample of 23,294 tweets were collected within twenty-four days in December 2019 containing the keywords "BillGates" with 11,910 (51.12%) tweets or "GretaThunberg" with 11,384 (48.8%) tweets.

The second consists of the analysis of the network relationships of those who interact with Bill Gates or Greta Thunberg or talk about either of them, in order to investigate whether the networks of the two influencers overlap and their followers and referrers share their aims of working actively to provide a better future for society with their own social network and followers.

To build a wider network of interactions and gather an extensive number of accounts keen on the topic that drives Bill Gates and Greta Thunberg activities we added to the 23,294 tweets an additional extract of 15,000 tweets that contain the words "sustainable" or "sustainability" within the same period of observation. This makes a total sample of 38,294 tweets.

From a technical point of view, the extraction of data was made developing our own python script that connects to the premium search tweets 30-day API that provides a rolling 30 days of access to its historical data and also allows us to apply filters to the extract, such as date, hashtag, user account, etc. For this research we only applied a filter using the keywords: "BillGates" or "GretaThunberg" in the first extract and the keywords: "sustainable" or "sustainability" in the second extract.

These gathered tweets were stored in a json file that was processed and analyzed using our own developed python scripts that employ Natural Language Processing (NLP) libraries for sentiment analysis and word cloud construction. Finally, the file was also processed with the Gephi software. Gephi is an open source software for exploring and manipulating networks that was developed by Bastian, Heymann and Jacomy (Bastian *et al.* 2009). In our research we use this software for the identification of communities and relationship among users that generate and interact with tweets that contain the keywords "BillGates", "GretaThunberg", "sustainable" and "sustainability".

2.2 Sentiment Analysis

After the extract, transformation and load (ETL), we use Natural Language Processing (NLP) and machine learning methods (ML) to perform sentiment analysis and word cloud visual representations.

Sentiment analysis is performed using the lexicon-based sentiment analysis and classification, a popular method for measuring the polarity of sentiment of a collection of documents. In this research we apply the Valence Aware Dictionary for Sentiment Reasoning (VADER). VADER is a rule-based model that is able to manage a wide variety of content generated in the form of tweets, and compute its sentiment polarity. VADER handles more than 7,000 items and its associated sentiment intensity measures that were validated by humans in advance before being incorporated into the sentiment lexicon dictionary (Ribeiro *et al.* 2016; Becken *et al.* 2017). VADER is robust and widely used among the scientific community and it is able to outperform individual human raters (Hutto and Gilbert 2014).

The VADER NLP method evaluates each of the single words of a tweet written in the English language and returns a metric score for the sentiment of the tweet which ranges from −1 (strongly negative sentiment) to +1 (strongly positive sentiment). We have applied the following criteria to classify this score within three clusters of sentiments: Tweets with scores from −1 to −0.05 are considered negative, with scores from −0.05 to 0.05 are considered neutral and higher than 0.05 are considered positive. We perform the same process for each of the 23,294 tweets stored in our json file.

Hence, we score whether the conversations of Bill Gates and Greta Thunberg link to positive, neutral or negative sentiments in the network community.

2.3 Word Cloud Analysis

A word cloud is a visual representation of text which is developed based on the frequency of usage of each word in the data collection. Word cloud analysis was performed to understand the most relevant topics and concepts linked to both influencers and validate whether there is some degree of overlapping among them or not.

In addition to this, we apply a clusterization, a process entailing the development of word cloud analysis in conjunction with the sentiment analysis (NLP). Hence, we identify the most relevant topics that raise positive or negative sentiments among the people who mention or interact with content related to Bill and Greta on Twitter.

For this purpose, we have used in our python code several existing python libraries such as matplotlib, pandas and wordcloud, that are widely used among the scientific community and data scientists. We configure the word clouds to show the four-hundred most repeated words and word-phrases of the total sample of tweets first, and later for the two clusters of positive and negative sentiment tweets, obtaining six different word clouds. The greater the size of the word or word-phrase in the word cloud the higher the frequency.

2.4 Network Analysis

The network analysis uses Gephi, an open source software for network analysis and visualization. It allows for the exploration and visualization of large networks of any kind, providing features such as high-quality layout algorithms, clustering, sample filtering by specific characteristics of the network and statistics of the network as a whole but also the nodes, edges and the dynamic of the social network (Bastian *et al.* 2009).

Feeding Gephi software with the sample of tweets collected in the first stage of this research, we have analyzed the dynamics of the accounts that contributed with tweets that contain at least one of the names Bill Gates or Greta Thunberg or the keywords "sustainable" or "sustainability", and also the accounts that acted as prescribers and retweeted these contents within the period of observation.

Our aim is to create a network that shows how many accounts retweeted content from an account with tweets that contain the lists of words and to draw the picture of the communities which are interested in these topics. For this purpose, we use the ForceAtlas2 a continuous graph layout algorithm; "ForceAtlas2 is a force directed layout: it simulates a physical system in order to spatialize a network. Nodes repulse each other like charged particles, while edges attract their nodes, like springs. These forces create a movement that converges to a balanced state. This final configuration is expected to help the interpretation of the data." (Jacomy *et al.* 2014). This network will allow us to understand how communities interact and how to define their taxonomy.

3 Results

From the influencer point of view, sentiment analysis can provide advice and recommendations on how to deliver their message, who are the recipients and how they receive it. The word cloud gives us a sense of the dynamics of both influencers and their referees and their main issues, as Figs. 2 and 3 show. In both cases, climate change is one of the main topics of discussion. It is also interesting to realize that while in the case of Bill Gates it is just one of the many issues associated with his activism, as can be seen in the webpage of the Bill and Melinda Gates Foundation (https://www.gatesfoundation.org), there are many other concerns. They relate to other projects of the Foundation: sustainability, education, empowerment, poverty and partnerships. On the other hand, the Greta Thunberg word cloud representation is a fight between those in favor or those against the climate crisis (not change) and sustainability.

The difference accentuates the profile as "one topic only" activism of Greta Thunberg, whose interaction relates mostly to that issue. This specialization seems to have a double effect, on the one hand all the references are focused on it, but in addition there is strong disagreement on the issue that may hinder other messages that she may want to get through.

Bill Gates sends many other messages, but in the current situation, climate change has a special urgency, as most of the negative sentiment keywords relate to it. As (Suh *et al.* 2010) point out the need for social content and the meta-information contained in them helps to evaluate the information. In the latter, the context is derived from the prior references of the value of the influencer and its behavior and the intersection on

Positive, negative or neutral sentiment word cloud

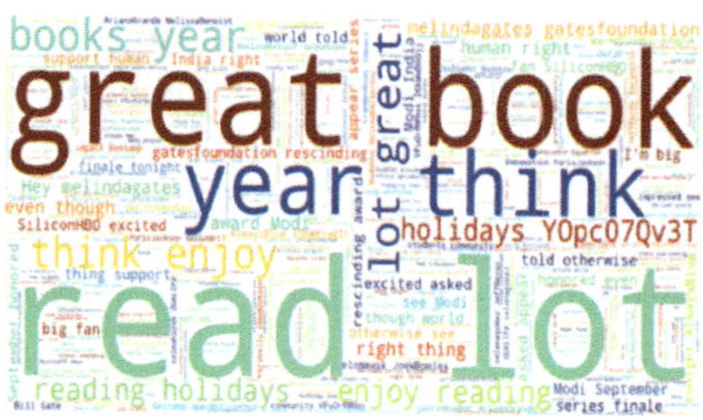

Positive sentiment word cloud

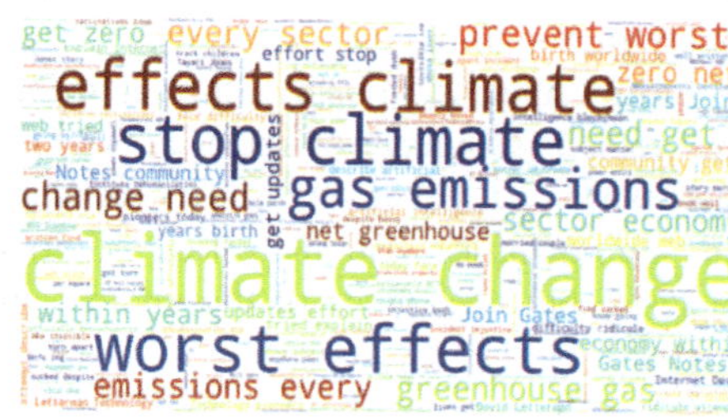

Negative sentiment word cloud

Fig. 2. Word cloud for 400 most repeated words in Tweets where "Bill Gates" is mentioned.

Positive, negative or neutral sentiment word cloud

Positive sentiment word cloud

Negative sentiment word cloud

Fig. 3. Word cloud for 400 most repeated words in Tweets where "Greta Thunberg" is mentioned.

the issue, a theory that derives from the early seminal work of Katz (1957). As Satell (2014) point out "the fundamental problem with influencer marketing is not that some people aren't more influential than others, but that there is little, if any, evidence that influencer strategies—other than celebrity endorsement—are viable". Social influencers are, in one way or another, celebrities and the difference between them is who retweet whom, which will allow us to understand how information is diffused in Twitter (Bernstein *et al.* 2010).

When looking at the positive sentiment keywords in the word cloud, the Gates results rely on many of their foundation's achievements and projects. On the other hand, Thunberg relies more on her own achievements and how they affect her activism. Looking through the tweets, the difference between the two influencers is large. While the former relates to positive images of altruism in the whole range of the topic, the latter reflects an image of social activism on Climate Change, reflecting in each case what Satell (2014) says "…if you want things to spread, forget about special people with 'rare qualities'. Be interesting …" to your interest group. In this case, the goal is the same, but the choice of the interest group is diverse, attracting a different set of crowds.

It is then worthwhile to analyze the effect of these marketing strategies on general sentiment (Fig. 4). When rating the 11,910 tweets extracted containing "Bill Gates" by their sentiment, neutral-positives represent 79.06%. The conversation around Bill Gates is often more positive and optimistic about the words seen above, while in Greta Thunberg's case a more negative sentiment is generated; 40.92% of the tweets where her name appears are classified as negative. As the word cloud shows, it may be because Greta Thunberg warns about the future negative consequences of climate change, asking governments and industries for a radical change in their behavior, and there are groups of users who react negatively to that message. With the same notions, Bill Gates' tweets focus on construction, development and education from a more positive perspective throughout his own foundation, avoiding rebuttal from third parties.

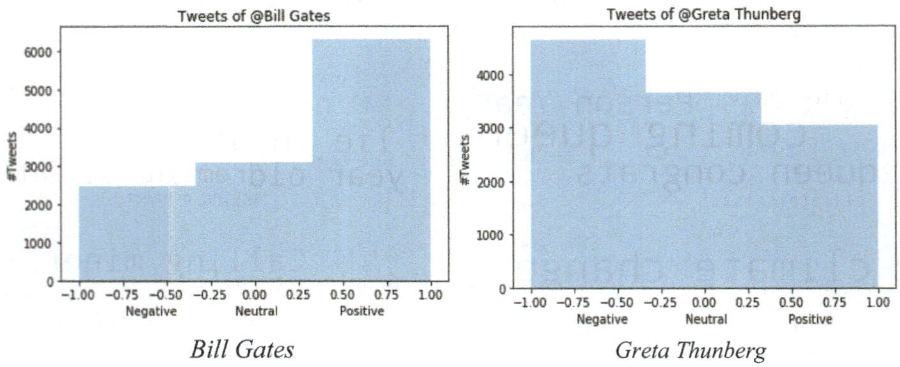

Bill Gates *Greta Thunberg*

Fig. 4. Sentiment analysis for Bill Gates and Greta Thunberg in Twitter

Why this difference? The answer again lies in who retweets whom. A naïve analysis may present both of them (Bill and Greta) sharing audiences and followers who may be willing to interact with either one. Working under the hypothesis that, if am interested or worried about climate change as an individual, I would follow both Greta and Bill and would retweet content from both of them. We test this hypothesis drawing on the network of accounts that generated or retweeted the 38,500 tweets of our sample that contains the keywords under research (Fig. 5). While there is a great deal of conversation about them and/or climate change or sustainability, their respective communities do not interact. This means that Bill Gates and Greta Thunberg have their own audiences that retweet their content or generate new content which mentions them. Hence, the characteristics and profile of the two influencers and the tone and message of their tweets also have an impact on the kind of audiences, followers and referrers they have.

Whole social network Zoom in

Fig. 5. Social Network Analysis (SNA) for Bill Gates (purple node) and Greta Thunberg (green node) in Twitter

The description of the topology of the network in Fig. 5 is as follows: The number of nodes is 36,875 and the number of edges is 22,725. Nodes are both accounts that create the tweets and accounts that interacted with these tweets, acting as referrers, spreading the message in form of a retweet. This means that the average degree of the network, that is the measure of connectivity among the accounts, is 0.616. This proves that, apart from the two influencers and their audiences that retweet their contents, there are many small isolated communities having conversation about them and sustainability (grey spots in the image). This is also validated by the average clustering coefficient of the single nodes which is 0.001, which is very low but an expected figure as we are working with a network where the interactions among users consist of retweets. The average path length of the edges that connect the nodes is 1.037, meaning that one account that acts as referee retweets content from an account that talks about Bill or Greta, but there is not much impact far away from the referee. This is also validated when we see that the network diameter, that is the shortest distance between the most distant accounts in the network, is just 4.

The modularity, with a value of 0.977, allows us to identify the different communities in the network, that are represented by the different colors in Fig. 5. Hence, there is a strong community structure, where the accounts of the different communities are strongly connected with the main contributor (out-degree centrality measure equals 1,901 for Bill Gates and 1,476 for Greta Thunberg) but the communities as a whole are not very connected amongst themselves. The modularity is represented in Fig. 5 by the different colors.

This directed network betweenness centrality, closeness centrality and eccentricity are calculated using Brandes algorithm (Brandes 2001). Betweenness centrality represents how often a node appears on shortest paths between nodes in the network, reaching in our network a maximum value of 234.

Closeness centrality provides us information about the accounts that are able to spread information in a very efficient way in the network, only 18.87% of the accounts in this network have the maximum value of 1. Finally, eccentricity is the distance from a given starting node to the farthest node from it in the network, with a maximum value of 4 in this network.

4 Discussion

How politically active influencers interact and how the political agenda is set has changed enormously over the last few years. The relevance of the different topics is nowadays more a community effort of interest-groups than an ideological issue, and therefore, how a topic becomes relevant is up to media and social media (Newman 2002; Corner and Pels 2010). Social networks have become what the forum was in ancient Rome: "Blame the people who hail him when he speaks in the Forum of the 'new, wonderful good society' which shall now be Rome" This quote, doubtfully attributed to Cicero[1], instantly make us think about Social Media and current politics. We have developed a method to discover how two top political influencers spread a topic on Twitter and how the network sees the same topics. The goal was to expose different marketing strategies for social influencers that allows us to evaluate the impact in each case.

As we have seen in the previous sections, the different strategy works well for each of the influencers. As Greta Thunberg posts in a tweet the 6th of January 2020: "unless we start to focus everything on this [climate change], our targets [on carbon emissions] will soon be out of reach". Therefore, there is a need to be aware immediately about the issue raised, making her only goal to reach that objective. In that sense, her social exposure is strictly aimed at that, reaching both loyal followers and discontents. Our method shows how the millions of her fans and detractors build an ecosystem that is completely separate from that of Bill Gates.

[1] Actually, it belongs to Florida Supreme Court Justice Millard F. Caldwell who in 1965 wrote and attributed it to Cicero.

Bill Gates' position is different. In an interview with CNN's Fareed Zakaria in February the eighteenth, 2019, he pushed for change, but not a "radical change". He and his wife have devoted their foundation to many goals, among them beating climate change through research, awareness and more traditional political lobbying. This affects how users perceive the message, increasing its credibility but reducing its urgency, allowing for more sense of authority (Arora *et al.* 2019).

The results of this research show the benefits and robustness of the method used. In the future the results will be improved with the addition of more tweets in a longer period of observation to avoid the impact of seasonality effects.

References

Arora, A., et al.: Measuring social media influencer index-insights from Facebook, Twitter and Instagram. J. Retail. Consumer Serv. **49**, 86–101 (2019). https://doi.org/10.1016/j.jretconser.2019.03.012

Bakshy, E., et al.: Everyone's an influencer: quantifying influence on Twitter. In: Proceedings of the Fourth ACM International Conference on Web Search and Data Mining, WSDM 2011, pp. 64–71. https://doi.org/10.1145/1935826.1935845

Bastian, M., et al.: Gephi: an open source software for exploring and manipulating networks. In: Third International AAAI Conference on Weblogs and Social Media (2009). http://citeseerx.ist.psu.edu/viewdoc/summary?doi=10.1.1.172.7704. Accessed 7 Jan 2020

Brandes, U.: A faster algorithm for betweenness centrality. J. Math. Sociol. **25**(2), 163–177 (2001)

Becken, S., et al.: Monitoring the environment and human sentiment on the Great Barrier Reef: assessing the potential of collective sensing. J. Environ. Manag. **203**, 87–97 (2017). https://doi.org/10.1016/j.jenvman.2017.07.007

Bernstein, M.S., et al.: Eddi: interactive topic-based browsing of social status streams. In: Proceedings of the 23nd Annual ACM Symposium on User Interface Software and Technology, pp. 303–312 (2010). https://doi.org/10.1145/1866029.1866077

Castells, M.: The Information Age: The Rise of the Network Society. Blackwell, Malden (1996)

Corner, J., Pels, D.: Media and the Restyling of Politics Consumerism, Celebrity and Cynicism. SAGE (2010)

Ellis, E.: Greta Thunberg's Digital Rise Calls Back to a Pre-Digital Era | WIRED', Wired, pp. 12–18 (2019). https://www.wired.com/story/greta-thunberg-social-media/. Accessed 5 Jan 2020

Giachanou, A., Crestani, F.: Like it or not. ACM Comput. Surv. **49**(2), 1–41 (2016). https://doi.org/10.1145/2938640

Hutto, C.J., Gilbert, E.: VADER: a parsimonious rule-based model for sentiment analysis of social media text. http://sentic.net/. Accessed 7 Jan 2020

Jacomy, M., et al.: ForceAtlas2, a continuous graph layout algorithm for handy network visualization designed for the Gephi software. PLoS One. Public Libr. Sci. **9**(6). https://doi.org/10.1371/journal.pone.0098679

Joyce, M., Mary, C.: Digital Activism Decoded: The New Mechanics of Change. International Debate Education Association (2010)

Katz, E.: The two-step flow of communication: an up-to-date report on an hypothesis. Public Opin. Q. **21**(1, Anniversary Issue Devoted to Twenty Years of Public Opinion Research), 61. https://doi.org/10.1086/266687

Newman, B.I.: The role of marketing in politics. J. Polit. Market. **1**(1), 1–5. https://doi.org/10.1300/j199v01n01_01

Van Noorden, R.: Online collaboration: scientists and the social network. Nature 126–129 (2014). https://doi.org/10.1038/512126a

Ribeiro, F.N., et al.: SentiBench - a benchmark comparison of state-of-the-practice sentiment analysis methods. EPJ Data Sci. SpringerOpen **5**(1) (2016). https://doi.org/10.1140/epjds/s13688-016-0085-1

Satell, G.: 3 Reasons to kill influencer marketing. Harvard Bus. Rev. (9), 2–6. https://hbr.org/2014/09/3-reasons-to-kill-influencer-marketing. Accessed 6 Jan 2020

Shah, D.V., et al.: The personalization of politics: political identity, social media, and changing patterns of participation. Ann. Am. Acad. Polit. Soc. Sci. **644**(1), 6–19 (2012). https://doi.org/10.1177/0002716212451428

Suh, B., et al.: Want to be retweeted? Large scale analytics on factors impacting retweet in Twitter network. In: 2010 IEEE Second International Conference on Social Computing. http://apiwiki.twitter.com/. Accessed 5 Jan 2020

Uzzi, B., Dunlap, S.: How to build your business plan. Harvard Bus. Rev. **83**(12), 51. www.hbr.orgorcall800-988-0886.www.hbr.org. Accessed 5 Jan 2020

Yue, L., Chen, W., Li, X., Zuo, W., Yin, M.: A survey of sentiment analysis in social media. Knowl. Inf. Syst. **60**(2), 617–663 (2018). https://doi.org/10.1007/s10115-018-1236-4

Unanticipated Consequences of Interactive Marketing: Systematic Literature Review and Directions for Future Research

Elvira Ismagilova[1(✉)], Yogesh Dwivedi[2], and Nripendra Rana[1]

[1] Faculty of Management, Law and Social Sciences, University of Bradford, Bradford, UK
{e.ismagilova,n.p.rana}@bradford.ac.uk
[2] Emerging Markets Research Centre, School of Management, Swansea University, Swansea, UK
y.k.dwivedi@swansea.ac.uk

Abstract. Internet and social media have created new opportunities and challenges for marketing practices. This research provides a comprehensive analysis of the unanticipated consequences of interactive marketing. The current study focuses on a number of aspects of interactive marketing research such as consumer-to-consumer and consumer-to-company communications, consumer brand engagement, impact of social influencers and online buzz, impact of online advertisement, companies adoption and use of new technologies by companies, consumer empowerment by digital technologies, complain handling, impact of mobile advertising, co-creation, and impact of social media marketing. This research provides a valuable synthesis of the relevant literature. The findings of this study could be used as an informative framework for both academics and practitioners.

Keywords: Interactive marketing · Unanticipated consequences · Literature review

1 Introduction

Internet and social media have created new opportunities and challenges for marketing practices. It was expected that new tools would enable "very powerful, very inexpensive, and very intrusive direct marketing" (Deighton and Kornfeld 2009). The predictions were right to some degree. However, they had some consequences which marketers did not expect (Mangold and Faulds 2009; Xiang and Gretzel 2010). The surprise was, that instead of empowering only companies, new technologies empowered consumers.

Thanks to the new technologies consumers received peer-to-peer tools such as eBay, Youtube, Facebook, blogs and information search tools (e.g. Google and Wikipedia). Mobile platforms provided consumers with connectivity, context-aware search, and the ability to tag and annotate physical spaces with digital information that could be retrieved and used by other consumers later.

F. J. Martínez-López and S. D'Alessandro (Eds.): *Advances in Digital Marketing and eCommerce*, SPBE, pp. 91–98, 2020.
https://doi.org/10.1007/978-3-030-47595-6_12

The technologies allowed consumers to engage with brands directly. Customer engagement has been linked to various brand performance indicators such as sales growth, customer involvement in product development, customer feedback and referrals. Social media allows customers to review, comment, create and share content across numerous online networks. Customers got direct access to companies, brands, and marketers thanks to social media. This brings both, challenges and opportunities to marketers. Nowadays, companies have to engage with customers in real-time and manage a high amount of customer data.

A number of studies conducted a comprehensive literature review on digital/social media studies (Lamberton and Stephen 2016; Leung et al. 2013) and the consequences of new technologies (Deighton and Kornfeld 2009). For example, Lamberton and Stephen (2016) conducted a thematic analysis of the research on digital, social media and mobile marketing (DSMM) published from 2000 to 2015. The main themes which emerged were DSMM as a facilitator of individual expression, DSMM as a decision support tool and DSMM as a market intelligence source. However, these studies became outdated or did not focus on the consequences of new technologies for both, marketers and consumers. Thus, the aim of this paper is to provide a review of studies that focused on the unanticipated consequences of the new technologies for both, companies and consumers. The findings of this study can provide an informative framework for research on the consequences of new technologies for academics and practitioners.

The rest of the paper is structured as follows. Section 2 offers a brief overview of the methods used to identify relevant studies to be included in this review. The next section synthesises the studies identified in the previous section and provides a detailed overview. Section 4 outlines the limitations of current studies and presents direction for further research. Finally, Sect. 5 discusses the key aspects of the research, outlining the limitations of the current paper.

2 Literature Search Method

This study used cited reference search for Deighton and Kornfeld's (2009) articles on Scopus database to identify studies for the literature review. The search returned 152 articles.

3 Literature Synthesis

The studies which focused on unanticipated consequences of interactive marketing were divided into the following themes: consumer-to-consumer and consumer-to-company communications, consumer brand engagement, impact of social influencers and online buzz, impact of online advertisement, companies adoption and use of new technologies by companies, consumer empowerment by digital technologies, complain handling, impact of mobile advertising, co-creation, and impact of social media marketing.

3.1 Consumer-to-Consumer and Consumer to Company Communication

Some studies focused on consumer-to-consumer and company to consumers communications, by looking at consumers' motivations to engage in this type of communications and examining its positive/negative effect (Gheorghe et al. 2018; Song et al. 2016). Song et al. (2016) studied the interaction effects of consumers' endorsements on marketer-generated content and user-generated content posts in the social media brand community of a popular Asian fashion retailer. Particularly, the study focused on UGC, consumer endorsement passive endorsements (likes) and active endorsements (commenting on a post). It was found that active endorsements positively moderate the effects of marketer-generated content in inducing consumers' expenditure. Nevertheless, it was found that passive endorsements negatively moderated marketer-generated content. It made it less effective in inducing expenditure. However, for UGC the results were the opposite. Additionally, the study found that active endorsements via social-tagging on brand fans lead to more spending (the recipients of social-tags spent 6 dollars more than non-recipients in this week).

Some studies focused on consumer engagement with the company/brand (Harrigan et al. 2018; Scarpi 2010; Rohm et al. 2013). Nowadays customers voluntarily and intentionally engage in online relationships with brands via social media. Consumer brand engagement refers to consumer's cognitive, emotional and behavioral activity around specific consumer/brand interaction.

Scarpi (2010) investigated the impact of the size of brand communities on consumer behavior towards the brand and company. By using the data from a survey the findings show that small communities operate differently from larger ones with regard to numerous aspects and possible strengths and weaknesses. It was found that members of small communities develop higher community loyalty, brand loyalty in small communities stems more from community loyalty than from brand effect. Small communities engage in word of mouth for the community more than in word of mouth for the brand.

3.2 Impact of Social Influencers and Online Buzz

Another group of studies focused on the impact of social influencers and online buzz (Keel et al. 2019). For example, Keel et al. (2019) studied the impact of online buzz on internet Initial Public offerings. It was found that high levels of buzz in the year prior to the offering are associated with higher company valuations at the IPO and for the following two years. The findings suggest that online buzz serves as a costly state falsification signal that is not cheap talk. It acts as a risk reducer for the underwriter and presents qualitative information about the issuer.

Van Norel et al. examined how celebrity Tweet messages can be used to improve a damaged companies reputation and the way how this messaged should be designed and what celebrities should be used. By using an experiment it was found that celebrities' tweets can repair a positive public opinion about companies. It was found that an intelligent celebrity, who has the best fit with the topic has the best impact.

3.3 Impact of Online Advertisement

Some studied examined the impact of online advertisements have on consumers and companies (Ahmed et al. 2019; Acquisti and Spiekermann 2011). Ahmed et al. (2019) investigated the effectiveness of online digital media advertising as a strategic tool for building brand sustainability by looking at the impact of various channels. It was found that the channels of digital media advertising have a positive and significant influence on the effectiveness of online digital media which creates brand sustainability in the context of fast-moving consumer goods and services sectors in Pakistan. Acquisti and Spiekermann (2011) aimed to investigate the impact of interruptive advertising on consumers' willingness to pay for products bearing the advertiser's brand. By using a controlled experiment it was found that the ads significantly lowered the willingness to pay or goods associated with the advertising brand. It is important for practitioners to be aware of the negative consequences of this type of advertising as it can result in a negative attitude towards the brand.

3.4 Impact of Social Media Marketing

Some scholars were focusing on the impact of social media marketing (Corduan 2017). The study by Yazdanparast et al. (2016) found that brand-based SMM is important in impacting consumers' attitudes towards brands. It was found that attitude toward SMM of brands positively associated with perceived quality of the brand, perceived value for the cost of the brand, perceived uniqueness of the brand and willingness to pay a price premium aim for the brand.

Consumers might consider advertising on social media as intrusive and violating their personal life. Thus, new forms of advertising are introduced. Bóveda-Lambie and Hair focused on invertising - forms of non-intrusive marketing that consumers invite into their lives and how it can influence the consumer-brand relationship, through the results of self-brand connections. By conducting surveys it was found that consumers view social media invertising more favorably and less intrusive than social media advertising. However, the study did not find a support that consumer invertising interactions with brands develop stronger self-brand connections than when they don't interact with the brand in social media.

3.5 Impact of Mobile Advertising

The next group of studies investigated the impact of mobile advertising (Enwereuzor, 2017; Sinkovics et al. 2012). Enwereuzor (2017) examined consumers' experience of unsolicited mobile advertising in the context of Nigeria. The results obtained from 12 semi-structured interviews revealed that consumers experience negative feelings when they get such advertisements. These negative feelings center on annoyance and irritation, disturbance, lack of interest due to loss of money after receiving such calls, suspicion of fraudulent activities, and disappointment.

Sinkovics et al. (2012) investigated factors influencing the perception of mobile advertisement in two countries, Japan and Australia. By using the data collected from surveys, it was found that infotainment and credibility are key factors influencing advertising value for both, Australian and Japanese consumers. However, it was found that Japanese consumers are more irritated by mobile advertising in comparison with Australian consumers. For both countries, it was found that advertising value positively affects attitude towards advertising.

3.6 Adoption and Use of New Technologies by Companies

Some studies focused on the adoption and use of new technologies by companies (Rogers and Clark 2016). For example, Rogers and Clark (2016) proposed a conceptual model for context-aware B2B sales-CABS. Context-aware B2B selling is defined as "the integration of information about the customer's situation with business intelligence to enable meaningful recommendations and communications throughout the sales process" (p.6). This application of technology can help to facilitate co-creation value between seller and buyer by providing access to timely and relevant information about operational needs. It can help to link the supplier sales activity to the customer buying cycle.

3.7 Consumer Empowerment

Some scholars focused on consumer empowerment (Buehler and Maas 2018; Malthouse and Shankar 2009). Malthouse and Shankar (2009) state that consumers got the power to be protected from unwanted marketing communication by using spam filters, digital video records, caller id, and do-not-call/mail lists.

Buehler and Maas (2018) investigated consumer empowerment in the relationship between consumers and service providers. By using the self-efficacy theory the study explained the impact of consumer empowerment on perceived performance risk in insurance decision making. The study used survey data from 487 consumers in Switzerland who recently decided on an insurance service. By using SEM for data analysis, it was found that consumer empowerment consists of perceived self-efficacy and perceived controllability. Both showed a significant impact on perceived performance risk. It was also found that customers' involvement in the purchase process moderates the effect of self-efficacy on perceived performance risk. Based on the result of this study companies could use consumer empowerment for risk reduction strategy. Consumers with self-efficacy and controllability beliefs perceived significantly less performance risk. Future research should investigate the long-term effect on consumer-perceived empowerment on the customer journey.

3.8 Complain Handling

Another group of studies focused on the way how companies handle companies from consumers (Tarnovskaya and Biedenbach 2018). For example, the study by Tarnovskaya and Biedenbach (2018) aims to explore brand meaning negotiation between different groups of stakeholders in the case of corporate rebranding failure. The study particularly focuses on the dynamic process of brand meaning creation by multiple stakeholders during corporate rebranding in the digital environment. The study analyses the case of Gap which rebranding lasted for only one week in 2010 and was reversed because of strong negative reactions by multiple stakeholders. By using an ethnography the study found that the polarisation of brand meanings, in which both antagonistic and supportive forms co-exist, has a determinable impact on the outcome of corporate rebranding.

3.9 Co-creation

Co-creation is defined as customer participation in numerous stages of production and use processes via the use of operant resources (e.g. knowledge, skills, and effort). Co-creation has a number of benefits such as consumer engagement, an increase in sales, consumer satisfaction. However, co-creation creates challenges such as consumer interactivity and dealing with the implications of failed co-created products and services. The number of studies focused on co-creation (Sugathan et al. 2017; France et al. 2015). For example, the study by Sugathan et al. (2017) aims to understand consumers' evaluation of failure, their subsequent attributions, their expectancy of success, and their willingness to co-create in the future. By employing two independent empirical studies the authors found that an increase in the degree of co-creation increases internal failure attribution and reduces firm failure attribution. Customers are no longer just passive purchasers of the brand but are active participants in creating brand experiences. France et al. (2015) developed a conceptual model for brand co-creation from a customer perspective. The proposed model shows that brand engagement, brand self-congruity and category involvement affect brand co-creation which in turn affects brand knowledge and brand value.

4 Limitations and Directions for Future Research

Studies in the context of interactive marketing have the following limitations. First, the majority of studies focused on the benefits of new technologies for companies but did not look extensively on the challenges faced by companies adopting social media especially in the context of b2b companies. Future research can investigate the dark side of social media use on companies such as an excessive number of requests on social media, which can lead to the reduction of the responsiveness. Second, most of the studies use a cross-sectional approach to collect the data. Future research can use a longitudinal approach to advance understanding of the consequences of interactive marketing over time. Third, current studies were conducted in China (e.g. Alden et al. 2016), USA (Yazdanparast et al. 2016), India (Sugathan et al. 2017). It is advised that future research is conducted in other countries as findings can be different due to the culture and social media adoption rate. Future studies should pay particular attention to other emerging markets (such as Russia, Brazil, and South Africa) as they suffer from the slow adoption rate of social media marketing. Some companies in these countries still rely more on traditional media for advertising their products and services, as they are more trusted in comparison with social media channels (Ali et al. 2016). Additionally, the majority of studies (e.g. Scarpi 2010) use quantitative methods to collect the data. It is advised that future studies should use a mix of quantitative and qualitative research techniques to explore new consequences of interactive marketing and get new consumer insights. Finally, more research is needed on unanticipated consequences of the use of artificial intelligence in marketing on consumers and companies.

5 Conclusion

The aim of this research was to provide a systematic review of the literature on the unanticipated consequences of interactive marketing for companies and consumers. As a result, this research synthesised the existing knowledge in the field and provided directions for future studies. Based on the literature review the unanticipated consequences can be divided into two groups: positive and negative. Positive unanticipated consequences include 1) Positive impact of online buzz on the value of IPO 2) Consumers became active participants in creating brand experience 3) Co-creation has a positive effect on brand knowledge and brand value 4) Celebrities can improve company's damaged reputation by using tweet messages. Negative consequences include: 1) Negative consequences of consumer endorsement (e.g. making marketing-generated content less effective) 2) Creation of antibranding images by consumers which could be seen by everyone 3) Interruptive advertising online has a negative effect on consumers' willingness to pay for products bearing in the advertisement 4) Unsolicited mobile advertising leads to negative feelings.

This study has a number of limitations. First, only publications from the Scopus database were included in the literature analysis and synthesis. Second, this research did not use weight analysis and meta-analysis. In order to provide a broader picture of the research and reconcile the conflicting findings of the existing studies, it is recommended that future research should contact these 2 types of analyses. It will advance knowledge in the interactive marketing domain.

References

Acquisti, A., Spiekermann, S.: Do interruptions pay off? Effects of interruptive ads on consumers' willingness to pay. J. Interact. Market. **25**(4), 226–240 (2011)

Ahmed, R.R., Streimikiene, D., Berchtold, G., Vveinhardt, J., Channar, Z.A., Soomro, R.H.: Effectiveness of online digital media advertising as a strategic tool for building brand sustainability: evidence from FMCGs and services sectors of Pakistan. Sustainability **11**(12), 3436 (2019)

Alden, D.L., Kelley, J.B., Youn, J.B., Chen, Q.: Understanding consumer motivations to interact on brand websites in the international marketplace: evidence from the US, China, and South Korea. J. Bus. Res. **69**(12), 5909–5916 (2016)

Ali, Z., Shabbir, M.A., Rauf, M., Hussain, A.: To assess the impact of social media marketing on consumer perception. Int. J. Acad. Res. Account. Finance Manage. Sci. **6**(3), 69–77 (2016)

Buehler, P., Maas, P.: Consumer empowerment in insurance: effects on performance risk perceptions in decision making. Int. J. Bank Market. **36**(6), 1073–1097 (2018)

Corduan, A.: Cultural diversity in international social public relations. In: International Conference On Social Media, Wearable and Web Analytics (Social Media), pp. 1–5. IEEE, June 2017

Deighton, J., Kornfeld, L.: Interactivity's unanticipated consequences for marketers and marketing. J. Interact. Market. **23**(1), 4–10 (2009)
Enwereuzor, I.K.: Capturing consumers' experiences of unsolicited mobile advertising. Telematics Inform. **34**(7), 948–960 (2017)
France, C., Merrilees, B., Miller, D.: Customer brand co-creation: a conceptual model. Market. Intell. Plann. **33**(6), 848–864 (2015)
Gheorghe, I.R., Purcărea, V.L., Gheorghe, C.M.: Consumer eWOM communication: the missing link between relational capital and sustainable bioeconomy in health care services. Amfiteatru Econ. **20**(49), 684–699 (2018)
Harrigan, P., Evers, U., Miles, M.P., Daly, T.: Customer engagement and the relationship between involvement, engagement, self-brand connection and brand usage intent. J. Bus. Res. **88**, 388–396 (2018)
Keel, A.L., Lending, C.E., Marshall, B.: The impact of online buzz on internet IPO valuation. J. Strateg. Market. 1–23 (2019, in press)
Lamberton, C., Stephen, A.T.: A thematic exploration of digital, social media, and mobile marketing: research evolution from 2000 to 2015 and an agenda for future inquiry. J. Market. **80**(6), 146–172 (2016)
Leung, D., Law, R., Van Hoof, H., Buhalis, D.: Social media in tourism and hospitality: a literature review. J. Travel Tour. Market. **30**(1–2), 3–22 (2013)
Malthouse, E., Shankar, V.: A closer look into the future of interactive marketing. J. Interact. Market. **23**(2), 105–107 (2009)
Mangold, W.G., Faulds, D.J.: Social media: the new hybrid element of the promotion mix. Bus. Horiz. **52**(4), 357–365 (2009)
Rogers, B., Clark, L.: CABS: a conceptual model for context-aware B2B sales applications. J. Res. Interact. Market. **10**(1), 50–66 (2016)
Rohm, A., Kaltcheva, V.D., Milne, G.R.: A mixed-method approach to examining brand-consumer interactions driven by social media. J. Res. Interact. Market. **7**(4), 295–311 (2013)
Scarpi, D.: Does size matter? An examination of small and large web-based brand communities. J. Interact. Market. **24**(1), 14–21 (2010)
Sinkovics, R.R., Pezderka, N., Haghirian, P.: Determinants of consumer perceptions toward mobile advertising—a comparison between Japan and Austria. J. Interact. Market. **26**(1), 21–32 (2012)
Song, J., Goh, K.Y., Phan, T.Q.: Consumers' endorsement effects on marketer and user-generated content in a social media brand community. In: PACIS, p. 349, June 2016
Sugathan, P., Ranjan, K.R., Mulky, A.G.: Atypical shifts post-failure: Influence of co-creation on attribution and future motivation to co-create. J. Interact. Market. **38**, 64–81 (2017)
Tarnovskaya, V., Biedenbach, G.: Corporate rebranding failure and brand meanings in the digital environment. Market. Intell. Plann. **36**(4), 455–469 (2018)
Xiang, Z., Gretzel, U.: Role of social media in online travel information search. Tour. Manag. **31** (2), 179–188 (2010)
Yazdanparast, A., Joseph, M., Muniz, F.: Consumer based brand equity in the 21st century: an examination of the role of social media marketing. Young Consumers **17**(3), 243–255 (2016)

Consumer Adoption of Online-to-Offline Food Delivery Services: A Conceptual Model

Ou Wang(✉)

Waikato Management School, University of Waikato, Hamilton, New Zealand
ou.wang@waikato.ac.nz

Abstract. There is a dramatic growth in the market of Online-To-Offline food delivery services (O2O-FDS) recently. A need exists for the stakeholders of food and catering industries to better understand the market of O2O-FDS in order to create suitable marketing strategies and promotion policies for this promptly changing e-commerce era. However, there is a lack of understanding of the significant factors influencing the consumer adoption of O2O-FDS. This study develops a conceptual model to help systematically understand those important factors. The model is developed based on a literature review concerning the O2O-FDS topic and other relevant topics in food marketing and consumer behaviour. It shows that the O2O-FDS adoption is significantly influenced by *food choice motives, socio-demographics, innovation-adoption characteristics,* and *APP-service quality.*

Keywords: Consumer · O2O · Food delivery service · Conceptual model · E-commerce

1 Introduction

A decade or so ago, we entered the era for e-commerce food shopping. Today, the process speeds up, and new e-commerce modes appear and grow dramatically in food consumption and marketing. As a traditional e-commerce mode, Business-to-Consumer (B2C) food shopping has experienced a quick growth in the past decade (Wang and Somogyi 2018). However, its defect is obvious in food marketing; mainly suitable for packaged foods, rather than fresh foods and cooked meals (Wang and Somogyi 2018). Online-To-Offline Food Delivery Services (O2O-FDS) is one of the emerging modes to supplement the role of B2C in e-commerce food shopping. The O2O-FDS digitalises traditional offline food delivery services with information technologies for mobile payment and meal ordering (Wang et al. 2020). Consumers can use O2O-FDS platforms to order and to make payment for meals from local restaurants or other food service sectors, with those meals delivered to them (Wang et al. 2020). This could hardly come true through the B2C platforms.

The explosion of O2O-FDS first appears in developing countries due to their low logistics and labour costs, cheap mobile devices and services and huge population bases in contrast with developed countries. China is the best case in this scope and leads the O2O-FDS revolution in the world (Cho et al. 2019; Xiao et al. 2018). China's market size of O2O-FDS reached 35 billion US dollars in 2018, doubled the value in

F. J. Martínez-López and S. D'Alessandro (Eds.): *Advances in Digital Marketing and eCommerce*, SPBE, pp. 99–105, 2020.
https://doi.org/10.1007/978-3-030-47595-6_13

2015 (Thibaud 2019; Tong et al. 2020). Internet giants i.e. Uber Eats are trying to copy China's success globally and the O2O-FDS market shares increase quickly in other corners of the world including developed countries i.e. U.S. and South Korea (Eadicicco 2019; Roh and Park 2019; Wang et al. 2020). This trend results into an increased importance for the stakeholders of food and catering industries to better understand the O2O-FDS market, in particular its consumer behaviour, in order to create marketing strategies and promotion policies that meet this promptly changing e-commerce era.

A number of studies have been conducted to explore important factors that influence consumer adoption of B2C food shopping (Wang and Somogyi 2018; Wang et al. 2020). The B2C food shopping is significantly influenced by innovation-adoption characteristics, food choice motives, consumer segments, socio-demographic characteristics, reference effect, and food categories (e.g. Hansen 2005; 2008; Heng et al. 2018; Wang and Somogyi 2018; Wang et al. 2020). While only a few studies could be found related to food consumer behaviour on the O2O-FDS, most published in 2018 and 2019 and half using China as their research location due to the large market size and fast development of the O2O-FDS industry in China (Wang et al. 2020). These new findings are scattered and there is a lack of systematically understanding of the significant factors influencing the consumer adoption of O2O-FDS.

To address the gap, this study will develop a conceptual model to help systematically understand the important factors that have effects on the O2O food delivery shopping behaviour. In order to achieve our goal, this conceptual paper provides a literature review concerning the O2O-FDS topic as well as other relevant topics in food marketing and consumer behaviour.

2 Selection of the Relevant Consumer Studies with O2O-FDS

Published articles were used as a base to develop a conceptual model with the factors influencing consumer adoption for O2O-FDS. The articles were selected through the Google Scholar. The relevant journal articles were recognized by using the following key words: "Consumer" and [O2O OR Online to offline] and [food delivery]. Furthermore, the following criteria were hired to select relevant articles: 1) the research provided information on the consumer adoption of O2O-FDS; 2) the research was published in an academic journal and its full-text was available for review; 3) the research was an empirical study. Based on these criteria, 10 articles were finally selected for in-depth analysis shown in Table 1.

Most of the 10 studies were conducted in Asian emerging countries including China, India, Indonesia and Malaysia. This is in line with the reality that the O2O-FDS market has the first explosive growth in developing countries due to the far lower logistics and labour costs, cheaper mobile devices and services and larger population than developed countries (Cho et al. 2019; Xiao et al. 2018). While two studies were found to use samples from a developed country- South Korea. This corresponds that the O2O-FDS market share has started to speed up among developed countries after the explosion in developing countries (Eadicicco 2019; Roh and Park 2019; Wang et al. 2020).

Table 1. Overview of selected studies about the consumer adoption of O2O-FDS

No.	Author	Research location	Data collection approach	Sample size	Respondent type
1	Wu et al. (2015)	China	Survey	260	University students
2	Yeo et al. (2017)	Malaysia	Survey	224	University students
3	Kang and Namkung (2019)	South Korea	Survey	351	Consumers
4	Cho et al. (2019)	China	Survey	311	Consumers
5	Lee et al. (2019)	South Korea	Survey	340	Consumers
6	Ray et al. (2019)	India	Survey	395	Consumers
7	Roh and Park (2019)	South Korea	Survey	500	Consumers
8	Suhartanto et al. (2019)	Indonesia	Survey	405	Consumers
9	Xu and Huang (2019)	China	Experiment	477	University Students
10	Wang et al. (2020)	China	Survey	954	Consumers

3 The Conceptual Model for Consumer Adoption of O2O-FDS

As shown in Fig. 1, a conceptual model is developed based on the findings from the 10 studies in Table 1. It indicates the significant factors that influence consumers on their adoption of O2O-FDS. Only those factors which have statistically significant effects on the O2O-FDS adoption are involved in this model. The consumer adoption is composed of two stages with consumers' general attitudes and their consumption behaviours (e.g. real consumption or consumption intentions) towards O2O-FDS (Wang et al. 2020). The attitude is consumers' summary evaluations (positive or negative) of the O2O-FDS and it has strongly significant influences on their consumption or consumption intentions of food products through the O2O-FDS platforms (Cho et al. 2019; Kang and Namkung 2019; Wang et al. 2020; Yeo et al. 2017). This indicates that those factors with direct effects on the O2O-FDS attitudes have indirect influences to the O2O-FDS consumption through the O2O-FDS attitudes (Wang et al. 2020).

Based on theories in the e-commerce food shopping behaviour, those significant factors can be grouped into four types: food choice motives, socio-demographics, innovation-adoption characteristics, and APP-service quality (Wang and Somogyi 2018; Wang et al. 2020). The following sub-sections will discuss the effects of those important factors on the O2O-FDS adoption by each of the four factorial types.

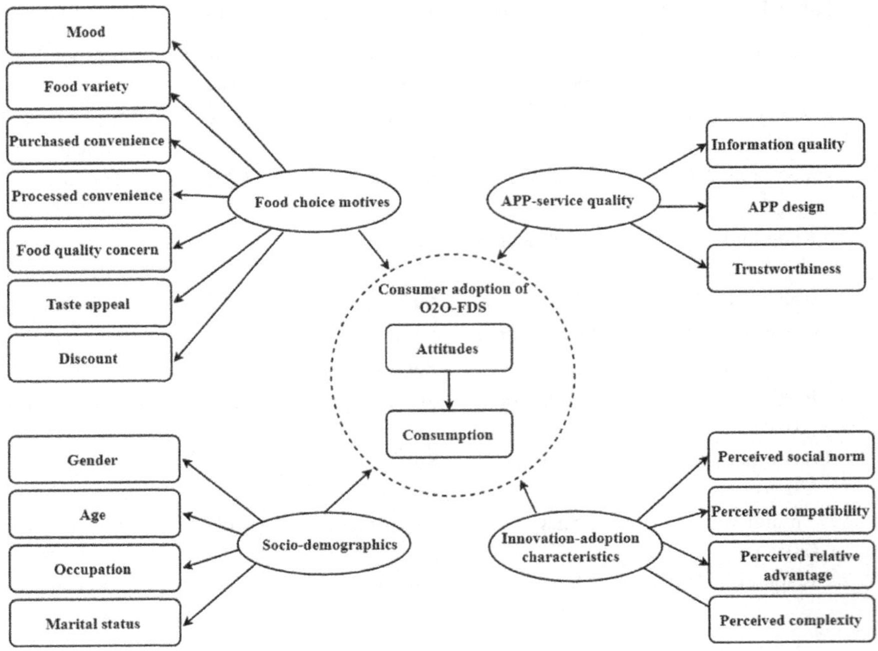

Fig. 1. Conceptual model of the important factors for consumer adoption of O2O-FDS

3.1 Food Choice Motives and the O2O-FDS Adoption

Steptoe et al. (1995) indicate nine important motives for consumers' daily food choices. These nine food choice motives (FCMs) include *health, mood, convenience, sensory appeal, natural content, price, weight control, familiarity* and *ethical concern.* Scholars have associated these FCMs with many kinds of dietary attitudes and consumption behaviours in order to recognize significant motives that have effects on it i.e. consumer adoption of traditional food, sustainable foods, and social-network-related dietary quality (Wang et al. 2020).

A recent study by Wang et al. (2020) has systematically recognized consumers' FMCs related to e-commerce food shopping by using both qualitative and quantitative methods. That include *taste appeal, value for money, cheap, variety, safety concern, quality concern, processed convenience, purchase convenience, others' reviews* and *discount.* The study has also explored associations between these FCMs and the consumer adoption of O2O-FDS, and found that *quality concern, processed convenience, purchase convenience,* and *taste appeal* have significant influences on consumers' attitudes or consumptions towards the O2O food delivery shopping. Furthermore, other studies confirm the significant associations between the O2O-FDS adoption and the FCMs *quality concern, processed convenience,* and *purchase convenience* (Cho et al. 2019; Roh and Park 2019; Suhartanto et al. 2019; Yeo et al. 2017). In addition, *mood (or hedonic motivation), food variety* and *discount* are also important FCMs for the O2O-FDS adoption found by three studies (Cho et al. 2019; Ray et al. 2019; Yeo et al. 2017).

In sum from the findings, those consumers who attach more importance to the food choice concerning *food quality, purchase convenience, processed convenience, available food variety, discount* and *mood enhancement*, are more likely to adopt O2O-FDS than other consumers. While those consumers who attach more importance to the food choice with *taste appeal* are less likely to adopt O2O-FDS than others.

3.2 Innovation-Adoption Characteristics and the O2O-FDS Adoption

Hansen (2005) indicates a five-factorial construct for innovation-adoption characteristics that have effects on consumers' e-commerce food shopping behaviours. The five factors include *perceived social norm* (i.e. the peer pressures on an individual's adoption of e-commerce food shopping), *perceived compatibility* (i.e. if the e-commerce food shopping is in line to an individual's lifestyle and values), *perceived relative advantage* (i.e. the superiority of e-commerce food shopping in comparison with offline ones such as time or money saving), *perceived complexity* (i.e. the usage complexity of the e-commerce food shopping services), and *perceived risk* (e.g. the usage risk such as payment and exchange problems) (Hansen 2005; Wang and Somogyi 2018). A lot of studies have fully or partly confirmed the important influences of consumers' innovation-adoption characteristics on their adoption of B2C food shopping (Wang and Somogyi 2018; Wang et al. 2020).

There is still a lack of studies to systematically and fully explore effects of the five innovation-adoption characteristics on the O2O-FDS adoption. While some of the 10 studies partly confirms the significant effects related to *perceived social norm, perceived compatibility, perceived relative advantage* and *perceived complexity*. Although researchers use different terms including *perceived usefulness, post-usage usefulness, performance expectancy, customer experience* and *perceived value*, all these factors should belong to the scope of consumers' *perceived relative values* based on measurement contents used in their studies which are related to time saving, money saving or receiving e-coupons and all have positive influences on the O2O-FDS adoption (Kang and Namkung 2019; Lee et al. 2019; Ray et al. 2019; Roh and Park 2019; Suhartanto et al. 2019; Wu et al. 2015; Yeo et al. 2017). This term replacement also appears for *perceived social norm* (i.e. social influence), *perceived compatibility* (i.e. habit and the prior online purchase experience) and *perceived complexity* (i.e. mobile anxiety and the 'perceived ease of use' as a reverse measurement); which *perceived social norm* and *perceived compatibility* have positive effects, while *perceived complexity* has a negative effect on the O2O-FDS adoption (Kang and Namkung 2019; Lee et al. 2019; Ray et al. 2019; Roh and Park 2019; Wu et al. 2015; Yeo et al. 2017).

3.3 Socio-demographics and the O2O-FDS Adoption

Some socio-demographic characteristics have been confirmed with the significant effects on consumers' adoption of B2C food shopping, including *age, marital status, gender, occupation, income, educational level* and *household-size* (Wang and Somogyi 2018; Wang et al. 2020). Regarding the O2O-FDS adoption, only 2 of the 10 studies provide the empirical findings in this scope. Wang et al. (2020) point out that those consumers who have a *male gender*, a *younger age*, a *higher level position*, and/or are *married* or *unmarried but with a partner*, are more willing to adopt O2O-FDS than their counterparts with a *female gender*, an *older age, a lower level position*, and/or being *single*. Another study by Roh and Park (2019) mentions that *married consumers* are more inclined towards converting their convenience-seeking-motivation into the adoption of O2O-FDS.

3.4 App-Service Quality and the O2O-FDS Adoption

The rise of O2O-FDS is mainly driven by the high smartphone penetration and the mature of mobile payment technology (Wang et al. 2020). The service quality of mobile apps has therefor direct effects on consumer experiences with the O2O-FDS provided by it. Such effects have been explored by 5 of the 10 studies. The findings show a three-factorial construct of the app-service quality perceived by consumers for O2O-FDS including *information quality, app design* and *trustworthiness* (Cho et al. 2019; Kang and Namkung 2019; Lee et al. 2019; Ray et al. 2019; Xu and Huang 2019). *Information quality* refers to the degree that the accuracy, adequacy, timeliness, understandability and accessibility of information provided by a O2O-FDS app fits with consumers' expectations (Kang and Namkung 2019; Lee et al. 2019; Xu and Huang 2019). A good *APP design* represents the effective design for issues that support the easy usage or understanding to consumers e.g. logic, payment, warranty, the food and restaurant listing, food and consummatory images, and message sidedness (Cho et al. 2019; Kang and Namkung 2019; Ray et al. 2019; Xu and Huang 2019). *Trustworthiness* is the degree that consumers trust into the information provided by a O2O-FDS APP, and the operational capability and reputation of its operator (Cho et al. 2019; Kang and Namkung 2019). In general, a high *app-service quality* will enhance the O2O-FDS adoption by consumers.

4 Conclusion

This study is the first to develop a conceptual model related to the important influencing factors for consumer adoption of O2O-FDS. There are four types of factors that have statistically significant influences on the O2O-FDS adoption including food choice motives, socio-demographics, innovation-adoption characteristics, and APP-service quality. The findings have significant academic contributions and provide reliable materials for researchers to design their future studies related to the O2O-FDS consumer behaviours i.e. developing and testing a confirmatory model in the scope (Wang and Somogyi 2018).

Further, it also has important managerial and policy contributions. By the model, food producers, markers and policy-makers can comprehensively understand consumer behaviours in terms of adoption of O2O-FDS. This can help them to develop effective marketing strategies and promotion policies for selling their food products and services in O2O-FDS platforms e.g. selling their food products and services to right consumer segments (male, young, married consumers…) and promoting it to meet true consumer needs (high quality, taste appeal, purchase/processed convenience…).

References

Cho, M., Bonn, M.A., Li, J.J.: Differences in perceptions about food delivery apps between single-person and multi-person households. Int. J. Hosp. Manag. **77**, 108–116 (2019)

Eadicicco, L.: Uber sees its burgeoning food delivery service as a massive opportunity (2019). https://www.businessinsider.com.au/uber-ipo-filing-reveals-details-of-uber-eats-food-delivery-service-2019-4?r=USandIR=T. Accessed 9 Jan 2020

Hansen, T.: Consumer adoption of online grocery buying: a discriminant analysis. Int. J. Retail Distrib. Manag. **33**(2), 101–121 (2005)

Hansen, T.: Consumer values, the theory of planned behaviour and online grocery shopping. Int. J. Consum. Stud. **32**(2), 128–137 (2008)

Heng, Y., Gao, Z., Jiang, Y., Chen, X.: Exploring hidden factors behind online food shopping from Amazon reviews: a topic mining approach. J. Retail. Consum. Serv. **42**, 161–168 (2018)

Kang, J.W., Namkung, Y.: The information quality and source credibility matter in customers' evaluation toward food O2O commerce. Int. J. Hosp. Manag. **78**, 189–198 (2019)

Lee, S.W., Sung, H.J., Jeon, H.M.: Determinants of continuous intention on food delivery apps: extending UTAUT2 with information quality. Sustainability **11**(11), 3141 (2019)

Ray, A., Dhir, A., Bala, P.K., Kaur, P.: Why do people use food delivery apps (FDA)? A uses and gratification theory perspective. J. Retail. Consum. Serv. **51**, 221–230 (2019)

Roh, M., Park, K.: Adoption of O2O food delivery services in South Korea: the moderating role of moral obligation in meal preparation. Int. J. Inf. Manag. **47**, 262–273 (2019)

Steptoe, A., Pollard, T.M., Wardle, J.: Development of a measure of the motives underlying the selection of food: the food choice questionnaire. Appetite **25**(3), 267–284 (1995)

Suhartanto, D., Helmi Ali, M., Tan, K.H., Sjahroeddin, F., Kusdibyo, L.: Loyalty toward online food delivery service: the role of e-service quality and food quality. J. Foodserv. Bus. Res. **22**(1), 81–97 (2019)

Thibaud: The food delivery market in greater China in 2019 (2019). https://daxueconsulting.com/o2o-food-delivery-market-in-china/. Accessed 9 Jan 2020

Tong, T., Dai, H., Xiao, Q., Yan, N.: Will dynamic pricing outperform? Theoretical analysis and empirical evidence from O2O on-demand food service market. Int. J. Prod. Econ. **219**, 375–385 (2020)

Wang, O., Somogyi, S.: Consumer adoption of online food shopping in China. Br. Food J. **120** (12), 2868–2884 (2018)

Wang, O., Somogyi, S., Charlebois, S.: Food choice in the e-commerce era: a comparison between Business-To-Consumer (B2C), Online-To-Offline (O2O) and new retail. Br. Food J. (2020, in press)

Wu, T.J., Zhao, R.H., Tzeng, S.Y.: An empirical research of consumer adoption behavior on catering transformation to mobile O2O. J. Interdisc. Math. **18**(6), 769–788 (2015)

Xiao, L., Fu, B., Liu, W.: Understanding consumer repurchase intention on O2O platforms: an integrated model of network externalities and trust transfer theory. Serv. Bus. **18**(4), 731–756 (2018)

Xu, X., Huang, Y.: Restaurant information cues, Diners' expectations, and need for cognition: experimental studies of online-to-offline mobile food ordering. J. Retail. Consum. Serv. **51**, 231–241 (2019)

Yeo, V.C.S., Goh, S.K., Rezaei, S.: Consumer experiences, attitude and behavioral intention toward online food delivery (OFD) services. J. Retail. Consum. Serv. **35**, 150–162 (2017)

Role of Digital Relationships in the Marketing of Higher Education: An Exploratory Analysis from New Zealand

Surej P. John(✉)

School of Business, Eastern Institute of Technology, Napier, New Zealand
spjohn@eit.ac.nz

Abstract. The adoption and growth of innovative digital marketing technologies have helped the businesses to embrace relationship marketing strategies in their markets. Relationship marketing strategies are intended to provide sustainable competitive advantages through identifying, developing and maintaining value-creating relationships among its stakeholders, and marketing strategies of higher education were no exception. The current study examines the role of relationship marketing approaches in digital marketing and promotion of educational exports in New Zealand. Based on a systematic review of the literature published between 2000 and 2018, the current study examines the evolution and growth of relationship marketing approaches in the marketing theory and practice. Findings suggest that trust, commitment and service orientation are the critical success factors and growth drivers of relationship marketing approaches in higher education. The study is expected to provide valuable insights for digital marketers particularly those involved in the digital marketing and promotion of higher education exports.

Keywords: Relationship marketing · Digital marketing · Higher education

1 Introduction to Relationship Marketing Paradigm

Relationship marketing is regarded as one of the most debated topics among marketing academics for the past three decades from both a conceptual and empirical perspective. Egan (2003) noted that relationship marketing is "the major trend" in marketing and probably the most controversial discussion topic in management literature during the last decades of this century. Looking back into the literature, relationship marketing is defined as "*an integrated effort to identify, maintain, and build up a network with the individual consumers and to continuously strengthen the network for the mutual benefit of both sides, through interactive, individualized and value-added contacts over a long period of time*" (Shani and Chalasani 1992, p. 34). The definition pointed out the need for businesses to build long-lasting relationships with customers for mutual benefits. However, others argued for a wide and comprehensive face to the relationship marketing approaches in the literature (Christopher et al. 1991; Gummesson 1997). According to Morgan and Hunt, relationship marketing refers to all activities that help a business to establish, develop and maintain successful relational exchanges between its

F. J. Martínez-López and S. D'Alessandro (Eds.): *Advances in Digital Marketing and eCommerce*, SPBE, pp. 106–113, 2020.
https://doi.org/10.1007/978-3-030-47595-6_14

stakeholders including suppliers, buyers, internal (e.g. employees) and external stakeholders like competitors (Morgan and Hunt 1994).

According to the Nordic School of Thought, the management of relationships through various service-oriented activities rather than the traditional marketing mix differentiates relationship marketing from conventional marketing approaches. The Nordic School of Thought suggested three core processes, through which business relationships are to be managed. These include i) the interaction process; ii) the dialogue or communication process and iii) the value process (Gronroos 1997; 2004). Gronroos suggested that "*management of interaction between customers is the core of relationship marketing as the exchange of product is the core of a transaction marketing*" Gronroos (2004, p. 102). The strength of the relationship increases in an interaction process when various types of contacts between the supplier and customers occur over time. Further to interaction, communication is identified as another significant process in relationship marketing. An Integration of various marketing communication activities including advertisements, sales promotions, direct marketing is essential to facilitate the development, maintenance and enhancement of stakeholder relationships in businesses. Finally, customer value generation process indicates the development of customer value in an exchange. Customers should be able to perceive the value of the product or service they have consumed and this perceived value should be equal to or greater than their perceived sacrifice to acquire the product.

2 Educational Tourism and Online Marketing

Educational tourism is a fast-growing tourism activity in which participants travel to a destination either individually or as a group with the prime objective of obtaining a learning experience (Abubakar et al. 2014). Today educational tourists play a significant role in enhancing the tourism industry around the world, particularly among OECD nations. International students represent more than 5% of the entire United States higher education population in 2019. US hosts more than 1 million international students during 2018/19 which contributed to $44.7 billion to the US economy (IIE 2020). According to the recent statistics, New Zealand hosted approximately 110,000 international student travellers during 2017, generating NZ$4.4 billion to the New Zealand economy (Education 2018). Today education exports are the fourth largest export sector of New Zealand (ICEF 2018). Further, "New Zealand spends a comparatively large share of its national wealth on educational institutions" (OECD 2019a, p. 1) and thus presents a good focus for this study. Of all the students enrolled in the twenty-seven formal tertiary education institutions (8 universities and 19 polytechnics) in NZ, 50% came from China and India, with others travelling from as far abroad as Canada, Saudi Arabia and Russia (OECD 2019b). Despite its growing significance, very few studies focus their attention on international student travellers. The study is aimed to investigate the marketing efficiencies of higher educational institutions in New Zealand. In particular, the study examines the factors that are critical for the success of digital marketing strategies of higher educational institutions.

The rapid development of higher educational institutions, increasing mobility and co-integration of intellectual markets, reduced public funding, government regulations and moreover increased competition force higher educational institutions including universities to adopt international marketing strategies in order to promote and advertise themselves in the national and global educational market. With the rise of the internet and other digital technologies, destination marketers (DMs) increasingly use various forms of digital channels such as websites, blogs, and social media to communicate with current and prospective tourists through online posts (Shu and Scott 2014). Since social media-based marketing efforts are found to have a direct effect on user's brand awareness, brand image and overall brand equity, marketers are increasingly using those channels for digital marketing and promotion, and education marketing is no exception. Most higher education institutions have already integrated social media applications into their marketing programs in order to reach, interact with and attract future potentials students (Constantinides and Stagno 2011). In New Zealand, all university websites provide links to their social media networks which allow its current and potential students to share information with each other and getting engaged online. Research suggests that students use social media sites of educational institutions for various reasons. These include social engagement (e.g. view pictures and videos of facilities, finding friends, etc.), information search (e.g. search information about university and study options, read reviews and comments etc.) and content contribution (e.g. sharing pictures and videos, providing opinions and reviews etc.). Even though the potential of social media as an effective marketing and promotional channel is quite evident in the literature, it is incoherent and still lacks clarity in defining the nature of collaborative relationships exist between educational providers and its customers over electronic channels. Current study argues that relationship marketing theories best fit with the digital marketing objectives of the higher education providers. In a tertiary education setting, relationship marketing involves identifying, building and maintaining relationships between the educational provider and its stakeholders. The literature identifies the relationships between three customer groups significant for the success of digital marketing: alumni, current and potential students (Constantinides and Stagno 2011).

3 Methodology

Based on the grounded theory principles, the current study analyzed the contents of relationship marketing articles published in leading marketing journals for the past two decades. Out of 634 peer-reviewed and full papers available with the subject topic "relationship marketing" in ABI/INFORM database between the periods 1 January 2000 and 31 December 2018, a final sample of 132 articles were selected for content analysis after screening for subject relevance and contributions to relationship marketing theory and practice. NVivo version 12 was used for content analyses including open coding, category and thematic development based on the grounded theory foundations. Content analysis of 132 articles published during the last two decades revealed four factors that are critical to the success of any relationship marketing practice in online marketing of higher education. These include trust, commitment, service and technology. Figure 1 presents the major themes derived from our content analysis

Fig. 1. Themes identified from the content analyses of relationship marketing literature

4 Relationship Marketing Strategies for Educational Exports

Trust

Trust refers to the "*confidence in exchange partner's reliability and integrity*" (Morgan and Hunt 1994, p. 23). In the context of higher education, the role of trust encompasses the exchange and interaction of the institution with its current and potential students, alumni and other stakeholders. In an online space, user's engagement and involvement with the brand is related to their perceived trust. The literature identifies that online users' involvement and engagement over digital channels will lead to customer trust and online word of mouth activities (Islam and Rahman 2016). We argue that marketers should develop innovative strategies for encouraging user's engagement over digital channels. For educational marketing, social media channels could design various content categories including displays of current and future programs and offerings, sweepstakes, contests and games, collecting student feedback, infotainment, online enrolments, and other institutional branding activities. These content management strategies are expected to have a positive effect on online customer engagement which in turn influence their perceived trust towards the educational provider.

Commitment

Seller's commitment to develop and maintain profitable relationships with customers and other stakeholders is central to the future of relationship marketing initiatives. The commitment in relationship marketing context may be defined as "*seller's enduring desire to maintain a valued relationship with its stakeholders*" (Verma et al. 2016, p. 209). In order to develop and maintain a valued relationship, sellers must be prepared and committed to investing significant financial resources for the development and implementation of both market and marketing resources including internal digital infrastructure, new products and brands, channels and strategic partnerships (Srinivasan and Moorman 2005). Active participation and presence in the social networks and apps, email marketing, digital ads, viral campaigns, digital brand experiences, mobile marketing, and other online channels including websites, blogs and games may reflect the commitment of universities in developing and maintaining online relationships with current and potential students, alumni and other key stakeholders in education.

Service Orientation

The current study identifies marketer's service orientation as the third critical success factor of relationship marketing. Vargo and Lusch (2004, p. 2), defined service as "*the application of specialized competences (knowledge and skills) through deeds, processes, and performances for the benefit of another entity competences or the entity itself*". Having an efficient service system may help marketers to differentiate themselves from competitors and capture customers trust and loyalty. Service systems refer to the amalgamation of people, technology, organizations and shared information with the intention of value co-creation (Maglio and Spohrer 2008). More importantly, customers do not buy goods services, but they render services which create value for them (Vargo and Lusch 2004). Customer service is regarded as the process which provides various forms of benefits including time, place and form utilities for the customers during the pre-sale, sale and post-sale transactions (Christopher et al. 1991). Most businesses have realized the co-creator role played by customers in the value creation process and have provided innovative ways to serve customer needs. Digital marketing applications including websites, online communities, social media, mobile applications etc. can help marketers to relate with and engage customers online in the value co-creation process (Steinhoff et al. 2018). For example, social media can be effectively used for five phases of digital marketing activities in the context of educational tourism (Chan and Guillet 2011). These include 1) attracting potential students, 2) engaging with the current and potential students, 3) retaining alumni, 4) learning (e.g. student feedback, review, surveys etc.) and finally 5) relating with students and other online users. Executing these phases with a service-oriented view will help the current and potential students to develop a positive attitude towards the institutions which in turn influence their behaviour and loyalty. Table 1 presents the three relationship marketing drivers and its implications in the digital marketing practices of higher education.

Table 1. Factors influencing the success of digital relationships in higher education marketing

RM drivers	RM strategic objectives	Recommendations to enhance relationship marketing
Trust	Build confidence in the reliability and integrity of partners	Encourage staff and students to share their teaching and learning experience via posts or tweets in social media
	Increase the users' involvement in digital channels	Develop games and contests for online users. Offer promotions and incentives for viral posts
	Develop confidence that the educational provider is competent and will perform the specific tasks in the right professional standard	Use the online channels for promoting the academic achievements and recognitions received
	Develop confidence that the education provider will perform the job effectively and reliably	Collect the student feedback on various academic activities including teaching and learning and present the results to the wider public through digital media
Commitment	Develop and maintain a positive relationship with current and potential students	Maintain active participation in social media channels through regular updates and posts. Provide timely updates on scholarship information and research grants for current and potential students
	Enhance student experience	Use email and mobile marketing tools to provide timely feedback to students
	Enhance student experience	Offer integrated digital channels for reserving student counselling and other support services
Service Orientation	Enhance the value proposition offered to the customers	Promote courses offered, programs, study options and costs through digital channels. Information about scholarships, internal and external grants, internships and job opportunities may enhance potential students' perceived benefits
	Increase customer awareness and knowledge of the services offered	Distribute pictures, videos and other visuals of academic and non-academic activities
	Enhance customer's ability to search for and collect relevant information	Invest in digital infrastructure and online advertisements to reach potential customers more efficiently
	Enhance the value co-creation process in the education sector	Invest in digital marketing resources that can help listen to the voice of current students. Developing interactive websites, mobile applications, online communities, social media etc. can help marketers to relate with and engage customers online

5 Conclusion

The research provides new insights into the digital relationships in the marketing of higher education by examining its conceptual scope, digital marketing practices and extant marketing research. However, the scope of this paper is limited to examining the digital relationship marketing growth drivers in the context of educational tourism. Even though the roles of trust, commitment and service orientation in online relationship marketing are identified, its influence on various business stakeholders as well as diverse marketing communication channels is still under-examined. These limitations mark potential research opportunities for future studies.

References

Abubakar, A.M., Shneikat, B.H.T., Oday, A.: Motivational factors for educational tourism: a case study in Northern Cyprus. Tourism Manag. Perspect. **11**, 58–62 (2014). https://doi.org/10.1016/j.tmp.2014.04.002

Chan, N.L., Guillet, B.D.: Investigation of social media marketing: how does the hotel industry in Hong Kong perform in marketing on social media websites? J. Travel Tourism Mark. **28** (4), 345–368 (2011). https://doi.org/10.1080/10548408.2011.571571

Christopher, M., Payne, A., Ballantyne, D.: Relationship marketing: bringing quality customer service and marketing together (1991)

Constantinides, E., Stagno, M.C.Z.: Potential of social media as instruments of higher education marketing: a segmentation study. J. Mark. High. Educ. **21**(1), 7–24 (2011). https://doi.org/10.1080/08841241.2011.573593

Education New Zealand: International student enrolments are down but value holds. EducationCounts (2018). https://enz.govt.nz/news-and-research/media-releases/international-student-enrolments-are-down-but-value-holds/

Egan, J.: Back to the future: divergence in relationship marketing research. Mark. Theory **3**(1), 145–157 (2003). https://doi.org/10.1177/1470593103003001008

Gronroos, C.: Interaction dialogue value processes of relationship marketing. In: Proceedings of the Fifth International Colloquium on Relationship Marketing (1997)

Gronroos, C.: The relationship marketing process: communication, interaction, dialogue, value. J. Bus. Ind. Mark. **19**(2), 99–113 (2004). https://doi.org/10.1108/08858620410523981

Gummesson, E.: Relationship marketing as a paradigm shift: some conclusions from the 30R approach. Manag. Decis. **35**(4), 267–272 (1997). https://doi.org/10.1108/00251749710169648

ICEF: Education now New Zealand's fourth-largest export sector. ICEF Monitor (2018). https://monitor.icef.com/2018/11/education-now-new-zealands-fourth-largest-export-sector/

IIE: The number of International Students in the United States Hits All-Time High. Institute of International Education (2020). https://www.iie.org/Why-IIE/Announcements/2019/11/Number-of-International-Students-in-the-United-States-Hits-All-Time-High

Islam, J.U., Rahman, Z.: Linking customer engagement to trust and word-of-mouth on Facebook brand communities: an empirical study. J. Internet Commer. **15**(1), 40–58 (2016). https://doi.org/10.1080/15332861.2015.1124008

Maglio, P.P., Spohrer, J.: Fundamentals of service science. J. Acad. Mark. Sci. **36**(1), 18–20 (2008). https://doi.org/10.1007/s11747-007-0058-9

Morgan, R.M., Hunt, S.D.: The commitment-trust theory of relationship marketing. J. Mark. **58** (3), 20–38 (1994). https://doi.org/10.1177/002224299405800302

OECD: Education at a glance 2019. OECD (2019a)

OECD: Education GPS. OECD (2019b)

Shani, D., Chalasani, S.: Exploiting niches using relationship marketing. J. Consum. Mark. **9**(3), 33–42 (1992). https://doi.org/10.1108/07363769210035215

(Lavender) Shu, M., Scott, N.: Influence of social media on Chinese students' choice of an overseas study destination: an information adoption model perspective. J. Travel Tourism Mark. **31**(2), 286–302 (2014). https://doi.org/10.1080/10548408.2014.873318

Srinivasan, R., Moorman, C.: Strategic firm commitments and rewards for customer relationship management in online retailing. J. Mark. **69**(4), 193–200 (2005). https://doi.org/10.1509/jmkg.2005.69.4.193

Steinhoff, L., Arli, D., Weaven, S., Kozlenkova, I.V.: Online relationship marketing. J. Acad. Mark. Sci. (2018). https://doi.org/10.1007/s11747-018-0621-6

Vargo, S.L., Lusch, R.F.: Evolving to a new dominant logic for marketing. J. Mark. **68**(1), 1–17 (2004). https://doi.org/10.1509/jmkg.68.1.1.24036

Verma, V., Sharma, D., Sheth, J.: Does relationship marketing matter in online retailing? A meta-analytic approach. J. Acad. Mark. Sci. **44**(2), 206–217 (2016). https://doi.org/10.1007/s11747-015-0429-6

Digital Marketing Strategies in Educational Tourism: A Social Media Perspective

Surej P. John(✉)

School of Business, Eastern Institute of Technology, Napier, New Zealand
spjohn@eit.ac.nz

Abstract. The prime objective of this study is to examine how international student travellers are engaged and involved in the digital marketing communication efforts of educational export providers. Based on an online survey conducted among international student travellers in New Zealand, the study identified critical factors influencing the success of digital marketing communication, particularly through social media networks. The four significant factors that influence online user's adoption and use of marketing information are found to be argument quality, source credibility, user involvement and audience engagement. Further, the current study examined the mediating roles of audience involvement dimensions including transportation, parasocial interaction and identification as well as audience engagement dimensions including cognitive, emotional and behavioural engagement in social media marketing communication process. Further to its contributions to the marketing literature, the study provides valuable implications to the educational export providers and other destination marketers.

Keywords: Social media marketing · Audience engagement · Audience involvement · Educational tourism

1 Social Media Marketing and Educational Tourism

Marketing communication channels have experienced a huge revolution over the past two decades after the advent of the internet. As of October 2019, four billion, four hundred and eighty thousand people access the internet around the world which is more than half (58.8%) of the global population (Internet World Stats 2019). Among the digital global population, nearly 3.7 billion people are active social media users (Statista 2019a). Today, with 2.45 billion monthly users, Facebook remains the world's largest social media network (Statista 2019b). Current literature in digital marketing suggests the potential of social media in reaching consumers and their social communities as well as building personal relationships with them. Social media has become a popular marketing and promotional channel due to its ability to integrate five functional properties. These include 1) information provision, 2) collaboration, 3) communication, 4) interactivity and finally its potential to conduct transactions (Hays et al. 2013, p.212). As a result, the power for creation, consumption and distribution of an overall brand image has transferred from the hands of marketers to consumers online connections and their electronic word of mouth (Erkan and Evans 2016). Due to the

F. J. Martínez-López and S. D'Alessandro (Eds.): *Advances in Digital Marketing and eCommerce*, SPBE, pp. 114–121, 2020.
https://doi.org/10.1007/978-3-030-47595-6_15

proliferation of digital communication channels including social media, consumers are hyper-informed, and highly connected than ever, with more opportunities to engage and interact with brands. Today, Social media is widely used for marketing applications including advertisements, public relations, branding, customer management. Understanding the factors influencing the information adoption process in social media communication will help the marketing practitioners to reach their target market more efficiently. Efficient usage of digital marketing channels brings many value-added benefits to marketers including automation, personalisation, target marketing, enhanced interaction and improved customer loyalty. Therefore, it is essential for marketers to understand how to efficiently use digital marketing channels in their marketing processes.

This paper focuses on the digital marketing strategies of educational tourism providers. Educational tourism involves programs in which people travel to a destination either individually or in a group with the primary objective of acquiring knowledge and learning experience. According to the US Department of Commerce, more than 1 million international students in the United States contributed $44.7 billion to the US economy in the year 2018 (IIE 2020). Educational export is the third-largest export industry in Australia contributing $32.2 billion in 2018 (Australian Bureau of Statistics 2018). In New Zealand, educational exports have contributed more than $5 billion to its economy and are the fourth largest export sector supporting more than 50,000 jobs (New Zealand Education 2018). Despite the growing significance of educational tourism in the social and economic development of a nation, little research has been done on this topic particularly in the context of marketing. Social media is a very relevant marketing communication medium as 'educational tourism' is an information-intensive industry where online users (current and potential student tourists) obtain information about various travel destinations, educational providers, accommodation facilities, tours and attractions which may assist them in their overall travel planning process. Despite the explosive growth and popularity of social media channels, surprisingly only a few studies have investigated its influence on student communities, one of the largest online user communities by age group. Besides, we have a limited understanding of the factors influencing the adoption of marketing communication over social media. To address the links between educational travel, tourism and digital marketing, the current study examines how social media posts (both user-generated and firm generated) influence online users' attitude towards destinations and their travel intentions by addressing the roles of argument quality, source credibility, and audience engagement and audience involvement in marketing communications.

2 Argument Quality and Source Credibility

An extensive review of literature based on the technology adoption and communication frameworks suggested two factors; 1) argument quality and 2) source credibility are critical to the online user's acceptance and further adoption of online information (Petty and Cacioppo 1986; Sussman and Siegal 2003). Argument quality indicates the persuasive strength of arguments in social media posts (Bhattacherjee and Sanford 2006). It reflects the relevance, sufficiency, accuracy, currency, value, and overall usefulness of the information received (Filieri et al. 2015). The quality of available information helps the audience to be able to think critically and analyse the merits and relevance of the information prior to making a decision (Bhattacherjee and Sanford 2006). According to the Information Adoption Model, argument quality influences an individual's central route of persuasion (Sussman and Siegal 2003). In other words, argument quality influences user perception while they process and adopt information.

Source credibility in online communication refers to the extent to which an information source is perceived to be trustworthy, competent and believable and is regarded as an effective peripheral cue in the information adoption process (Petty and Cacioppo 1986). According to Stephenson et al. (2001), source credibility influences audience engagement by strengthening message processing or elaboration. This happens when an online audience who follow peripheral cues are influenced by the source's attractiveness, charisma, likeability and credibility (Sussman and Siegal 2003). When the audience finds that the quality of the transmitted message is inadequate for them to form an attitude regarding a product or service, they may rely on external cues of communication including the trustworthiness, reliability, integrity and character of the source of communication. Therefore, the higher the perceived credibility of the information communicated; the greater will be the adoption of information among its audience.

3 Audience Engagement and Involvement

In the context of digital marketing, audience engagement and involvement may be regarded as similar concepts, however, they exhibit some significant differences. While online engagement indicates the emotional state of mind and level of attention among the online audience, online involvement indicates their interactional dimensions. The current study proposes that online engagement is an antecedent of audience involvement in digital marketing communication. Online engagement can be defined as the audience's motivational state of mind and an internal emotion occurs due to their interactive and co-creative customer experience with online contents communicated. Engagement enables and encourages the users to interact with the media and brand. Extant research suggests that engagement is a multi-dimensional construct with cognitive, an affective and behavioural dimensions (Hollebeek 2013; Hollebeek and Macky 2019). While cognitive engagement refers to the audience's brand-related thought and mental elaboration in digital communication, emotional engagement indicates the level of the audience's affection towards the brand (Hollebeek and Macky 2019). Emotional engagement measures the level of energy, effort and time spent by consumers in a consumer-brand communication (Harrigan et al. 2018). In short, online user's engagement with brand social media pages may lead to behaviours including reviewing firm's products and services, sharing product/brand experience with other networks with similar interests, and expressing loyalty or criticisms.

Audience involvement refers to the "*degree to which audience[s] engage in reflection upon, and para-social interaction with, certain media programs, resulting in overt behavioural change*" (Fu et al. 2016, p.38). Audience involvement indicates the level of interaction between the audience and the media. Digital marketing channels, particularly social media have significantly extended the breadth and depth of customer-brand interactions (Schivinski et al. 2016). The interactive nature of social media helps online customers to establish conversations with their focal brands in online communities and getting involved in content generation and value creation processes (Sashi 2012). According to the literature, audience involvement in communication is associated with three different processes which are 1) transportation, 2) parasocial interaction, and 3) Identification (Igartua 2010; Schramm and Wirth 2010; Seo et al. 2018). To examine the influence of the above-discussed variables on social media user's online perception and resulting behaviour, the current study proposes various hypothetical relationships as demonstrated in Fig. 1.

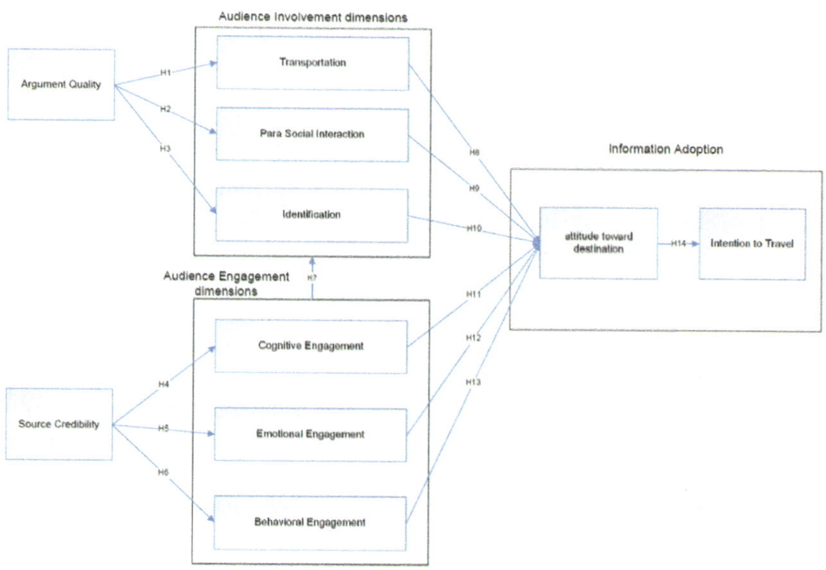

Fig. 1. Conceptual model for social media engagement and Involvement

4 Methodology

To shed more light into the growing educational tourism segment, the current research investigates the characteristics of social media posts that influence the international student's perceived destination image and their intention to travel to that destination. An online survey was developed using Qualtrics and distributed to full-time international students in eight universities and nineteen polytechnics in New Zealand. A snowball sampling technique was employed to collect the data promptly. Out of 450 questionnaire links distributed via email during December 2017, 252 responses were received from which 233 were found to contain data useful for analysis after screening for missing data, skewness, and kurtosis. To ensure the content validity and reliability of the measures, all the items were carefully selected based on the existing literature. Five items for measuring argument quality were adapted from Cheung et al. (2008), four items for source credibility were taken from Yoon and Kim (2016), four items each for measuring cognitive, emotional and behavioural engagement dimensions were adapted from the works of Demangeot and Broderick (2016) and Scott and Craig-Lees (2010). Five items were used for measuring transportation (Fu et al. 2016; Green and Brock 2000), and four items each used for para-social interaction Schramm and Wirth (2010) and identification Cohen (2001) dimensions of audience involvement. Five items for measuring destination image were adapted from Fu et al. (2016) and Park et al. (2017). Items for measuring online users travel intentions were adapted from the works of Abubakar et al. (2014) and Park et al. (2017). The validity of the proposed conceptual model and fourteen hypotheses were tested using structural equation modelling techniques using AMOS version 21 (Ho 2006).

5 Key Findings and Implications

More than 85% of respondents admitted that they have researched a target destination prior to travel through pictures and videos on Facebook, 65% on YouTube, and 56% on Instagram, nearly 40% on Snap Chat and through movies. Nearly 41% of the respondents spend 1–3 h per day on the above media types while another 30% spend 3–5 h per day. Results suggest that argument quality, source credibility, audience involvement and engagement are significant predictors of online user's attitude formation and behavioural intention. Structural path analyses suggest that argument quality strongly influences online user's transportation, para-social interaction, and identification dimensions of online involvement. Further, results indicate that source credibility is strongly related to both cognitive and behavioural dimensions of social media engagement, however, results could not support the influence of source credibility on online users' emotional engagement. Our results indicated a significant role of transportation dimension in online communication. Path analysis suggests that argument quality is strongly related to transportation ($\beta = 0.53$) which in turn positively influence users perceived destination image ($\beta = 0.20$). Results suggest that all three dimensions of user involvement have a direct effect on online information adoption. While both cognitive and behavioural engagement dimensions are positively related to audience perception formation, the relationship between emotional engagement and destination image was not supported. The key findings are presented in Table 1.

Table 1. Structural path estimates of the conceptual model

Path	*Independent variable*	*Dependent variable*	*β*
1	Argument quality	Transportation	0.526***
2	Argument quality	Para social interaction	0.396***
3	Argument quality	Identification	0.209***
4	Source credibility	Cognitive engagement	0.514***
5	Source credibility	Emotional engagement	NS
6	Source credibility	Behavioural engagement	0.465***

(*continued*)

Table 1. *(continued)*

Path	*Independent variable*	*Dependent variable*	*β*
7	Audience engagement	Audience involvement	0.508***
8	Transportation	Destination image	0.203**
9	Para social interaction	Destination image	0.189***
10	Identification	Destination image	0.272***
11	Cognitive engagement	Destination image	0.157***
12	Emotional engagement	Destination image	NS
13	Behavioural engagement	Destination image	0.205***
14	Destination image	Intention to travel	0.444***

NS-Not supported, ** $p < 0.05$; *** $p < 0.005$

The study addresses the link between marketing communication, higher education and tourism by examining the factors influencing the adoption and use of social media posts among international student travellers in New Zealand. Results suggest that the quality of the contents posted in social media sites are critical for enhancing user involvement. Content types such as pictures and videos should be designed in such a way that they could take the audience away from their mundane reality to an attractive imaginary study destination. The results confirm the narrative transportation theory (Green and Brock 2000). Results indicate the role of information sources in marketing communication. Source credibility is found to be directly influencing both cognitive and behavioural engagement dimensions in social media marketing. Users prefer to engage more with the online contents if they could identify and verify the information sources. For example, communicating with students through social media posts (e.g. pictures and videos of the campus facilities) enables them to interact with the educational providers by commenting, reviewing, expressing likes or dislikes, sharing the contents with others in the communities. To establish a trusting relationship with potential online users, the credibility of the information provided by both marketers and other online users is essential. Social media may be effectively used for disseminating information regarding the ranking and reputation of the educational institution, reviews and recommendations from current students about the program offerings, tuition fees, living costs and other expenses, availability of scholarships, jobs and immigration prospects after graduation which are influencing a student's choice of an educational destination abroad through diverse content types.

The current study provides valuable insights about social media marketing strategies, however, its scope was limited to educational tourism context in New Zealand. Since the data for this research is collected only from international student travellers, the application of key findings may be limited among wider tourism segments. Another issue to be addressed is its conceptual framework. The study focused only on two major determinants of online information adoption in digital marketing; argument quality and source credibility. An individual's adoption and use of online marketing communication may be influenced by other factors including social and cultural environment of the audience, types of digital devices used for communication, characteristics of the audience including personality, language and so on. These limitations mark potential research opportunities for future studies.

References

Abubakar, A.M., Shneikat, B.H.T., Oday, A.: Motivational factors for educational tourism: a case study in Northern Cyprus. Tourism Manag. Perspect. **11**, 58–62 (2014)

Australian Bureau of Statistics: Export income to Australia from international education activity in 2016–17 (2018). https://internationaleducation.gov.au/research/research-snapshots/pages/default.aspx. Accessed 1 April 2019

Bhattacherjee, A., Sanford, C.: Influence processes for information technology acceptance: an elaboration likelihood mode. MIS Q. **30**(4), 805–825 (2006)

Cheung, C.M.K., Lee, M.K.O., Rabjohn, N.: The impact of electronic word-of-mouth: the adoption of online opinions in online customer communities. Internet Res. **18**(3), 229–247 (2008)

Cohen, J.: Defining identification: a theoretical look at the identification of audiences with media characters. Mass Commun. Soc. **4**(3), 245–264 (2001)

Demangeot, C., Broderick, A.J.: Engaging customers during a website visit: a model of website customer engagement. Int. J. Retail Distrib. Manag. **44**(8), 814–839 (2016)

Erkan, I., Evans, C.: Social media or shopping websites? The influence of eWOM on consumers' online purchase intentions. J. Mark. Commun. **7266**(May), 1–17 (2016)

Filieri, R., Alguezaui, S., McLeay, F.: Why do travelers trust TripAdvisor? Antecedents of trust towards consumer-generated media and its influence on recommendation adoption and word of mouth. Tour. Manag. **51**, 174–185 (2015)

Fu, H., Ye, B.H., Xiang, J.: Reality TV, audience travel intentions, and destination image. Tour. Manag. **55**, 37–48 (2016)

Green, M.C., Brock, T.C.: The role of transportation in the persuasiveness of public narratives. J. Pers. Soc. Psychol. **79**(5), 701–721 (2000)

Harrigan, P., Evers, U., Miles, M.P., Daly, T.: Customer engagement and the relationship between involvement, engagement, self-brand connection and brand usage intent. J. Bus. Res. **88**, 388–396 (2018). (November 2017)

Hays, S., Page, S.J., Buhalis, D.: Social media as a destination marketing tool: its use by national tourism organisations. Curr. Issues Tourism **16**(3), 211–239 (2013)

Ho, R.: Handbook of Univariate and Multivariate Data Analysis and Interpretation with SPSS. Chapman and Hall/CRC, London (2006)

Hollebeek, L.D.: The customer engagement/value interface: an exploratory investigation. Australas. Mark. J. **21**(1), 17–24 (2013)

Hollebeek, L.D., Macky, K.: Digital content marketing's role in fostering consumer engagement, trust, and value: framework, fundamental propositions, and implications. J. Interact. Mark. **45**, 27–41 (2019)

Igartua, J.J.: Identification with characters and narrative persuasion through fictional feature films. Communications. Eur. J. Commun. Res. **35**(4), 347–373 (2010)

IIE: Number of International Students in the United States Hits All-Time High (2020). https://www.iie.org/Why-IIE/Announcements/2019/11/Number-of-International-Students-in-the-United-States-Hits-All-Time-High. Accessed 16 Jan 2020

Internet World Stats: Internet Usage Statistics (2019). https://www.internetworldstats.com/stats.htm. Accessed 17 Jan 2020

New Zealand Education: International education contributes $5.1 billion to New Zealand (2018). https://enz.govt.nz/news-and-research/ed-news/international-education-contributes-5–1-billion-to-new-zealand/. Accessed 4 Mar 2020

Park, S.H., Hsieh, C.M., Lee, C.K.: Examining Chinese college students' intention to travel to japan using the extended theory of planned behavior: testing destination image and the mediating role of travel constraints. J. Travel Tourism Mark. **34**(1), 113–131 (2017)

Petty, R., Cacioppo, J.: The elaboration likelihood model of persuasion. Adv. Exp. Soc. Psychol. **19**, 123–205 (1986)

Sashi, C.M.: Customer engagement, buyer-seller relationships, and social media. Manag. Decis. **50**(2), 253–272 (2012)

Schivinski, B., Christodoulides, G., Dabrowski, D.: Measuring consumers' engagement with brand-related social-media content: development and validation of a scale that identifies levels of social-media engagement with brands. J. Advertising Res. **56**(1), 64–80 (2016)

Schramm, H., Wirth, W.: Testing a universal tool for measuring parasocial interactions across different situations and media: findings from three studies. J. Media Psychol. **22**(1), 26–36 (2010)

Scott, J., Craig-Lees, M.: Audience engagement and its effects on product placement recognition. J. Promot. Manag. **16**(1–2), 39–58 (2010)

Seo, Y., Li, X., Choi, Y.K., Yoon, S.: Narrative transportation and paratextual features of social media in viral advertising. J. Advertising **47**(1), 83–95 (2018)

Statista: Global digital population as of October 2019 (2019a). https://www.statista.com/statistics/617136/digital-population-worldwide/. Accessed 17 Jan 2020

Statista: Number of monthly active Facebook users worldwide as of 4th quarter 2018 (in millions) (2019b). https://www.statista.com/statistics/264810/number-of-monthly-active-facebook-users-worldwide/. Accessed 26 Mar 2019

Stephenson, M.T., Benoit, W.L., Tschida, D.A.: Testing the mediating role of cognitive responses in the elaboration likelihood model. Commun. Stud. **52**(4), 324–337 (2001)

Sussman, S.W., Siegal, W.S.: Informational influence in organizations: an integrated approach to knowledge adoption. Inf. Syst. Res. **14**(1), 47–65 (2003)

Yoon, D., Kim, Y.K.: Effects of self-congruity and source credibility on consumer responses to coffeehouse advertising. J. Hospitality Mark. Manag. **25**(2), 167–196 (2016)

Extension of META-UTAUT for Examining Consumer Adoption of Social Commerce: Towards a Conceptual Model

Prianka Sarker(✉), D. Laurie Hughes, and Yogesh K. Dwivedi

School of Management, Emerging Markets Research Centre (EMaRC), Swansea University Bay Campus, Swansea SA1 8EN, UK
{937449,d.l.hughes,y.k.dwivedi}@swansea.ac.uk

Abstract. Social commerce is a relatively new subset of digital commerce where buying and selling is transacted via social media interaction. This study attempts to evaluate the suitability of a number of models/theories for understanding the factors affecting consumer adoption of social commerce. This paper first highlights the limitations of alternative theories and then discusses the strengths of the selected theory. Besides the core model, two external variables (Trust and Risk) are considered for extending the selected model for gaining a more comprehensive understanding of antecedents affecting the consumer's adoption behaviour.

Keywords: Social commerce · Adoption · TAM · Meta-UTAUT

1 Introduction

Social commerce generally refers to the activities and transactions of e-commerce via the social media environment using web 2.0 software (Liang and Turban 2011).

Due to the rapid growth and adoption of social media, different brands and businesses are taking advantage of this technology to understanding consumer needs. From the consumer's perspective, review and rating, recommendation and referrals, forums and communities help customers in decision making when purchasing via social commerce (Featherman and Hajli 2016). From the seller perceptive, businesses and brands can reach across borders at a global scale. Moreover, marketing and promotional activities become more accessible and reachable using digital media. Businesses quickly understand consumers' demand and opinion through review, rating and feedback. This helps businesses to improve their products and services (Oragui 2020).

Social commerce is a powerful tool for businesses and customers supported by the attention from scholars in the development of different areas of social commerce. From a literature analysis perspective, the majority of studies seem to have focused their efforts to examine antecedents of intention to adopt with limited attempts to understand social commerce adoption behaviour. Moreover, very few studies have advanced established adoption theories such as UTAUT. In order to provide a basis for further theoretical advances on this topic, this study aims to present a review of theories and constructs utilized to examine social commerce adoption. The study also aims to

F. J. Martínez-López and S. D'Alessandro (Eds.): *Advances in Digital Marketing and eCommerce*, SPBE, pp. 122–129, 2020.
https://doi.org/10.1007/978-3-030-47595-6_16

propose a conceptual model by identifying and integrating external constructs (trust and perceived risk) with an established adoption model. It is noted that the constructs and hypotheses we considered have also been utilized in other technology adoption studies. The relevance and importance of those constructs for understanding social commerce are discussed in this study. The study will be concluded by highlighting the limitations and potential avenues for future research.

2 Literature Searches

The literature search was undertaken using Scopus database and the following set of keywords: "Social commerce" S-Commerce" OR "F–Commerce" AND "Adoption" OR "Acceptance" OR "Usage" OR "Use Behaviour" OR "Intention" OR "Purchase". This keywords-based search was allowed in title, abstracts, and keywords of the search outputs. This search returned 184 articles. In order to focus on more salient work, we eliminated the conference papers, internet and other sources and only considered journal articles. Further filtering was conducted for identifying 111 quantitative studies, which were published between 2006 to 2019.

3 Dominant Theories of Social Commerce Adoption

Several adoption theories and models have been used in social commerce studies. In this review, we are presenting and reviewing the frequently utilised theories and models. Table 1 has presented some examples of the theory/models that are discussed further. As shown in Table 1, the main focus of existing studies has been to examine intention as dependent variables regardless as to which theory has been utilised. These studies exhibit limited efforts to examine the actual behaviour and post-adoption-related variables as dependent variables.

Table 1. Frequently used Theories/Models in social commerce

Theory/Model	Source	Country	Highlights
TAM	Biucky and Harandi (2017)	Iran	The model explained 7% of the variance in intention to use and 20% of the variance in perceived usefulness
TAM	Kim and Noh (2012)	South Korea	The model explained 65.7% variance in the perceived usefulness of social commerce
S-O-R model	Li (2017)	Taiwan	The model explained 65.4% of the variance in buying intention
Trust transfer theory	Lin et al. (2017)	China	The model explained 38.5%of the variance in social shopping intention and 36.7% of the variance in social sharing intention
Social support theory	Hajli et al. (2015)	UK	The model explained 30% of the variance in the intention to buy and 28% of the variance in social commerce construct
Social presence theory	Hassan et al. (2018)	Pakistan	The model explained 40.6% variance in trust-in-marketplace and 46.3% variance in social commerce purchase intention

Technology acceptance model (TAM) is the most dominant theory that has been used in social commerce research. A total of 14 studies have utilised TAM to understand antecedents of social commerce purchase intention. The main criticisms of TAM include its over utilisation, integration with similar theories and its parsimonious nature as a limitation for understanding complex issues such as social commerce adoption (Slade et al. 2015).

Within social commerce studies, the Stimulus- Organism-Response (S-O-R) model is the second most frequently utilised model. The S-O-R model has initially been used for understanding consumer behaviour within a store environment. Therefore, it is also considered as a potential model for social commerce consumer behaviour. Within social commerce research, a total of 10 studies have used the S-O-R model for understanding various aspects, including purchase intention. However, the model is that it is too broad and does not provide a specific list of constructs/variables; hence many studies use different constructs to represent stimulus, organism and response, which makes it challenging to assess theoretical advances.

Social support theory is an appropriate theory in the context of social commerce. People come across online communities to obtain social support. Social support is defined as perceived care and support of members of a group (Cobb 1976), where individuals find supportive resources in relationships developed with a friend in the community (Wellman and Wortley 1990). Nine studies that have used social support theory have also examined the role of other constructs such as relationship quality, perceived value for determining continuance participation behaviour. This suggests that using only the role of social support is not sufficient for understanding social commerce adoption.

Other theories that have been utilised for understanding social commerce adoption research include trust transfer theory (used in 11 studies), social presence theory (eight studies) and social exchange theory (used in six studies). Also, there are other dominant adoption theories (such as UTAUT, UTAUT2, and Meta-UTAUT) have not been utilised to a great extent. As these theories provide a more comprehensive view of adoption antecedents, they should be utilised by future studies to gain a better understanding of the antecedents of social commerce adoption.

4 Theoretical Model Selection

After carefully filtering the literature review, we found that the constructs of UTAUT are useful for examining the actual behaviour. However, UTAUT does not include a construct such as attitude, which is an essential consumer-related attribute (Dwivedi et al. 2006; 2019; Rana et al. 2013). Due to this, we considered Meta-UTAUT (Dwivedi et al. 2019) that includes the attitude construct as a basis for building a conceptual model for this study. There are several reasons for using Meta UTAUT. Meta-UTAUT shows that attitude plays a vital role in the acceptance and use of IT/IS by having a direct impact on behavioural intention as well as on use behaviour. Another reason for giving preference to Meta-UTAUT over UTAUT is that meta-UTAUT does not require the use of certain moderators. Past studies that have utilised UTAUT justified non-inclusion of moderators and excluded them from the development and testing of their theoretical models. As Meta-UTAUT provides moderator less alternative to UTAUT, it was selected as an appropriate base theory for this research. However, some aspects are lacking within this theory, which necessitates consideration of external constructs. Hence, the next section discusses and selects appropriate external constructs for integration with Meta-UTAUT.

5 Model Extension and Hypotheses Development

A review of the social commerce literature suggests that some of the variables relevant and essential to this domain are not part of the original Meta-UTAUT model. We argue that Trust and Perceived Risk should be considered as additional external constructs to be integrated with Meta-UTAUT. Trust and Perceived Risk are seen in various technology adoption studies as well as these two constructs have also been frequently utilised in social commerce studies. Table 2 lists the significant and non-significant relationship of the Meta-UTAUT constructs (performance expectancy, effort expectancy, social influence, facilitating condition attitude), trust and perceived risk with behavioural intention/purchase intention. The role of Trust and Risk is discussed, and associated hypotheses are proposed below.

Table 2. Relationship of the Constructs of Meta UTAUT

IV	DV	Significant	No	Non-sig	No
Trust	PI	Hajli et al. (2015), Gibreel et al. (2018), Makmor et al. (2018), Kim (2013), Hajli (2017), Lee and Choi (2014), Vongsraluang and Bhatiasevi (2017), Hassan et al. (2018), Li (2017), Zhao et al. (2019), Lin et al. (2017), Ng (2013), Tarmedi et al. (2018)	14	Williams (2018)	1
PR	BI	Farivar et al. (2017; 2018), Biucky and Harandi (2017)	3	Williams (2018), Gan and Wang (2017), Tello et al. (2018)	3
PE	PI	Lee and Choi (2014), Kim and Noh (2012), Biucky and Harandi (2017), Shin (2013), Williams (2018), Gatautis and Medziausiene (2014)	7	Gibreel et al. (2018)	1
PE	Attitude	Shin (2013), Cho and Son (2019)	2		
SI	BI	Gatautis and Medziausiene (2014), Sheikh et al. (2017), Farivar et al. (2017), Chen and Shen (2015), Li and Ku (2018)	5	Sheikh et al. (2017),	2
Attitude	PI	Yeon et al. (2019), Lin and Wu (2015), Hajli and Sims (2015), Cho and Son (2019), Shin (2013)	5		
EE/PEOU	BI	Gatautis and Medziausiene (2014), Sheikh et al. (2017), Biucky and Harandi (2017), Kim (2013), Featherman and Hajli (2016)	5	Sheikh et al. (2017)	2
FC	BI	Gatautis and Medziausiene (2014), Sheikh et al. (2017), Lin and Wu (2015), Hajli et al. (2015)	4		

Legend: **IV:** Independent variable; **DV:** Dependent variable; **PI**: Purchase intention; **BI:** Behavioural intention; **PR:** Perceived risk; **PE:** Perceived expectancy; **PU:** Perceived Useful; **SI:** Social influence; **EE:** Effort expectancy; **PEOU:** Perceived ease of use; **FC:** Facilitating condition.

5.1 Trust

Trust is a complicated aspect to define traditionally and treated both as a unitary and multidimensional concept (Mcknight and Chervany 2001). Trust is one of the essential aspects of e-commerce studies. This is because when rules are not satisfactory, consumers reduce the risk by relying on trust (Gefen and Straub 2004). Personal data security and reliability are also anticipated as factors in the middle of trust on the internet (Alshibly 2015). Due to the necessity of trust, 15 social commerce studies have hypothesised effect of trust on behavioural intention, which includes 14 studies that have established a significant positive relationship with purchase intention. This suggest that trust is a vital element of online based transactions. Many other technology acceptance studies have also integrated trust and risk (Kapoor et al. 2014; Slade et al. 2014; 2015; Weerakkody et al. 2017) and found a significant relationship. For example, Slade et al. (2015) found positive significant between trust in provider and intention to use mobile payment. Also, Beldad and Egner (2017) examined trust in continuously used of fitness app and found a significant positive result. Considering importance of trust in electronic transactions and its consistent role in significantly influencing consumer intention, the following hypothesis is proposed: ***Trust significantly influences consumer's behavioural intention to adopt social commerce.***

5.2 Perceived Risk

According to Beaty et al. (2013), the Perceived risk is the uncertainty involved in the process of buying services or product. In social commerce, consumers can share product information with the community and explore the experience with others, which may lead to intrusion of privacy (Herrando et al. 2017). Risk related to product quality and originality, vendors/seller's authenticity and payment can influence consumer behaviour. Considering risk as an important element of technology adoption, many studies examined this construct. For example, Roy et al. (2012) explored perceived risk and found negative significant effect on internet banking adoption. Also, in social commerce studies risk has been hypothesised with behavioural intention in the limited number of times and three studies found negative significant and three found negative non-significant relationship. Therefore, this is suggesting that further work needs to be conducted to clarify and establish the role of this construct for influencing behavioural intention. Literature provides empirical evidence that the higher the risk lower the intention of adopting social commerce-related applications. Considering these points - the following hypothesis is proposed: ***Perceived risk negatively influence consumer's behavioural intention to adopt social commerce.***

6 Conclusion

Social commerce is emerging as an active research area, and in the last few years, different areas of social commerce have been explored. We have found that TAM, S-O-R model and social support theory have been widely used within social commerce adoption research. However, they pose certain limitations towards further theoretical advances on this emerging topic. For this reason, this study proposed an alternative theory (Meta-UTAUT) as a base model due to the advantages offered by this model, as discussed in this paper. However, due to lack of space, we could not elaborate on the core model (Meta-UTAUT). Therefore, future studies will elaborate on these factors and analyse the model for greater understanding. We have proposed to integrate constructs such as trust and perceived risk as an integral addition to the Meta-UTAUT model. However, there are some other constructs; for example, hedonic motivation, cost, innovativeness can also be relevant for understanding social commerce adoption. Future studies on this topic should also consider those variables. Furthermore, future studies should focus on examining role of actual behaviour. Also, empirical studies should be conducted to test Meta-UTAUT model along aforementioned external variables.

References

Alshibly, H.H.: Customer perceived value in social commerce: an exploration of its antecedents and consequences. J. Manag. Res. **7**(1), 17–37 (2015)

Beaty, T.H., Taub, M.A., Scott, A.F., Murray, J.C., Marazita, M.L., Schwender, H., Mangold, E.: Confirming genes influencing risk to cleft lip with/without cleft palate in a case–parent trio study. Hum. Genet. **132**(7), 771–781 (2013)

Biucky, S.T., Harandi, S.R.: The effects of perceived risk on social commerce adoption based on TAM model. Int. J. Electron. Commer. Stud. **8**(2), 173–196 (2017)

Chen, J., Shen, X.L.: Consumers' decisions in social commerce context: an empirical investigation. Decis. Support Syst. **79**(1), 55–64 (2015)

Cho, E., Son, J.: The effect of social connectedness on consumer adoption of social commerce in apparel shopping. Fashion Text. **6**(1), 14–15 (2019)

Dwivedi, Y.K., Rana, N.P., Jeyaraj, A., Clement, M., Williams, M.D.: Re-examining the unified theory of acceptance and use of technology (UTAUT): towards a revised theoretical model. Inf. Syst. Front. **21**(3), 719–734 (2019)

Dwivedi, Y.K., Khan, N., Papazafeiropoulou, A.: Consumer adoption and usage of broadband in Bangladesh. In: AMCIS 2006 Proceedings, p. 426 (2006)

Farivar, S., Turel, O., Yuan, Y.: A trust-risk perspective on social commerce use: an examination of the biasing role of habit. Internet Res. **27**(3), 586–607 (2017)

Farivar, S., Turel, O., Yuan, Y.: Skewing users' rational risk considerations in social commerce: an empirical examination of the role of social identification. Inf. Manag. **55**(8), 1038–1048 (2018)

Featherman, M.S., Hajli, N.: Self-service technologies and e-services risks in social commerce era. J. Bus. Ethics **139**(2), 251–269 (2016)

Gan, C., Wang, W.: The influence of perceived value on purchase intention in social commerce context. Internet Res. **27**(4), 772–785 (2017)

Gatautis, R., Medziausiene, A.: Factors affecting social commerce acceptance in Lithuania. Procedia-Soc. Behav. Sci. **110**, 1235–1242 (2014)

Gefen, D., Straub, D.W.: Consumer trust in B2C e-Commerce and the importance of social presence: experiments in e-Products and e-Services. Omega **32**(6), 407–424 (2004)

Gibreel, O., AlOtaibi, D.A., Altmann, J.: Social commerce development in emerging markets. Electron. Commer. Res. Appl. **27**(2), 152–162 (2018)

Hajli, N., Sims, J.: Social commerce: the transfer of power from sellers to buyers. Technol. Forecast. Soc. Chang. **94**(1), 350–358 (2015)

Hajli, N., Shanmugam, M., Powell, P., Love, P.E.: A study on the continuance participation in on-line communities with social commerce perspective. Technol. Forecast. Soc. Chang. **96** (2), 232–241 (2015)

Hajli, N., Sims, J., Zadeh, A.H., Richard, M.O.: A social commerce investigation of the role of trust in a social networking site on purchase intentions. J. Bus. Res. **71**, 133–141 (2017)

Hassan, M., Iqbal, Z., Khanum, B.: The role of trust and social presence in social commerce purchase intention. Pak. J. Commer. Soc. Sci. **12**(1), 111–135 (2018)

Herrando, C., Jiménez-Martínez, J., Martín-De Hoyos, M.J.: Passion at first sight: how to engage users in social commerce contexts. Electron. Commer. Res. **17**(4), 701–720 (2017)

Kapoor, K.K., Dwivedi, Y.K., Williams, M.D.: Innovation adoption attributes: a review and synthesis of research findings. Eur. J. Innov. Manag. **17**(3), 327–348 (2014)

Kim, D.: Under what conditions will social commerce business models survive? Electron. Commer. Res. Appl. **12**(2), 69–77 (2013)

Kim, S., Noh, M.J.: Determinants influencing consumers' trust and trust performance of social commerce and moderating effect of experience. Inf. Technol. J. **11**(10), 1369–1380 (2012)

Lee, H., Choi, J.: Why do people visit social commerce sites but do not buy? The role of the scarcity heuristic as a momentary characteristic. KSII Trans. Internet Inf. Syst. **8**(7), 125–127 (2014)

Li, C.Y.: How social commerce constructs influence customers' social shopping intention? An empirical study of a social commerce website. Technol. Forecast. Soc. Chang. **45**(2), 342–345 (2017)

Li, C.Y., Ku, Y.C.: The power of a thumbs-up: will e-commerce switch to social commerce? Inf. Manag. **55**(3), 340–357 (2018)

Liang, T.P., Turban, E.: Introduction to the special issue social commerce: a research framework for social commerce. Int. J. Electron. Commer. **16**(2), 5–14 (2011)

Lin, C.S., Wu, S.: Exploring antecedents of online group-buying: social commerce perspective. Hum. Syst. Manag. **34**(2), 133–147 (2015)

Lin, J., Yan, Y., Chen, S.: Understanding the impact of social commerce website technical features on repurchase intention: a Chinese guanxi perspective. J. Electron. Commer. Res. **18** (3), 225–226 (2017)

Makmor, N., Alam, S.S., Aziz, N.A.: Social support, trust and purchase intention in social commerce era. Int. J. Supply Chain Manag. **7**(5), 572–581 (2018)

McKnight, D.H., Chervany, N.L.: What trust means in e-commerce customer relationships: an interdisciplinary conceptual typology. Int. J. Electron. Commer. **6**(2), 35–59 (2001)

Mendoza-Tello, J.C., Mora, H., Pujol-López, F.A., Lytras, M.D.: Social commerce as a driver to enhance trust and intention to use cryptocurrencies for electronic payments. IEEE Access **6**, 50737–50751 (2018)

Ng, C.S.P.: Intention to purchase on social commerce websites across cultures: a cross-regional study. Inf. Manag. **50**(8), 609–620 (2013)

Oragui, D.: Social Commerce: 8 Benefits for Your Business. [online] Blog.salesandorders.com. https://blog.salesandorders.com/social-commerce-benefits. Accessed 16 Jan 2020

Rana, N.P., Dwivedi, Y.K., Williams, M.D.: Evaluating alternative theoretical models for examining citizen centric adoption of e-government. Transforming Gover.: People, Process Policy **7**(1), 27–49 (2013)

Roy, S.K., Kesharwani, A., Bisht, S.S.: The impact of trust and perceived risk on internet banking adoption in India. Int. J. Bank Mark. **30**(4), 303–322 (2012)

Cobb, S.: Social support as a moderator of life stress. Psychosom. Med. **38**(5), 300–314 (1976)

Sheikh, Z., Islam, T., Rana, S., Hameed, Z., Saeed, U.: Acceptance of social commerce framework in Saudi Arabia. Telematics Inform. **34**(8), 1693–1708 (2017)

Shin, D.H.: User experience in social commerce: in friends we trust. Behav. Inf. Technol. **32**(1), 52–67 (2013)

Slade, E.L., Williams, M.D., Dwivedi, Y.K.: Devising a research model to examine adoption of mobile payments: an extension of UTAUT2. The Marketing Review **14**(3), 310–335 (2014)

Slade, E., Williams, M., Dwivedi, Y., Piercy, N.: Exploring consumer adoption of proximity mobile payments. J. Strateg. Mark. **23**(3), 209–223 (2015)

Tarmedi, E., Sulastri Sumiyati, S., Dirgantari, P.D.: Factors affecting customer trust and their impact on customer behavioural intention: a study of social commerce in Indonesia. Pertanika J. Soc. Sci. Humanit. **23**(2), 35–36 (2018)

Vongsraluang, N., Bhatiasevi, V.: The determinants of social commerce system success for SMEs in Thailand. Inf. Dev. **33**(1), 80–96 (2017)

Weerakkody, V., Irani, Z., Kapoor, K., Sivarajah, U., Dwivedi, Y.K.: Open data and its usability: an empirical view from the Citizen's perspective. Inf. Syst. Front. **19**(2), 285–300 (2017)

Wellman, B., Wortley, S.: Different strokes from different folks: community ties and social support. Am. J. Sociol. **96**(3), 558–588 (1990)

Williams, M.D.: Social commerce and the mobile platform: payment and security perceptions of potential users. Comput. Hum. Behav. 105557 (2018). (in press)

Yeon, J., Park, I., Lee, D.: What creates trust and who gets loyalty in social commerce? J. Retail. Consum. Serv. **50**(2), 138–144 (2019)

Zhao, J.D., Huang, J.S., Su, S.: The effects of trust on consumers' continuous purchase intentions in C2C social commerce: a trust transfer perspective. J. Retail. Consum. Serv. **50**(2), 42–49 (2019)

The Effect of Web Advertising Visual Design on Online Purchase Intention: Insights on Generations Y and Z

Luisa M. Martinez[1(✉)], Teresa V. Neves[2], and Luis F. Martinez[2]

[1] IPAM Lisboa and UNIDCOM/IADE, Universidade Europeia, Lisbon, Portugal
luisa.martinez@universidadeeuropeia.pt
[2] Nova School of Business and Economics, Universidade Nova de Lisboa, Lisbon, Portugal
{21972,luis.martinez}@novasbe.pt

Abstract. Web advertising is a fast-growing industry in which brands fight for the attention of the most attractive consumers: Millennials and Centennials. This study aims to test the impact of Web Advertising Visual Design (WAVD) on the consumers' Online Purchase Intention (OPI) and, simultaneously, analyze if such influence differs across those generations. Participants (N = 318) filled in an online questionnaire. Data revealed a direct impact of visual design on consumers' OPI as well as an indirect impact via Attitude Toward the Brand (ATB). Moreover, results showed that generations Y and Z do not differ significantly in their intentions, although Centennials exhibit a higher coefficient for the influence of WAVD on OPI. Regarding the theoretical implications, the results tend to confirm the Theory of Visual Rhetoric and partially confirm the Theory of Reasoned Action. Managerial implications and research limitations are also discussed.

Keywords: Web advertising · Visual design · Online Purchase Intention · Brand attitude · Generation Y · Generation Z

1 Introduction

Although several entertainment and media segments are facing a decline in growth rates, Internet advertising stands out with its continuous expanding market – specially as consumer demand for Internet access rises across the globe (PwC 2017). As high-speed mobile connections are becoming increasingly available – and affordable – to more and more consumers, it is vital for brands to better understand and to reach out to these connected customers in a personalized way. In such a competitive market, it is essential that companies give a careful consideration to Web Advertising Visual Design (WAVD) in order to be able to accomplish their objectives within their target audience (Duffett 2015). Previous studies on visual design have focused on the influence that web advertising has on certain consumer reactions. Fewer have discussed the impact that WAVD could have on Online Purchase Intention (OPI) (Goodrich 2011; Shaouf et al. 2016). In their research, Shaouf et al. (2016) have considered an interesting potential

F. J. Martínez-López and S. D'Alessandro (Eds.): *Advances in Digital Marketing and eCommerce*, SPBE, pp. 130–140, 2020.
https://doi.org/10.1007/978-3-030-47595-6_17

impact of a direct effect of WAVD on OPI, complemented with an indirect effect, through a mediator influence of the consumer attitudinal responses to the visual design.

However, and despite the known disparities in effects between different groups of consumers (regarding gender or age), there seems to be a gap in the literature when trying to comprehend if this visual influence of an advertising differs across similar generations. Therefore, this study pretends to analyze the effects of WAVD on the consumer OPI and, furthermore, to understand if such stimuli can impact consumers from generations Y and Z differently. Researchers have studied the differences across the several generations that now co-exist in the market and have found several behavioral differences across them, which has been justifying a generational marketing target by brands (Higgins 1998; Williams and Page 2011). The Millennials (Generation Y) and the Centennials (Generation Z) are the most recent and allegedly similar ones regarding online behavior, as both generations could be considered as intrinsically digital natives. Despite their apparent resemblance, Generation Z studies are lacking, as this is the most recent generation and many of the Centennials are now entering the job market. Also, previous research has found that these two generations do not react in the same way to the same stimuli (e.g., Han et al. 2018; Priporas et al. 2017). Hence, one of the main purposes of this study is to understand if the influence that WAVD has on the consumer OPI differs between generations Y and Z.

2 Literature Review

2.1 Cohort Theory: Generations Y and Z

The cohort theory states that people born within the same period – thus raised in the same socio-economic and technologic environments and exposed to the same stimuli – will present similar consumer related needs, attitudes and demands (Jackson et al. 2011). Generation Y (also known as Millennials) was defined as the group of people born between 1977 and 1994 (Brosdahl and Carpenter 2011). Being exposed from the start to high acceptance for change and a significant respect for ethnic and cultural diversity, Millennials grew up in a time of immense and fast-paced change (Bolton et al. 2013; Williams and Page 2011). The strong fever for fast results is characteristic of Millennials, as well as their lack of concern with the why of things (Himmel 2008). The combination of all these factors to which Generation Y was exposed to resulted in open-minded individuals, highly efficient in multi-tasking, with a fast-paced spirit and with a strong goal orientation, being highly motivated to pursue their perceptions of success. As a summary, Williams and Page (2011) defined eight key values that best describe this generation: (1) choice; (2) customization; (3) scrutiny; (4) integrity; (5) collaboration; (6) speed; (7) entertainment; and (8) innovation. Next, Generation Z (also referred to as Tweens or Baby Bloomers) is composed by people born after 1994 (Williams and Page 2011). They are experiencing an environment where global terrorism and war are constants, alongside with school violence and economic uncertainty (Williams et al. 2010). These surrounding conditions are raising more conservative and traditional individuals than the previous generation, with a great value being given to security (Wellner 2000). On the other hand, they are also very savvy and high-tech people, accustomed to being constantly bombarded by digital notifications where everything, everywhere and everyone is only one click away. This combination resulted in global and diverse citizens, with four main characteristics, mentioned by Williams and Page (2011): (1) instant gratification; (2) success as guaranteed; (3) liberal social values; and (4) high appreciation for realness.

2.2 Social Media, Attitudinal Responses, and Purchase Intention

Both Generations Y and Z have image-driven individuals, people who make personal statements with their image (Himmel 2008). With a greater need for peer acceptance, individuals from both generations are virtually connected through social networks (Boyd and Ellison 2007). Several authors have begun to study the perceptions of online and of social media advertising (e.g., Delfanti and Arvidsson 2019; Duffett 2015). Online advertising can be measured through changes in the customers' attitudinal responses (Shaouf et al. 2016). Attitude can be defined as an overall feeling or evaluation of a certain subject, that can be an individual, an idea or an object (Fishbein and Ajzen 1975). There are two important attitudes to consider regarding customer responses: Attitude Toward Advertising (ATA) and Attitude Toward Brand (ATB). ATA was defined by MacKenzie and Lutz (1989) as the response obtained in a consumer with a singular advertisement and it is proven to directly influence the consumers' purchase intention of the advertised product (Suh and Yi 2006). ATB was defined by Phelps and Hoy (1996) as a predisposition to respond in a certain manner (favorable or unfavorable) to a particular brand. Other authors have studied these relationships in an online environment, establishing an influence of the consumers' attitudes in the impact the site stimuli have on their purchase intention (e.g., Korgaonkar and Wolin 2002; Stevenson et al. 2000). Also, OPI is the consumer's willingness to acquire a product or a service from an online retailer, through a website Cyr (2008). The intention of purchasing something has been proven to be related with the action of purchasing that same thing (Pavlou and Fygenson 2006). Therefore, the OPI is also an important key performance indicator that can predict the actual purchase amount that will result from a certain online stimulus (Elwalda et al. 2016; Shaouf et al. 2016). The right combination of visual stimuli in an online communication strategy is an important balance that advertisers are eager to comprehend.

2.3 Web Advertising Visual Design (WAVD)

Visual Design deals with aesthetic beauty of the web advertisement and is shown to have a crucial role in its success (Cho 1999). Cyr (2008) showed that aesthetic beauty positively affects the consumer's trust, when concerning the visual design of the web advertisement. Therefore, in an online context, a carefully designed WAVD may be a differentiating factor among thousands of advertisements (Pieters et al. 2010). From a variety of attention-grabbing tools (e.g., shapes, images, font type and size), color plays a vital role in capturing the attention and establishing a strong first-impression on potential consumers (Dreze and Zufryden 1997; Labrecque and Milne 2013). Some theories have arisen to explain this visual impact on consumer behavior. Scott (1994) proposed the theory of Visual Rhetoric (TVR), that states that visual elements (such as colors or images) can be used by an interested party as a message frame in an attempt to influence an audience. This TVR has been supporting models proposed by other authors to predict online consumer behaviors (e.g., Ganguly et al. 2009; Shaouf et al. 2016).

3 Model and Hypotheses

This paper aims to understand if there is any difference in the influence of WAVD on OPI when comparing generations Y and Z. For this purpose, a conceptual model was created in order to better assess the impact of WAVD on the consumer's attitudinal responses and OPI. Furthermore, the generation to which the consumer belongs to was used to moderate the relationship between the variables in this model. There are several models that try to predict behavioral intentions and their determinants. Accordingly, the Theory of Reasoned Action (TRA), proposed by Fishbein and Ajzen (1975), and its derivatives are widely accepted by theorists of several fields, including in online retailing (e.g., Elwalda et al. 2016; Pavlou and Fygenson 2006; Shaouf et al. 2016). TRA posits that the most important explanatory element of behavior is behavioral intention, rather than the subject's attitude toward the object at which the behavior is directed. Other authors have suggested models in accordance with this theory, using cognitive judgments such as ATA or ATB as intermediary variables that explain the effect of advertisements on OPI (MacKenzie and Lutz 1989; Shimp 1981).

Nonetheless, some authors have discussed the limitations of the TRA, suggesting that the visual appeal is able to impact the consumer's behavioral intentions, even without attitude or other cognitive judgments' influence (Sundar and Noseworthy 2014). The TVR defends that visual online stimuli impact consumer behavior as a 'direct effect' (e.g., Kabadayi and Gupta 2011). In their research, Shaouf et al. (2016) designed a new model that combined these two theories, complementing the direct effect of WAVD on OPI proposed by the TVR with its 'indirect effect', suggested by the TRA. The same reasoning was recreated in the model constructed in this paper, as following: (1) WAVD will influence OPI, based on the TVR (Scott 1994; Shaouf et al. 2016); and (2) cognitive responses such as ATA and ATB will impact OPI, as the TRA suggests (Fishbein and Ajzen 1975; Shaouf et al. 2016). Thus, the first set of hypotheses addresses these direct and indirect relations that WAVD has on OPI:

H1: WAVD will have a positive effect on a consumer's OPI;
H2: WAVD will positively influence a consumer's ATWA;
H3: ATWA will have a positive effect on a consumer's OPI;
H4: WAVD will positively affect a consumer's ATB;
H5: ATB will influence positively a consumer's OPI.

Regarding the moderating effect of the consumers' generation, recent literature suggests that Generation Z can be more impervious to a single ad due to constant information exposure (Priporas et al. 2017). Thus, a distinguishing visual design can easily stand out to the eyes of this generation. On the other hand, Generation Y is considered more impulsive than the older generations. However, this is also related with age characteristics since the same can be observed in Generation Z when comparing to

Generation Y (e.g., Williams and Page 2011). Therefore, we suggest the following hypotheses:

H6: Belonging to the younger Generation (Z) will emphasize the influence that WAVD has on OPI, when comparing to consumers belonging to Generation Y;
H7: Belonging to Generation Z will increase the impact that WAVD has on ATWA;
H8: Belonging to Generation Z will emphasize the effect that WAVD has on ATB.

This research seeks to extend the existing theory proposed by Shaouf et al. (2016). Therefore, a Structural Equation Model (SEM) was implemented due to its powerful casual-effect relations estimations between dependent and independent variables, while being simultaneously able to examine multiple dependence relationships. The proposed model was structured as presented in Fig. 1.

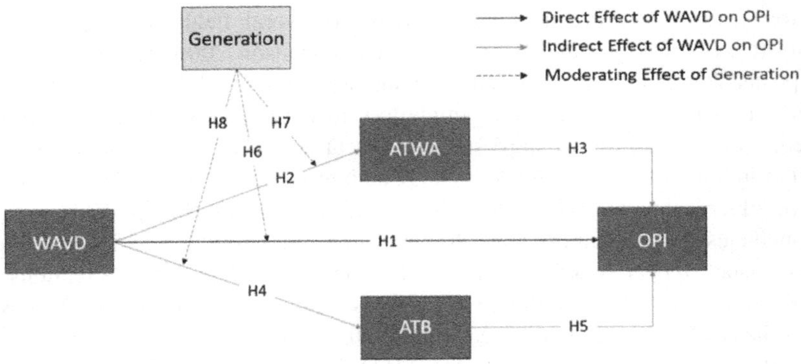

Fig. 1. Model configuration

4 Method

A web-based questionnaire was constructed using Qualtrics Surveys software. The questionnaire was divided into two parts. The first part intended to measure the general attitude the respondent had toward WAVD, without regarding any specific advertisement. It was also assessed how WAVD and the consumer's ATB and ATA could influence the OPI. The questions in this section consisted in statements to which respondents had to specify their level of agreement. The measurement scope was a five-points Likert scale, which ranged from "Strongly Disagree" (−2) to "Strongly Agree" (+2). This measurement scope has been used previously (e.g., Erkan and Evans 2016; Shaouf et al. 2016). The second part of the questionnaire aimed to measure the same attitudes toward the Design and the OPI but considering a specific web ad. To ensure that participants were responding based on the same stimuli, an advertising was included in the survey. The measurement scope was a seven-points Likert scale. This approach has been used before (e.g., Quintal et al. 2016). All scales were adapted from previous research (Wu et al. 2008; Zhang 1996). The questionnaire was shared on social media (Facebook) using a snowball sampling technique which resulted in 517 initial responses. Data quality pre-processing and exploration methods were applied to clean the data from inconsistent information. This process resulted in the removal of 184 incomplete or misfit responses. Hence, 318 valid responses (62% female) were considered for the analysis (39% Gen Y; 61% Gen Z).

Next, statistical analyses were performed regarding reliability and validity assessment. Cronbach's Alpha and Composite Reliability (CR) should be higher than 0.7. To complement these measures and confirm Convergent Validity, the average value of the squared loadings of all indicators used in the construct scale should be higher than 0.5 – this coefficient is called the Average Variance Extracted (AVE). Furthermore, discriminant validity can assess stronger relations of a construct with its indicators, in comparison with other constructs. Therefore, and according to Fornell-Larcker criterium, the AVE must be greater than the correlation of a specific construct with all the other constructs of the model to the square. Variance Inflation Factors (VIF) were the method used in order to examine the collinearity among constructs. This test analyzes how much does the variance of an estimated construct increase due to multicollinearity issues. The values it computes are compared against a threshold of 3, where higher values mean that multicollinearity issues probably exist. The relationships among variables were estimated through standardized regression weights, or estimated path-coefficients, and present values ranging between −1 and 1. In order to guarantee the model's suitability, several fit indexes were calculated and compared to a threshold of 0.9 (good fit).

5 Results

Regarding the model's reliability and validity, all variables presented coefficients higher than the respective thresholds, except the AVE (ATWA) that was slightly below 0.5. (.4816, which is relatively close to the threshold value). Therefore, considering that all other coefficients are comfortably coherent with the desired values, we can assume that the model is reliable and valid. All coefficients of the model's reliability measures are presented in Table 1.

Considering the model Fit Indexes, GFI was the only coefficient above the threshold of 0.9, with a value of .974. NFI, IFI and CFI all registered values very close to the required 0.9, with .888, .893 and .887 respectively. Despite being below the threshold, due to their proximity to the desired value they can still be considered reliable factors that show that this model is well suited. The AGFI coefficient, with a value of .613, was far below the required threshold of 0.9. On the other hand, the model's Chi-Square was 21.739 with 1 degree of freedom (and with a respective $p < .001$), which restores the model's reliability.

As mentioned above, a structural equation modeling (SEM) was used to assess the relationships between the proposed factors. Results obtained via AMOS 24 are depicted in Fig. 1 and include the following: (1) The model obtained suggests a positive impact of WAVD on OPI, in accordance with H1. The impact observed is significant ($\beta = .657$; $p < .001$); (2) Although WAVD is positively correlated with ATWA, this relation is not significant ($\beta = .018$; $p = .54$); (3) Although ATWA is

Table 1. Model reliability measures

(Threshold)	Cronbach's Alpha (>.7)	CR (>.7)	AVE (>.5)	$Corr^2_{(a;b)}$ ($<AVE_{(a;b)}$)	VIF (<3)
WAVD	.883	.9062	.5218	–	–
ATWA	–	–	.632	.002	1.252
ATB	–	–	.676	.017	1.332
OPI	–	–	.657	.161	1.114
ATWA	.790	.866	.4816	–	–
ATB	–	–	.702	.163	1.109
OPI	–	–	.506	.042	1.332
WAVD	–	–	–	–	1.219
ATB	.852	.87975	1.80437	–	–
OPI	–	–	.759	.100	1.272
WAVD	–	–	–	–	1.223
ATWA	–	–	–	–	1.045
OPI	.931	.9398	.7226	–	–
WAVD	–	–	–	–	1.015
ATWA	–	–	–	–	1.246
ATB	–	–	–	–	1.262

positively correlated to OPI, the effect is not significant ($\beta = .203$; $p = .118$); (4) WAVD is positively correlated with ATB, thus supporting H4 ($\beta = .077$; $p < .05$); and (5) ATB has a positive effect on OPI ($\beta = .428$; $p < .001$).

To assess the moderating effect of generation in this model and to see if the average OPI registered was different between generations, the first test computed was an ANOVA. Results revealed that the difference between the average OPI in each generation is significant, $F(1{,}316) = 20.982$, $p < .001$, suggesting that these generations are indeed influenced differently. Furthermore, a multi-group analysis (MGA) was performed to incorporate the generational moderating factor in this model. This analysis compared the previous estimations for the subsamples of each generation and assessed if such differences were significant: (6) WAVD registered an impact on OPI of $\beta = .497$ ($p < .001$) for generation Y while for generation Z the effect was stronger, with $\beta = .707$ ($p < .001$), in accordance with our predictions. However, the MGA showed that the χ^2 difference between models is of 1.691 ($p = .193$), thus not significant; (7) WAVD registered a null impact on ATWA considering only Generation Y and a $\beta = .06$ when analyzing Generation Z. The MGA however reported that the χ^2 difference is only .003, which is not significant ($p = .958$); and (8) WAVD has a positive effect on ATB for Generation Y with a $\beta = .13$, and a positive effect on Generation Z with $\beta = .12$. However, the MGA presented a χ^2 difference of .143, which is also not significant ($p = .705$).

6 Discussion

According to Huang and Benyoucef (2017), marketers should develop design strategies to ensure that their online platforms address the needs and wants of their customers. The hypothesis that WAVD have an important direct effect in the consumer's OPI (H1) was strongly supported, but the same was not verified for their indirect effect. In fact, WAVD's influence on ATWA was rather weak, failing to support H2, and ATWA's impact on OPI was not found, thus refuting H3. However, WAVD's effect on ATB was significant, confirming H4, and the hypothesis that ATB has an influence on OPI (H5) was supported by the data as well.

Overall, this research was able to provide a clear evidence that a more elaborated visual design (e.g. colors, font type and size, shapes, graphical information) has a direct effect on the consumer, resulting in a higher willingness to purchase the product. Contrary to previous research (Shaouf et al. 2016), this model established this influence without the intermediary effect of the consumer's attitudinal responses. Thus, we managed to contribute to solidifying the theory of Visual Rhetoric (Scott 1994) and providing relevant data for managers that a more carefully designed web advertisement immediately generates a higher purchase intention in consumers (particularly the ones who belong to generations Y and Z). This is certainly one of the key contributions of this research. On the other hand, the TRA was only partially confirmed by this model. We found that the visual aesthetics in advertising can positively influence the attitudinal response a consumer has towards a brand (ATB), which positively relates to the behavioral intention of purchasing a product from that brand. However, the same influence path flow was not verified for the attitudinal effect of an advertisement's perception. Therefore, the TRA was not supported when considering the impact an ATWA can have on OPI but it was verified regarding ATB and its positive effects. This also suggests that a poor design might damage the consumer's awareness of the brand more than the perception of that singular advertisement.

Regrettably, this model could not find a significant difference on the effects of WAVD on attitudinal responses or in OPI when comparing generations Y and Z. However, regarding a direct effect of WAVD on OPI, Generation Z revealed a higher coefficient than Generation Y (although this tendency was not significant in the Multi Group Analysis). Thus, this model is in accordance with previous literature, suggesting that these generations could indeed be influenced differently by the same stimuli. Furthermore, this study complements existing research by discarding the possibility that the visual aspects of an advertisement are one of such stimuli that can significantly induce these two different generations to have contrasting reactions.

Despite all these important conclusions and the statistic validations that support this model, this study was not exempt from limitations. The first recommendation for future research is to account for the influence that ATA has on ATB. It is shown that ATA can have a positive influence on ATB (Shaouf et al. 2016; Shimp 1981). Additionally, previous studies have found an important role of gender in these variables (Shaouf et al. 2016) and such effect was not included in this analysis. Also, research focused on aesthetics and web design could benefit from the use of eye-tracking tools, thus complementing self-reported survey measures (Hwang and Lee 2018; Pappas et al. 2018). Furthermore, the Multi Group Analysis used to study the generational moderating effect was performed under 0 degrees of freedom. This resulted in biased coefficients for the model's suitability. Finally, recent results in a study by Ko (2018) also showed that social identity cannot arouse users' social and commercial desires online. Further results could test the implication of social identity theories among generations Y and Z.

7 Conclusion

Overall, this research contributes to e-commerce literature by studying how consumers respond to a WAVD and what influence it can have on their OPI. Additionally, this study also contributes to the TVR and to the TRA, expanding both theories' implications in an online environment, by establishing a direct (and an indirect effect, via ATB) of the visual aesthetics of online advertising on the consumer's OPI. Moreover, this research sought to analyze how consumers in generations Y and Z react to the same visual stimuli, regarding their willingness to buy the advertised product. Thus, the results presented above have important managerial implications and provide guidance to managers when developing marketing strategies to reach out to young consumers.

Acknowledgments. This work was funded by Fundação para a Ciência e a Tecnologia (UID/ECO/00124/2013, UID/ECO/00124/2019 and Social Sciences DataLab, LISBOA-01-0145-FEDER-022209), POR Lisboa (LISBOA-01-0145-FEDER-007722, LISBOA-01-0145-FEDER-022209) and POR Norte (LISBOA-01-0145-FEDER-022209). The authors declare that they have no conflict of interest. All procedures performed in studies involving human participants were in accordance with the ethical standards of the institutional and/or national research committee and with the 1964 Helsinki declaration and its later amendments or comparable ethical standards. Informed consent was obtained from all individual participants included in the study.

References

Bolton, R.N., Parasuraman, A., Hoefnagels, A., Migchels, N., Kabadayi, S., Gruber, T., Solnet, D.: Understanding generation y and their use of social media: a review and research agenda. J. Serv. Manag. **24**(3), 245–267 (2013)

Boyd, D., Ellison, N.B.: Social network sites: definition, history, and scholarship. J. Comput. Mediat. Commun. **13**(2), 210–230 (2007)

Brosdahl, D.J.C., Carpenter, J.M.: Shopping orientations of US males: a generational cohort comparison. J. Retail. Consum. Serv. **18**(6), 548–554 (2011)

Cho, C.H.: How advertising works on the WWW: modified elaboration likelihood model. J. Curr. Issues Res. Advert. **21**(1), 33–50 (1999)

Cyr, D.: Modeling web site design across cultures: relationships to trust, satisfaction, and e-loyalty. J. Manag. Inf. Syst. **24**(4), 47–72 (2008)

Delfanti, A., Arvidsson, A.: Introduction to Digital Media, p. 178. Wiley Blackwell, Malden (2019)

Dreze, X., Zufryden, F.: Testing web site design and promotional content. J. Advers. Res. **37**(2), 77–91 (1997)

Duffett, R.G.: Facebook advertising's influence on intention-to-purchase and purchase amongst Millennials. Internet Res. **25**(4), 498–526 (2015)

Elwalda, A., Lü, K., Ali, M.: Perceived derived attributes of online customer reviews. Comput. Hum. Behav. **56**, 306–319 (2016)

Erkan, I., Evans, C.: The influence of eWOM in social media on consumers' purchase intentions: an extended approach to information adoption. Comput. Hum. Behav. **61**, 47–55 (2016)

Fishbein, M., Ajzen, I.: Belief, Attitude, Intention and Behavior: An Introduction to Theory and Research. Addison-Wesley, Reading (1975)

Ganguly, B., Dash, S.B., Cyr, D.: Website characteristics, trust and purchase intention in online stores: an empirical study in the Indian context. J. Inf. Sci. Technol. **6**(2), 22–44 (2009)

Goodrich, K.: Anarchy of effects? Exploring attention to online advertising and multiple outcomes. Psychol. Mark. **28**(4), 417–440 (2011)

Han, H., Xu, H., Chen, H.: Social commerce: a systematic review and data synthesis. Electron. Commer. Res. Appl. **30**, 38–50 (2018)

Higgins, K.T.: Generational marketing. Mark. Manag. **7**(3), 6–9 (1998)

Himmel, B.: Different strokes for different generations. Rent. Prod. News **30**(7), 42–46 (2008)

Huang, Z., Benyoucef, M.: The effects of social commerce design on consumer purchase decision-making: an empirical study. Electron. Commer. Res. Appl. **25**, 40–58 (2017)

Hwang, Y.M., Lee, K.C.: Using an eye-tracking approach to explore gender differences in visual attention and shopping attitudes in an online shopping environment. Int. J. Hum. Comput. Interact. **34**(1), 15–24 (2018)

Jackson, V., Stoel, L., Brantley, A.: Mall attributes and shopping value: differences by gender and generational cohort. J. Retail. Consum. Serv. **18**(1), 1–9 (2011)

Kabadayi, S., Gupta, R.: Managing motives and design to influence web site revisits. J. Res. Interact. Mark. **5**(2/3), 153–169 (2011)

Ko, H.-C.: Social desire or commercial desire? The factors driving social sharing and shopping intentions on social commerce platforms. Electron. Commer. Res. Appl. **28**, 1–15 (2018)

Korgaonkar, P., Wolin, L.D.: Web usage, advertising, and shopping: relationship patterns. Internet Res. **12**(2), 191–204 (2002)

Labrecque, L.I., Milne, G.R.: To be or not to be different: exploration of norms and benefits of color differentiation in the marketplace. Mark. Lett. **24**(2), 165–176 (2013)

MacKenzie, S.B., Lutz, R.J.: An empirical examination of the structural antecedents of attitude toward the ad in an advertising pretesting context. J. Mark. **53**(2), 48–65 (1989)

Pappas, I.O., Sharma, K., Mikalef, P., Giannakos, M.N.: Visual aesthetics of e-commerce websites: an eye-tracking approach. In: Proceedings of the 51st Hawaii International Conference on System Sciences (HICSS), Big Island, Hawaii (2018)

Pavlou, P.A., Fygenson, M.: Understanding and predicting electronic commerce adoption: an extention of the theory of planned behavior. MIS Q. **30**(1), 115–143 (2006)

Phelps, J.E., Hoy, M.G.: The Aad-Ab-PI relationship in children: the impact of brand familiarity and measurement timing. Psychol. Mark. **13**(1), 77–105 (1996)

Pieters, R., Wedel, M., Batra, R.: The stopping power of advertising: measures and effects of visual complexity. J. Mark. **74**(5), 48–60 (2010)

Priporas, C.-V., Stylos, N., Fotiadis, A.K.: Generation Z consumers' expectations of interactions in smart retailing: a future agenda. Comput. Hum. Behav. **77**, 374–381 (2017)

PwC: Perspectives from the Global Entertainment and Media Outlook 2017–2021: Curtain up! User experience takes center stage (2017). (www.pwc.com/outlook)

Quintal, V., Phau, I., Sims, D., Cheah, I.: Factors influencing generation Y's purchase intentions of prototypical versus me-too brands. J. Retail. Consum. Serv. **30**, 175–183 (2016)

Scott, L.M.: Images in advertising: the need for a theory of visual rhetoric. J. Consum. Res. **21** (2), 252–273 (1994)

Shaouf, A., Lü, K., Li, X.: The effect of web advertising visual design on online purchase intention: an examination across gender. Comput. Hum. Behav. **60**, 622–634 (2016)
Shimp, T.A.: Attitude toward the ad as a mediator of consumer brand choice. J. Advert. **10**(2), 9–48 (1981)
Stevenson, J.S., Bruner, G.C., Kumar, A.: Webpage background and viewer attitudes. J. Advert. Res. **40**(1–2), 29–34 (2000)
Suh, J.-C., Yi, Y.: When brand attitudes affect the customer satisfaction-loyalty relation: the moderating role of product involvement. J. Consum. Psychol. **16**(2), 145–155 (2006)
Sundar, A., Noseworthy, T.J.: Place the logo high or low? Using conceptual metaphors of power in packaging design. J. Mark. **78**(5), 138–151 (2014)
Wellner, A.S.: Generation Z. Am. Demogr. **22**(9), 60–64 (2000)
Williams, K.C., Page, R.A.: Marketing to the generations. J. Behav. Stud. Bus. **5**, 1–17 (2011)
Williams, K.C., Page, R.A., Petrosky, A.R., Hernandez, E.H.: Multi-generational marketing: descriptions, characteristics, lifestyles, and attitudes. J. Appl. Bus. Econ. **11**(2), 21–36 (2010)
Wu, S.I., Wei, P.L., Chen, J.H.: Influential factors and relational structure of Internet banner advertising in the tourism industry. Tour. Manag. **29**(2), 221–236 (2008)
Zhang, Y.: Responses to humorous advertising: the moderating effect of need for cognition. J. Advert. **25**(1), 15–32 (1996)

Optimizing the Digital Customer Journey – Improving User Experience by Persona-Based and Situation-Aware Adaptations

Christian Märtin[1(✉)], Pietro Asta[1], and Bärbel Bissinger[2]

[1] Faculty of Computer Science, Augsburg University of Applied Sciences, Augsburg, Germany
{Christian.Maertin,Pietro.Asta}@hs-augsburg.de
[2] Capgemini, Paris, France
Baerbel-Christine.Bissinger@capgemini.com

Abstract. This paper discusses a novel approach for combining persona-based and situation-aware software adaptation methods for individualizing some of the touch points of the digital customer journey and thereby optimizing customer experience and effectiveness of e-commerce applications. Our approach uses emotion recognition, eye-tracking, and other individual tracking methods for adapting interactive web applications by accessing a flexible adaptation framework at runtime. The framework provides model-based support and allows for individualization at runtime by applying situation-aware adaptations. The approach is demonstrated with examples from a commercial beauty-products e-business portal.

Keywords: Digital customer journey · Touch point individualization · Customer experience · Persona-based design · Situation awareness · Adaptive software

1 Introduction

One aspect of digitalization in marketing is the design of IT-based solutions for the steps or cycles of the customer journey (Følstad and Kvale 2018). The customer journey is the customer's interaction at several touch points with a service or several services of one or more service providers in order to achieve a specific goal (Halvorsrud et al. 2016). More focused on e-commerce or product purchasing, the customer journey can be defined as an iterative process that includes touch point based interactions with a provider or a business during the phases of the customer journey (Lemon and Verhoef 2016).

A generic customer journey is divided into the following five phases: *awareness,* where the customer is made aware of the product or service, favorability, where the interest of the customer is increased, so that the customer begins to take a closer look at the product and to inform herself about it, *consideration*, which increasingly triggers the customer's desire to own the product, *intent to purchase,* where the customer's

F. J. Martínez-López and S. D'Alessandro (Eds.): *Advances in Digital Marketing and eCommerce*, SPBE, pp. 141–148, 2020.
https://doi.org/10.1007/978-3-030-47595-6_18

intention to buy the product is being initiated, and, finally *conversion*, where the product will ultimately be bought by the customer. It also makes sense to add a *post purchase phase* to the customer journey. A distinction is made between direct and indirect touch points. The website, advertising spots and advertisement in general are understood as direct touch points. Indirect touch points for example include rating portals, user forums and blogs and can only be influenced to a limited extent by the provider.

Optimizing the customer journey is very important and necessary for the success of e-commerce providers. By using suitable tracking technologies, the behavior of consumers can be analyzed in real time. Analysis can also reveal all contact points created through advertising. Thanks to this knowledge, it is possible to identify optimization potential. This is done by uncovering relevant interdependencies between the channels used and the contact points (Bernecker 2017). At all touch points between the provider and the customer, one has to distinguish between the customer view and the provider view. It must be the provider's goal at every touch point, to create a situation that leads to optimum user experience (UX) for the potential customer (Stein and Ramaseshan 2016). UX in the customer journey is often described as customer experience (CX). CX aims at "a customer's cognitive, emotional, behavioral, sensorial, and social" reactions to the offerings of a provider or a business "during the customer's entire purchase journey" (Lemon and Verhoef 2016).

With our presented approach we intend to accompany task accomplishment of both, the provider and the customer. The provider is supported in reaching her goals for gaining the customers' interest or for raising purchase orders. The customer is experiencing an individualized interactive application environment that will allow for easier task accomplishment, e.g. finding the right product. The remainder of this paper is organized as follows:

- Section 2 gives an overview of related and previous work relevant to the scope of this paper and introduces the SitAdapt 2.0 system (Märtin et al. 2019) for situation-aware adaptations.
- Section 3 discusses two studies that evaluate the use of customer personas and situation-triggered adaptations in order to raise customer experience for the b2c part of an existing e-commerce portal for beauty products. It also describes automated persona-selection for new users.
- Section 4 concludes the paper and gives an outlook on our planned future work.

2 Related Work

In this paper, it is our goal to demonstrate, how generic business intelligence methods can be combined with persona-based design and situation-aware adaptation techniques to arrive at an overall optimization of the customer journey with a raised level of user experience and individuality. We therefore first discuss some of the methods from these disciplines that have influenced and inspired our own work.

2.1 Business Intelligence in E-Commerce

Whenever consumers enter the individual phases of the customer journey and get into contact with a provider through direct and indirect touch points, huge amounts of data – also referred to as big data – are produced and transmitted to the respective provider. In order to generate valuable knowledge from such data, business intelligence (BI) can be applied. BI combines the use of various methods and technologies that serve the collection, administration, evaluation and presentation of mainly external but also internal data in digital form (Gluchowski and Chamoni 2016). By using adequate tools data patterns, cross-connections and correlations can be discovered and trends can be predicted. Often, terms such as business analytics, data analytics, predictive analytics, people analytics, etc., are associated with business intelligence. In the focus of the applied analytical methods are data mining that uses statistical algorithms as well as the hypothesis-based online analytics processing (OLAP), which allows a multi-dimensional analysis of data. In (Cheng et al. 2012) the authors predicted for the now current generation of BI and analysis tools to focus on mobile and sensor-based content, location-awareness, person-centered and context-relevant analysis as well as mobile visualization techniques and HCI aspects.

Results from BI analysis can have impact on the design of e-commerce sites and provide insights on how to organize content parts, advertising, navigation and presentational aspects. In our approach the large quantities of user and situational data recorded by the SitAdapt 2.0 recording component (see Sect. 2.3) can be accessed by BI tools. Analysis results can therefore evolutionarily influence customer experience in all phases and for all direct touch points in future sessions.

2.2 Persona-Based Design

Another technique with positive impact on the customer journey and e-commerce in general can be the use of personas. In the context of this paper a "persona is an *archetype of a class of users* synthesizing goals and behavior patterns as well as skills, attitudes and environment. The user's characteristics […] must be effective for the design problem at hand." (De Marsico and Levialdi 2004). For each persona, an avatar is defined, that is equipped with authentic features such as name, photo, curriculum vitae, age, income, marital status, hobbies, education, etc. (Klünen 2019). In our approach to optimizing the customer journey, a persona represents a certain customer group of a provider. Most information required to design personas, as well as all knowledge about their preferences, result from expert analysis of existing customer data. The use of personas helps us to create a customized approach for specific customer groups, i.e. to work with specific visual, verbal and audio attributes. Also, persona-specific product preferences are taken into account. This allows the persona-specific tailoring of the marketing measures, in particular the choice of advertising material to be used, as well as the web design of the e-commerce site. Consequently, customer satisfaction can rise, and the customer may feel more comfortable, satisfied and happy, which in the best case leads to improved sales and better customer loyalty. A positive customer experience in turn has a favorable effect on the customer journey and the entire e-commerce site. Personas are currently a promising alternative and preliminary stage to more individualized advertising and adaptation techniques aimed at in the future.

Personas are also often used in human-computer interaction (HCI) and software engineering (Jahavery et al. 2009). In (McGinn and Kotamraju 2008) an alternative approach to finding personas is discussed: In order to reach specific HCI design goals, a survey was conducted with members of the different target groups, resulting in useful personas with attributes specific to tasks of each user group, but without organizational overhead.

2.3 Context- and Situation-Awareness

The concept of context-aware computing was first proposed for distributed mobile computing by (Schilit and Theimer 1994). In addition to technical aspects the definition of context also included environmental and social attributes. Later the term situation-awareness appeared in psychology and the cognitive sciences with the aim to support correct task accomplishment of human operators in complex situations by defining situation-dependent (Flach et al. 2004). In recent years interactive software has made huge steps towards understanding of and reacting to varying situations. To capture the individual requirements of a situation, (Chang 2016) proposes that a situation consists of an environmental context E that covers the user's operational environment, a behavioral context B that covers the user's social behavior by interpreting his or her actions, and a hidden context M that includes the users' mental states and emotions. A situation Sit at a given time t can thus be defined as $Sit = <M, B, E>_t$. A user's intention for using a specific software service for reaching a goal can then be formulated as temporal sequence $<sSit_1, Sit_2, \ldots, Sit_n>$, where Sit_1 is the situation that triggers the usage of a service and Sit_n is the goal-satisfying situation.

Our own work, the SitAdapt 2.0 system (Märtin et al. 2019) was inspired by (Chang 2016). It applies a model-based approach for designing and constructing web and mobile applications and is linking the domain and user interface models with a user-centric situation-aware runtime-adaptation component. The system (Fig. 1) uses a broad set of visual and other observation and monitoring tools and has been tested and evaluated for a number of applications from different e-business areas. All data recorded in a user session are stored in very fine-grained situation profiles (minimum time resolution: 1/60 s). SitAdapt 2.0 uses domain-independent and domain-specific resources for automating essential parts of the customer experience optimization process. Possible adaptations of the target web application are planned and pre-modeled at development time. At runtime they are triggered by situation rules and generated by activating and exploiting domain-dependent and independent HCI-patterns. For the approach presented in this paper we have combined SitAdapt 2.0 with persona-based design and user-tests in order to cover broad parts of the customer journey. Different aspects of our approach were evaluated by two independent user studies using the web-portal of a beauty products manufacturer[1]. Section 3 demonstrates part of the capabilities of the SitAdapt 2.0 system with some short examples. See (Märtin et al. 2019) for more structural and operational details.

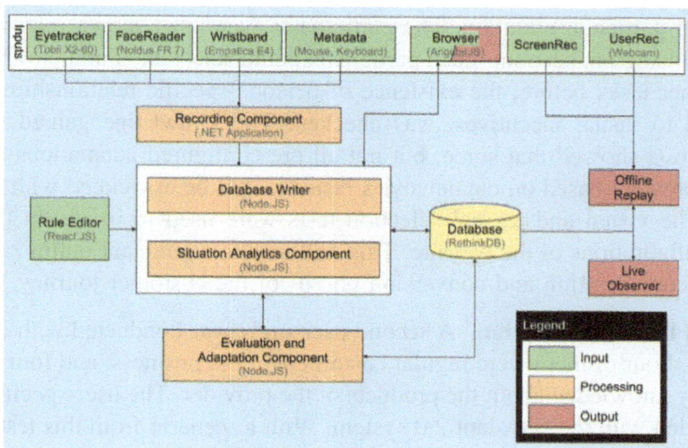

Fig. 1. Structure and components of the SitAdapt 2.0 system (Märtin et al. 2019).

3 From Personas to Situation-Aware Adaptations

Our co-operation partner has been using personas in digital marketing for a long time. The three recent personas were derived from customer data and refined in a workshop of the marketing and e-commerce teams. The personas reflect the company's main customer groups and are using the avatars Claudia, Sandra and Julia. Each persona profile contains a short biography as well as information on personality, age, buying behavior, e-commerce and web affinity, motivation to buy, and the preferred reference channels. A psychography is also included.

Persona Evaluation. In order to provide a justification for the pre-configured persona-specific web shop adaptations and to receive important information about product preferences, a usability test was carried out in our lab with 10 female test subjects, who represented the three persona-groups, but so far had not been customers of the company. Test scenarios were developed for gaining insights into product preferences as well as persona-specific visual and verbal design. For example, the test subjects had to simulate the shopping process as part of a test task and put products into their shopping cart. It was considered whether they would also buy the specific products intended for their persona-group. Which products are preferably bought by which persona had been

[1] Part of this work was carried out in cooperation with Dr. Grandel GmbH, Augsburg, Germany. We greatly acknowledge the opportunity to run the SitAdapt 2.0 tools and user tests on their enterprise e-business platform.

determined in advance by analyzing real customer data. In a different task the test candidates had to search the magazine on the company's website and spontaneously click on three articles that particularly appealed to them. It was checked, which articles were clicked on and whether subjects from the same persona-group chose the same articles. In addition, it was tested on which words and verbal approaches the said persons paid particular attention. The participants were also shown pictures from the company's Instagram account. Each participant could select any number of pictures. As with the other tasks before, the existence of persona-specific relationships, especially with regard to visual incentives, was checked. The knowledge gained through the laboratory tests showed that some, but not all pre-configured adaptations and product offerings that were based on data analysis results could be associated with the relevant personas. The visual and textual selection tests were used to re-design the persona-specific configurations of the website. This will lead to significant optimizations of the awareness, consideration and conversion phases of the customer journey.

Automated Persona Selection. A second user study was conducted with eight female participants. Four of them were regular customers of the business, and four of them did not have any knowledge about the products of the provider. The user-specific data were again recorded with the SitAdapt 2.0 system. With a scenario from this test it could be demonstrated, how observation and tracking of individual, but unknown customers can later be used to discover new personas and/or to map a new customer to an existing persona. Figures 2a and 2b show the eye-tracking heat maps of the two different user groups.

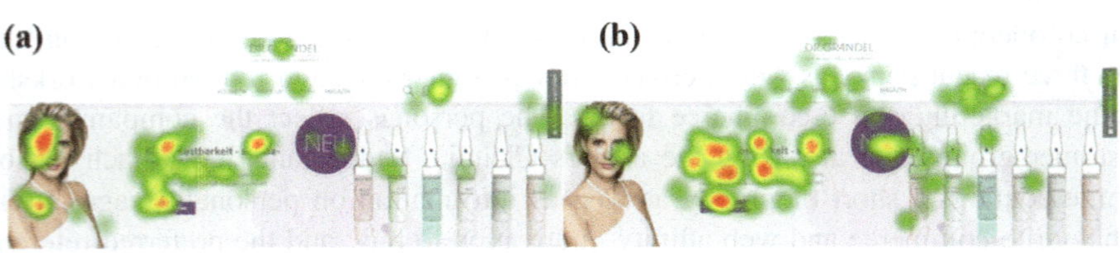

Fig. 2. a. and b.: Heatmaps of regular clients (a) and new users (b)

Situation-Aware Runtime Adaptations. Figure 3 shows the emotional reaction of one of the test subjects, when an unexpected visual appeared, after a button leading to some promotional action was pressed. The values of the basic emotions *happy* and *surprised* are reaching quite significant levels. These data are available in the SitAdapt 2.0 user profile, whereas the current situation (application meta-data, visuals, etc.) is recorded during the entire user session and stored in the situation profile. For all touch points that are visited during this session the information in the situation profile can be accessed at runtime. This combined information can be exploited by a SitAdapt 2.0 situation rule that triggers adaptations at runtime, e.g., for promoting a special offer:

Fig. 3. Emotional response to an unexpected image

```
<SituationRule> SpecialPromotion
       FOR N <Situationi> IN 3 s
                <Gaze_Tracking> Contains Field Promotion
                Image(Id) (>0)
                AND <Emotion> happy (>0.25)
                AND <Emotion> surprised (>0.20)
       <Action> SHOW AT 10 s Promotion1TextFUI
       <Action> WAIT Promotion1TextFUIInput
       <Action> LINK Promotion1TextFUIInput
                TaskModel PromotionProcessingTask(Promotion1)
```

If the user focuses on the image and after 3 s the emotions have changed to significant levels, a promotion dialog box is displayed in the user interface. The web application will wait for a user input and activate the promotion processing task specified in the task model.

4 Conclusion and Future Work

In this paper we have discussed a new software approach for accompanying and optimizing the customer journey that combines analysis of existing customers' data, persona-based design and situation-aware runtime adaptations in order to allow for better task accomplishment of both, the e-commerce provider, and the client. Two studies directed on measuring usability and user experience for a real-world b2c e-commerce portal for beauty products have demonstrated that a high-level of customer experience can be achieved, if the capabilities of the available tools are exploited consequently. The next step will be to get the SitAdapt 2.0 system from the lab into real life by using advanced camera-based visual tracking technology. The arising privacy and ethical issues will be handled by applying accepted principles of value sensitive design (Friedman and Hendry 2019).

References

Bernecker, M.: Customer Journey – die Reise des Kunden verstehen und nutzen! Deutsches Institut für Marketing (2017). https://www.marketing-institut.biz/blog/customer-journey

Chang, C.K.: Situation analytics: a foundation for a new software engineering paradigm. IEEE Comput. **49**, 24–33 (2016)

Chen, H., Chiang, R.H.L., Storey, V.C.: Business intelligence and analytics: from big data to big impact. MIS Q. **36**(4), 1165–1188 (2012)

De Marsico, M., Levialdi, S.: Evaluating web sites: exploiting user's expectations. Int. J. Hum Comput Stud. **60**(3), 381–416 (2004)

Flach, J.M., Mulder, M., Van Paassen, M.M.: The concept of situation in psychology. In: Banbury, S., Tremblay, S., (eds.) A Cognitive Approach to Situation Awareness: Theory and Applications, pp. 42–60. Ashgate Publishing, Oxon (2004)

Følstad, A., Kvale, K.: Customer journeys: a systematic literature review. J. Serv. Theory Pract. **28**(2), 196–227 (2018)

Friedman, B., Hendry, D.G.: Value Sensitive Design: Shaping Technology with Moral Imagination. MIT Press, Cambridge (2019)

Gluchwoski, P., Chamoni, P.: Analytische Informationssysteme, vol. 5. Springer, Heidelberg (2016)

Halvorsrud, R., Kvale, K., Følstad, A.: Improving service quality through customer journey analysis. J. Serv. Theory. Pract. **26**(6), 840–867 (2016)

Jahavery, H., Deichman, A., Seffah, A., Taleb, M.: A user-centered framework for deriving a conceptual design from user experiences: leveraging personas and patterns to create usable designs. In: Seffah, A., et al. (eds.) Human-Centered Software Engineering, pp. 53–81. Springer, London (2009)

Klünen, K.: Persona, Gablers Wirtschaftslexikon (2019). https://wirtschaftslexikon.gabler.de/definition/persona-119156

Lemon, K.N., Verhoef, P.C.: Understanding customer experience throughout the customer journey. J. Mark.: AMA/MSI Spec. Issue **80**, 69–97 (2016)

Märtin, C., Kampfer, F., Herdin, C., Yameni, L.B.: Situation analytics and model-based user interface development: a synergetic approach for building runtime-adaptive business applications. Complex Syst. Inf. Model. Q. CSIMQ (20), 1–19 (2019). https://doi.org/10.7250/csimq.2019-20.01

McGinn, J., Kotamraju, N.: Data-driven persona development. In: Proceedings of CHI 2008. ACM (2008)

Schilit, B.N., Theimer, M.M.: Disseminating active map information to mobile hosts. IEEE Netw. **8**(5), 22–32 (1994)

Stein, A., Ramaseshan, B.: Towards the identification of customer experience touch point elements. J. Retail. Custom. Serv. **30**, 8–19 (2016)

Influence of Source Credibility on Search for Information

Sonika Singh(✉)

UTS Business School, University of Technology Sydney, Ultimo, Australia
Sonika.singh@uts.edu.au

Abstract. The Internet is a prevalent source of product information for most consumers. To search for products consumer access information on manufacturer owned online information sources, social media and other third-party websites. However, fake content and information on social media and third party information websites is a growing problem and likely to influence credibility of the information source. This study seeks to examine the impact of source credibility on consumer's search effort.

Keywords: Consumer search · Source credibility · Information search · Digital media

1 Introduction

The Internet is a prevalent source of product information for most consumers. Globally, the average Internet user spends more than 16 hours per month online. Consumers spend a majority of their time on activities such as emailing, search and buying products. Internet search activity predominantly involves search for product information.

To search for products, consumers access information on manufacturer owned online information sources, social media and other third-party websites. However, fake content and information on social media and third party information websites is a growing problem. The increasing instances of fake information i.e. deliberately misinforming readers, influence consumer's perception of social media and third party websites as information sources. This brings into question the credibility of the source which is expected to influence search for products. Recent industry reports indicate that web traffic to sites which experienced instances of fake news has declined. This is especially high for news aggregator websites as compared to other websites.

There is substantial literature on search that examines how consumer characteristics influence the amount of search (Ratchford et al. 2003; Klein and Ford 2003; Moorthy et al. 1997; Punj et al. 1983), however, there is lack of research on how external information environment may impact consumer search behavior. This study contributes to existing literature by examining the impact of external information environment such as source credibility on consumer's search effort.

F. J. Martínez-López and S. D'Alessandro (Eds.): *Advances in Digital Marketing and eCommerce*, SPBE, pp. 149–152, 2020.
https://doi.org/10.1007/978-3-030-47595-6_19

2 Data

To examine the influence of source credibility on search, survey data is collected from 650 respondents using a consumer panel for two websites CNN and Amazon. CNN and Amazon were selected because these are one of the most popular and most visited websites for news and shopping products respectively. The survey data captured consumer perceptions of website credibility, information quality, reliability, security and time spent on a website as compared to other websites to search for information. Credibility was captured using Likert scale measures for scale items on the dimension of trustworthiness and expertise. The dependent variable in the study is search and operationalized as time spent on a website compared to other websites to search for information. This is Likert scale measure on a 7 point scale where 1 = totally disagree and 7 = totally agree. The focal independent variables are consumers' trust in third party websites as credible source of information (Likert scale measure on a 7 point scale where 1 = totally disagree and 7 = totally agree) and perception of third party websites as an information source for products (a Likert scale measure).

The mean descriptives in Fig. 1 and Fig. 2 indicate that consumers agree that they spend more time accessing content on CNN and Amazon as compared to other websites. The descriptives also indicate a high importance of source credibility for both CNN and Amazon.

CNN					
Variable	No. Obs	Mean	Std	Min	Max
Time spent on website	325	5.11	1.24	1	7
Source credibility	325	5.64	0.97	1	7
Information quality	325	4.86	1.70	1	7
Age	325	44	15	21	65
Income	325	72	41	25	150

Fig. 1. CNN descriptive statistics

AMAZON					
Variable	No. Obs	Mean	Std	Min	Max
Time spent on website	316	5.23	1.40	1	7
Source credibility	316	5.77	0.89	1	7
Information quality	316	4.88	1.57	1	7
Age	316	44	15	21	65
Income	316	73	41	25	150

Fig. 2. Amazon descriptive statistics

3 Results

Results from Fig. 3 and Fig. 4 indicate that source credibility has statistically significant impact on the relative time consumers spend on the focal website as compared to others.

DV=time spent on CNN compared to other websites
Adj R-squared=0.022

	Coef.	Std. Err.	t	P>|t|
Source credibility	**0.61**	0.06	9.57	0
Gender	-0.06	0.12	-0.53	0.6
Age	**-0.01**	0.00	-2.92	0.004
Income	0.00	0.00	-0.98	0.327
Intercept	2.36	0.40	5.87	0

Fig. 3. Regression results for CNN

DV=time spent on Amazon compared to other websites
Adjusted R squared=0.17

	Coef.	Std. Err.	t	P>|t|
Source credibility	**0.66**	0.08	7.93	0
Gender	0.03	0.15	0.21	0.831
Age	**-0.01**	0.01	-2.62	0.009
Income	0.00	0.00	-1.29	0.198
Intercept	2.18	0.51	4.27	0

Fig. 4. Regression results for Amazon

4 Conclusion and Discussion

Our preliminary results indicate that with the proliferation of fake news in digital media, source credibility plays a crucial role in consumer's search for information and is an important driver of the amount of time that consumers spend on a website. This finding is crucial to managers who should pay attention to the type and depth of information being displayed on the websites. Our data analysis is ongoing to further examine the drivers of credibility, and testing models that will best explain the data.

References

Klein, L.R., Ford, G.T.: Consumer search for information in the digital age: an empirical study of prepurchase search for automobiles. J. Interact. Mark. **17**(3), 29–49 (2003)

Moorthy, S., Ratchford, B.T., Talukdar, D.: Consumer information search revisited: theory and empirical analysis. J. Consum. Res. **23**(4), 263–278 (1997)

Punj, G.N., Staelin, R.: A model of consumer information search behavior for new automobiles. J. Consum. Res. **9**(4), 366–380 (1983)

Ratchford, B.T., Lee, M.S., Talukdar, D.: The impact of the Internet on information search for automobiles. J. Mark. Res. **40**(2), 193–209 (2003)

Assessing the Determinants of Millennials' Online Protective Behavior: How Their Protection Motivation Translates into Actual Use Behavior

Ana S. Medeiros[1], Luis F. Martinez[1(✉)], and Luisa M. Martinez[2]

[1] Nova School of Business and Economics, Universidade Nova de Lisboa, Lisbon, Portugal
{24081, luis.martinez}@novasbe.pt
[2] IPAM Lisboa and UNIDCOM/IADE, Universidade Europeia, Lisbon, Portugal
luisa.martinez@universidadeeuropeia.pt

Abstract. This research assesses the determinants of Millennials protection motivation (or security intentions) on their actual use behavior when navigating online, considering the protective measures they adopt. Accordingly, we propose a model integrating variables from two widely accepted behavioral theories, the Protection Motivation Theory and the Reasoned Action Approach. An online survey was conducted, relying on the responses of 236 participants from different nationalities, which were analyzed through hierarchical multiple regression. Results show a gap between security intentions and use behavior and indicate safety habit strength and actual control as significant predictors of Millennials' use behavior. By focusing not only on the users' behavioral intentions but also on their actual use behavior, this research seeks to extend the previous literature on the topic.

Keywords: Online security · Protection Motivation · Reasoned Action Approach · Security Intentions · Use Behavior

1 Introduction

Considering the strong impacts of cybercrime related activity, its causes, drivers, and effects have been widely studied (e.g., Anderson et al. 2013; Lagazio et al. 2014; Romanosky 2016). A review of the literature suggests that although cybersecurity is a very current and commonly studied topic, most research is centered on the implications for organizations (Saridakis et al. 2015). As mentioned above, unlike employees in a work setting, home users are not subject to training (Anderson et al. 2010), and often are not aware of the risks of using the Internet, as they do not have any knowledge preparation for their online journey (Kritzinger et al. 2010). Moreover, as stated by Anderson et al. (2010; p. 613), this type of user "represent[s] a significant point of weakness in achieving the security of the cyber infrastructure". Thus, home users are an interesting area of study.

F. J. Martínez-López and S. D'Alessandro (Eds.): *Advances in Digital Marketing and eCommerce*, SPBE, pp. 153–162, 2020.
https://doi.org/10.1007/978-3-030-47595-6_20

A study from the European Commission (2017) states that 51% of the European citizens do not feel well informed about cyber threats and, as mentioned above, 86% believe the risk of becoming a victim of cybercrime is currently increasing. These values reveal that most individuals do not feel prepared to face these current threats that result from their personal experiences, other persons' experiences, and the news media (Tsai et al. 2016). Furthermore, the user lack of knowledge relative to cybercrime touches upon another widely mentioned topic in the literature review which is cybercrime awareness. According to Dodge et al. (2007), varying awareness is hard to characterize due to the 'user's individual nature'. Since several models have been proposed to study the individual's threat perception (Kritzinger et al. 2010; Poepjes et al. 2012), it is noteworthy to instead analyze its influence on the user's behavioral intention and actual protective behavior. Current approaches include the Rational Choice Theory (RCT), the Reactance Theory, and the Justice Theory. As an alternative, Rogers (1975, 1983) has proposed the Protection Motivation Theory (PMT), which is based on the Theory of Reasoned Action (Fishbein et al. 1975).

2 Protection Motivation Theory

Commonly found in academic literature (e.g., Boss et al. 2015, the Protection Motivation Theory (PMT) seeks to explain the reasons that lead to protective behaviors and how individual users undertake those behaviors (Rogers 1975, 1983). The PMT has gained many supporters as it has been extended to understand the drivers for online safety behavior, namely in the context of individual users, as it accounts for the discrepancy between realizing threats and taking protective actions (Tsai et al. 2016). The model states that protective behaviors are motivated by Threat Appraisals, determined by the user's perceived vulnerability and susceptibility to risks, and Coping Appraisals, based on self-efficacy, response efficacy, and response costs associated with safe or adaptive behaviors. Also, Tsai et al. (2016), established a strong link between behavior intentions of home users and online habit strength, as in accordance with LaRose et al. (2007). Most published research seeks to comprehend and predict Security Awareness and, consequently, Security Intentions (e.g., Boss et al. 2015). However, there is a literature discrepancy related to security related behaviors. This translates into the absence of further research that analyzes how home user's Protection Motivation (or Security Intentions) convert into actual Use Behaviors when using the Internet. Boss et al. (2015) wrote about this issue, but even so, his study focuses mostly on Fear Appeals instead on the actual study of the individual's Use Behavior. Consequently, it is important to further comprehend the models that attempt to explain people's actual behavior, in order to understand the effect of behavioral intentions on the user's behavior. From the literature, the most important models for studying individual's behavior are the Theory of Reasoned Action (TRA) and the Theory of Planned Behavior (TPB), both of which aim to predict individual's behavior based on intentions and pre-existing attitudes (Fishbein and Ajzen 1975; Saridakis et al. 2015). From these theories, many more have been derived. One of the most widely studied is the Reasoned Action Approach (RAA).

3 Reasoned Action Approach

The Reasoned Action Approach (RAA) was first described by Fishbein and Ajzen (2010), the same authors of the Theory of Reasoned Action (Fishbein and Ajzen 1975) and the Theory of Planned Behavior (Ajzen 1991). The RAA has been commonly used to predict people's behavior in diverse areas, such as Health (Conner et al. 2017), Agriculture (Hulst et al. 2016) and Consumer Behavior (Liu et al. 2017). In terms of online behavior, its applications have been extended to the study of several areas ranging from online shopping behavior (Chang et al. 2005; Zhou et al. 2007), the adoption of social networks (Pinho et al. 2011), and online banking. According to this theory, Attitudes, Perceived Norms, and Perceived Control guide the user's behavioral intentions and actual behavior. Also, Behavioral Intention is stated to be the best single predictor for Use Behavior, since the strongest intentions have the greatest probability of transforming into actual behaviors. Equally, the RAA also states that Use Behavior is moderated by the variable Actual Control, which includes the user's skills, abilities, and environmental factors (Ajzen and Fishbein 2010). As stated in this theory, people are only able to perform a certain behavior if they have the requisite skills and abilities, and if there are no environmental constraints preventing them from acting on their specific behavioral intentions. In brief, intention is described as a strong predictor for Use Behavior. However, current literature is not able to fully explain the influence of Protection Motivation on Millennials' Use Behavior. Also, published literature does not consider other variables which might be influential at predicting Use Behavior applied to this field of study.

4 Development of the Research Hypotheses

Considering the gap identified in the literature review, the suggested research proposal focuses on understanding the influence of Protection Motivation (or Security Intentions) in the Use Behavior of home users in terms of the security measures they adopt. Also, it was considered that context and external factors such as age, gender, and experiences might have an influence in adopting certain security precautions (Ajzen and Fishbein 2010). For that reason, Cohort Theory was used, allowing for a greater understanding of the actual behavior of a specific generation as generational cohorts differ not only in age but also in education, relationship with peers, and past experiences (Ryder 1965). Therefore, for the purpose of this research we will follow the generational cohorts proposed by Brosdahl and Carpenter (2011). The cohorts considered are Baby Boomers (born from 1946 to 1960), Generation X (from 1961 to 1981), and Millennials (from 1981 to 2000). Moreover, knowing that Millennials are most likely to fall for cybercrime than any other generational cohort, we will focus this study on this specific generational cohort. Consequently, our research question should be formulated as: *How does Protection Motivation (or Security Intentions) affect Millennials' online Use Behavior? Specifically, which other factors may influence their Use Behavior?*

To respond to our research question, we combined variables from two models, the Protection Motivation Theory (PMT) and the Reasoned Action Approach (RAA), with the goal of analyzing the existence of discrepancies among Security Intentions and Use

Behavior and which other variables may influence Millennials Use Behavior, in the context of security precautions adopted by home computer users.

For the purpose of this research, Threat Severity was considered as a representative of Threat Appraisals, as some authors have already described it as an important predictor of Security Intentions (Zahedi et al. 2015). However, there are some contradictory research results on the significance of this variable as a predictor for Protection Motivation (Tsai et al. 2016). As for Coping Appraisals, the variables considered were: Response Costs, Response Efficacy, Subjective Norms, and Safety Habit Strength. Response Costs should evolve in the opposite direction of Protection Motivation, as individuals will show a greater intention to perform protective measures when costs are lower (Tsai et al. 2016). According to Response Efficacy, the more effective a behavior is perceived to be, the more individuals will intend to adopt it. Subjective Norms relate with the influence that individuals have on each other (Ajzen 1991). Safety Habit Strength is related with an individual's routine of performing protective behaviors (Tsai et al. 2016). This leads to hypotheses H_{1a}, H_{1b}, H_{1c}, H_{1d}, and H_{1e}, as follows.

H_{1a}: Threat Severity increases the Protection Motivation of Millennials.
H_{1b}: Response Costs decrease the Protection Motivation of Millennials.
H_{1c}: Response Efficacy increases the Protection Motivation of Millennials.
H_{1d}: Subjective Norms increase the Protection Motivation of Millennials.
H_{1e}: Safety Habit Strength increases the Protection Motivation of Millennials.

As we are considering Millennials' Protection Motivation, the model should also seek predict the user's overall Use Behavior in terms of the security measures he/she adopts when navigating online. The next step was to study the influence of Millennials' Protection Motivation on their Use Behavior. This leads to hypothesis H_2, as presented below.

H_2: Protection Motivation positively affects Millennials' online Use Behavior.

As for the RAA, it is described by the authors as a unified approach that accounts for any behavior, and should therefore also be applicable to our Research Question (Jansen et al. 2017). In 2017 Jansen and Schaik combined the PMT and RAA to study the precautionary behavioral intention in online banking, and concluded that the variables of the integrated model are strong predictors for that specific research topic. Following this rationale, by considering variables present in both the PMT and RAA, we expect that the model created has good explanatory power. As the main objective of this paper is to explain which variables may affect the Millennials' Use Behavior, the variable Actual Control was incorporated. Actual Control includes the user's relevant skills, abilities, and environment conditions that may act as barriers or facilitators for behavioral performance (Fishbein and Ajzen 2010). This leads to hypothesis H_3, presented below.

H_3: Actual Control positively influences Millennials' Use Behavior.

Considering the discrepancies between the user's Actual Control and what he/she perceives, it is also imperative to incorporate in the model a variable that translates the Perceived Control. In current literature this variable is described as the perception about being able to control one's own destiny, and thus, claim responsibility for one's own actions (Workman et al. 2008). Also, this variable has been incorporated by some authors in the PMT (Workman et al. 2008). A high Locus of Control may imply a greater sense of responsibility for online safety (Jansen et al. 2017). Based on this, we arrive at hypothesis H_4, as follows:

H_4: Locus of Control positively influences Millennials' Use Behavior.

Lastly, considering that a positive attitude toward a certain behavior is considered to positively influence that behavior (Fishbein and Ajzen 1975), the variable Attitude toward Online Safety (Attitude TOS) was incorporated in the model (Fig. 1). This leads to hypothesis H_5, as presented below:

H_5: Attitude toward Online Safety positively influences Millennials' Use Behavior.

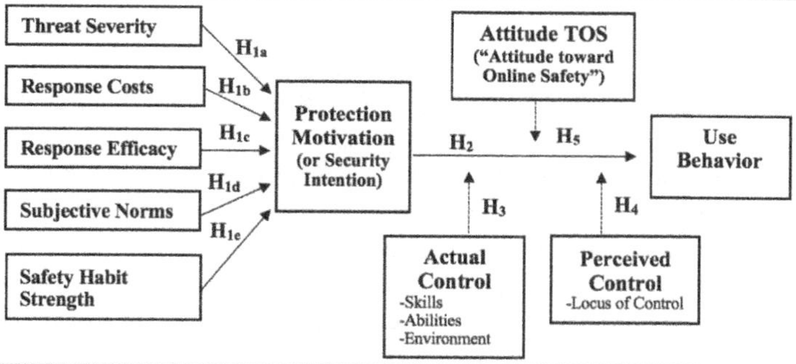

Fig. 1. The research model based on the Protection Motivation Theory (Rogers 1975) and the Reasoned Action Approach (Fishbein and Ajzen 2010).

5 Methodology

Our research was conducted through a web-based survey constructed with Qualtrics software. We considered 236 valid respondents (from 267): 71.6% were female and 26.4% were male; 75.8% had a Bachelor's degree or higher; 22 countries were represented in the sample (including 55.9% of respondents from Portugal, 9.3% from the USA, 5.1% from France, and 3.4% from Germany). The variable *Threat Severity* was modified from Liang and Xue (2010) and Tsai el al. (2016), and the items were measured using the same scale used by those authors; *Response Efficacy* was modified from literature of the same authors; *Subjective Norms* was adapted from the research of Anderson et al. (2010) and Tsai et al. (2016); *Response Costs* was based on the research of Liang and Xue (2010); *Safety Habit Strength* was adapted from Venkatesh et al. (2012) and Tsai et al. (2016); *Protection Motivation* (or *Security Intentions*) was modified from the research of Agarwal (2010), Liang and Xue (2010), and Tsai et al. (2016); *Actual Control* was self-developed according to the definition of Ajzen and Fishbein (2010); *Attitude toward Online Safety* was adapted from Mishra et al. (2014); *Locus of Control* was adapted from Workman et al. (2008); and, finally, *Use Behavior* was derived from the *Protection Motivation* variable, but focused on the user's current behavior instead of intentional behavior. For each variable, a Cronbach's Alpha was computed as a measure of reliability. The values obtained were greater than .70, which translates into a satisfactory level of internal consistency.

6 Results and Discussion

Previous research supports that variables such as Response Efficacy, Subjective Norms, Response Costs, and Safety Habit Strength could predict individual's intention to undertake protective measures when navigating online (Tsai et al. 2016). Similarly, our research suggests that Response Efficacy, Subjective Norms, and Safety Habit Strength are good predictors for Millennials' Protection Motivation. However, the same does not apply to Response Costs, considering that in our results this variable has little effect on Millennials' Security Intentions. As for the variable Threat Severity, past research is contradictory, as some authors believe that the variable has a negative significance when predicting Security Intentions (Tsai et al. 2016) and others state that the variable has no explanatory power. Our research suggests that this variable is not a significant predictor for Protection Motivation, as suggested by LaRose et al. (2007).

The main objective of this research was to understand the impact of Protection Motivation (or Security Intentions) on Millennials' Use Behavior when navigating online in terms of the protective measures they adopt. As described in hypothesis H_2, although Security Intentions positively influence Use Behavior, this research has found that there is a gap between the two variables, considering that Protection Motivation explains only partially the variation of Use Behavior (approximately 29.9%). This being the case, this research has also focused on explaining which factors may give rise to this variance between behavioral intentions and actual behavior. According to our findings, even though the variables Threat Severity, Response Efficacy, and Subjective Norms are good predictors for Protection Motivation (**Model 1**), the same does not apply when estimating Use Behavior. As seen in **Model 3** and **Model 4**, from the variables initially used in the PMT to estimate Protection Motivation, Safety Habit Strength revealed to be the only strong predictor for Use Behavior. These conclusions are rather interesting, meaning that Millennials do consider these five factors when deciding on a behavior. However, later on, Safety Habit Strength becomes the only significant factor they rely on when behaving in a certain manner. Results are shown in Tables 1 and 2.

Table 1. Regression with Protection Motivation as the dependent variable.

Variable	B	S.E.	β	T	Sig.
(constant)	.971				
Response Efficacy	.201	.074	.178	2.731	.007
Subjective Norms	.180	.052	.227	3.465	.001
Safety Habit Strength	.220	.047	.280	4.674	.00001
Response Costs	.015	.047	.020	.326	.745
Threat Severity	.148	.078	.117	1.904	.058
	R = .555		R^2 =. 309		Adjusted R^2 = .293

Table 2. Hierarchical multiple regression with *Use Behaviour* as the dependent variable.

Variable	Model 2					Model 3					Model 4				
	B	S.E.	β	T	Sig.	B	S.E.	β	T	Sig.	B	S.E.	β	T	Sig.
(constant)	1.576					1.120					.837				
Protection Motivation	.429	.057	.446	7.591	.00001	.243	.062	.252	3.909	.00001	.247	.067	.419	1.999	.00001
Response Efficacy						.048	.070	.044	.692	.490	.057	.076	.053	.753	.452
Subjective Norms						.051	.050	.067	1.024	.307	.053	.050	.070	1.060	.290
Safety Habit Strength						.298	.046	.394	6.473	.00001	.270	.052	.357	5.203	.00001
Response Costs						-.042	.044	-.560	-.956	.340	-.039	.044	-.053	-.887	.376
Threat Severity						-.013	.073	-.010	-.171	.864	.003	.075	.003	.042	.966
Actual Control											.117	.061	.126	1.932	.055
Locus of Control											-0.60	.048	-0.078	-1.246	.214
Attitude TOS											.013	.092	.011	.143	.886
	R=.446	R^2=.351	Adjusted R^2=.195			R=.593	R^2=.351	Adjusted R^2=.293			R=.603	R^2=.363	Adjusted R^2=.338		

Additionally, new factors were added to the analysis to optimize our ability to explain Use Behavior. As stated in hypothesis H_3, Actual Control was found to be a good predictor for Use Behavior, as it was able to increase our ability to explain the dependent variable to 36.3%. As shown by **Model 4,** the user's skills, abilities, and environment play an important role in explaining Use Behavior. Lastly, hypotheses H_4 and H_5 were not supported by **Model 4**, and consequently, Perceived Control (Locus of Control) and Attitude toward Online Safety are not able to further explain the variation of Use Behavior. However, as stated above, there is a positive correlation between Use Behavior and the two variables Attitude toward Online Safety ($r = 0.321, p < .01$) and Locus of Control ($r = 0.211$, $p < .01$), which can indicate that these variables may have been suppressed by the others.

7 Conclusion

This research was able to establish a gap between behavioral intention and actual behavior in terms of protective measures that Millennials adopt when navigating online. In addition, the model formulated was able to determine that Safety Habit Strength and Actual Control, which include individual's skills, abilities, and the environment factor, are significant when explaining Millennials' Use Behavior. One important limitation is that measuring Use Behavior can be quite challenging, as users might not be totally honest in the way they express their actual behavior. These findings can contribute to improving the overall security of the cyberspace as it becomes easier to influence Millennials adopting a safer online behavior.

Acknowledgments. This work was funded by Fundação para a Ciência e a Tecnologia (UID/ECO/00124/2013, UID/ECO/00124/2019 and Social Sciences DataLab, LISBOA-01-0145-FEDER-022209), POR Lisboa (LISBOA-01-0145-FEDER-007722, LISBOA-01-0145-FEDER-022209) and POR Norte (LISBOA-01-0145-FEDER-022209). The authors declare that they have no conflict of interest. All procedures performed in studies involving human participants were in accordance with the ethical standards of the institutional and/or national research committee and with the 1964 Helsinki declaration and its later amendments or comparable ethical standards. Informed consent was obtained from all individual participants included in the study.

References

Ajzen, I.: The theory of planned behavior. Organ. Behav. Hum. Decis. Process. **50**(2), 179–211 (1991)

Anderson, C.L., Agarwal, R.: Practicing safe computing: a multimethod empirical examination of home computer user security behavioral intentions. MIS Q. **34**(3), 613–643 (2010)

Anderson, R., Barton, C., Böhme, R., Clayton, R., van Eeten, M.J.G., Levi, M., Moore, T., Savage, S.: Measuring the cost of cybercrime. In: Böhme, R. (ed.) The Economics of Information Security and Privacy, pp. 265–300. Springer, Heidelberg (2013)

Boss, S., Galletta, D., Lowry, P., Moody, G., Polak, P.: What do systems users have to fear? Using fear appeals to engender threats and fear that motivate protective security behaviors. MIS Q. **39**(4), 837–864 (2015)

Brosdahl, D., Carpenter, J.: Shopping orientations of US males: a generational cohort comparison. J. Retail. Consum. Serv. **18**(6), 548–554 (2011)
Chang, M., Cheung, W., Lai, V.: Literature derived reference models for the adoption of online shopping. Inf. Manag. **42**(4), 543–559 (2005)
Conner, M., McEachan, R., Lawton, R., Gardner, P.: Applying the reasoned action approach to understanding health protection and health risk behaviors. Soc. Sci. Med. **195**, 140–148 (2017)
Dodge, R., Carver, C., Ferguson, A.: Phishing for user security awareness. Comput. Secur. **26**(1), 73–80 (2007)
European Commission: Resilience, deterrence and defence: building strong cybersecurity in Europe (2017). https://ec.europa.eu/digital-single-market/en/news/resilience-deterrence-and-defence-building-strong-cybersecurity-europe. Accessed 24 Sept 2018
Fishbein, M., Ajzen, I.: Belief, Attitude, Intention, and Behavior. Addison-Wesley Publishing Company, Reading (1975)
Fishbein, M., Ajzen, I.: Predicting and Changing Behavior: The Reasoned Action Approach. Taylor & Francis Group, New York (2010)
Hulst, F., Posthumus, H.: Understanding (non-)adoption of conservation agriculture in Kenya using the Reasoned Action Approach. Land Use Policy **56**, 303–314 (2016)
Jansen, J., Schaik, P.: Comparing three models to explain precautionary online behavioural intentions. Inf. Comput. Secur. **5**(2), 165–180 (2017)
Kritzinger, E., Solms, S.: Cyber security for home users: a new way of protection through awareness enforcement. Comput. Soc. **29**(8), 840–847 (2010)
Lagazio, M., Sherif, N., Cushman, M.: A multi-level approach to understanding the impact of cybercrime on the financial sector. Comput. Soc. **45**, 58–74 (2014)
LaRose, R., Rifon, N., Wirth, C.: Online safety begins with you and me: getting internet users to protect themselves. Paper presented at the 57th International Communication Association Conference (2007)
Liang, H., Xue, Y.: Understanding security behaviors in personal computer usage: a threat avoidance perspective. J. Assoc. Inf. Syst. **11**(7), 394–413 (2010)
Liu, Y., Segev, S., Villar, M.: Comparing two mechanisms for green consumption: cognitive-affect behaviour vs. theory of reasoned action. J. Consum. Mark. **34**(5), 442–454 (2017)
Mishra, D., Akman, I., Mishra, A.: Theory of reasoned action application for green information technology acceptance. Comput. Hum. Behav. **36**, 29–40 (2014)
Pinho, J., Soares, A.: Examining the technology acceptance model in the adoption of social networks. J. Res. Interact. Mark. **5**(2/3), 116–129 (2011)
Poepjes, R., Lane, M.: An information security awareness capability model (ISACM). In: Australian Information Security Management Conference (SECAU 2012) (2012)
Pinho, J., Soares, A.: Examining the technology acceptance model in the adoption of social networks. J. Res. Interact. Mark. **5**(2/3), 116–129 (2011)
Poepjes, R., Lane, M.: An information security awareness capability model (ISACM). In: Australian Information Security Management Conference (SECAU 2012) (2012)
Rogers, R.: A protection motivation theory of fear appeals and attitude change. J. Psychol. **91**(1), 93–114 (1975)
Rogers, R.: Cognitive and physiological processes in fear appeals and attitude change: a revised theory of protection motivation. In: Cacioppo, J.T., Petty, R.E. (eds.) Social Psychophysiology: A Sourcebook, pp. 153–177. Guilford Press, New York (1983)
Romanosky, S.: Examining the costs and causes of cyber incidents. J. Cybersecur. **2**(2), 121–135 (2016)
Ryder, N.: The cohort as a concept in the study of social change. Am. Sociol. Rev. **30**, 843–861 (1965)

Saridakis, G., Benson, V., Ezingeard, J., Tennakoon, H.: Individual information security, user behaviour and cyber victimisation: an empirical study of social networking users. Technol. Forecast. Soc. Change **102**, 320–330 (2015)

Tsai, H., Jiang, M., Alhabash, S., LaRose, R., Rifon, N., Cotten, S.: Understanding online safety behaviors: a protection motivation theory perspective. Comput. Secur. **59**, 138–150 (2016)

Venkatesh, V., Thong, J., Xu, X.: Consumer acceptance and use of information technology: extending the unified theory of acceptance and use of technology. MIS Q. **36**, 157–178 (2012)

Workman, M., Bommer, W., Straub, D.: Security lapses and the omission of information security measures: a threat control model and empirical test. Comput. Hum. Behav. **24**(6), 2799–2816 (2008)

Zahedi, F., Abbasi, A., Chen, Y.: Fake-website detection tools: identifying elements that promote individuals' use and enhance their performance. J. Assoc. Inf. Syst. **6**(16), 448–484 (2015)

Zhou, L., Dai, L., Zhang, D.: Online shopping acceptance model: a critical survey of consumer factors in online shopping. J. Electron. Commer. Res. **8**(1), 41–62 (2007)

The Effect of App Quality and Compatibility on Consumers' Omnichannel (OC) App Adoption and Loyalty: Comparison of US and Korean Consumers

Joonyong Park[1(✉)] and Renee B. Kim[2]

[1] School of Business, KISE, Hanyang University, Seoul, South Korea
hyjyphd@gmail.com

[2] School of Business, Hanyang University, Seoul, South Korea
Kimrby@hanyang.ac.kr, kimrby@gmail.com

Abstract. This paper proposes to empirically test a research model that evaluate the importance of selected antecedents of consumers' omnichannel shopping loyalty. In particular, this paper examines the influence of two variables (i.e. compatibility, omnichannel app quality) in understanding consumers' response to omnichannel retail service. Social cognitive theory and technology task fit theory are applied as theoretical frameworks, and the Technology Acceptance Model (TAM) is applied as a reference framework for the empirical research model. The proposed model is assessed with the partial least squares structural equation modeling (PLS-SEM), and the empirical data is collected from the U.S. and Korea. A web-based survey was developed to collect data from the U.S. and South Korean consumers who have experience using the OC apps. In total, 130 responses and 123 responses were used from the U.S. and South Korea, respectively for empirical analysis. This study finds the significant direct relationship of the 5 predictors (perceived quality of the OC app, perceived compatibility, perceived ease of use, perceived usefulness) with the key construct – consumer loyalty.

Keywords: Perceived quality of the OC app · Perceived compatibility · TAM · Loyalty

1 Introduction

One of the top priorities for change and innovation in the retail industry today is to enrich the customer experience by expanding resources and capabilities to develop an effective omnichannel strategy, while moving away from traditional channel and communication approaches for the new digital environment. Major retail firms around the world are adopting the digital transformation (omnichannel) to enhance customer experience by organically linking various customer contact channels (i.e. touch point) with customers, replacing the existing corporate-led and single store-oriented channel strategies. In particular, the retail firms are increasingly utilizing the mobile app to connect customers with their omnichannel services. For example, Wal-Mart has completely reorganized its mobile apps and websites to connect online and offline and enhanced its lifestyle-based

F. J. Martínez-López and S. D'Alessandro (Eds.): *Advances in Digital Marketing and eCommerce*, SPBE, pp. 163–178, 2020.
https://doi.org/10.1007/978-3-030-47595-6_21

customer buying experience. The mobile app has revamped the in-store maps to facilitate customers' shopping in offline stores, and to track product and inventory. In addition, Wal-Mart introduced the Mobile Express Returns program to enhance customers' convenience, which enables the returns of online purchases at the offline Wal-Mart stores. Other major retailers such as Macy's and Amazon Go are strengthening their omnichannel services by offering a mobile check-out service (Fig. 1).

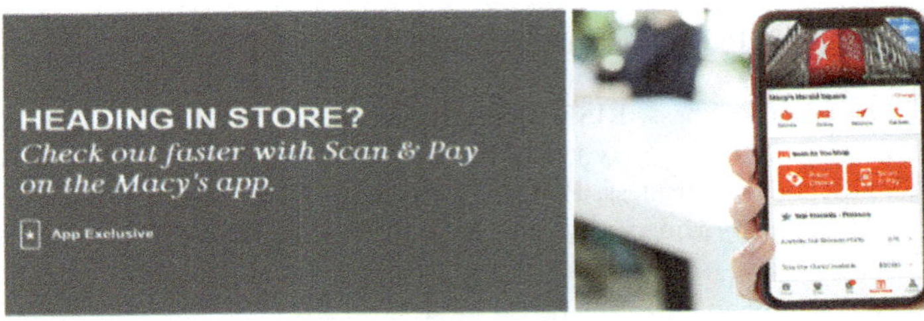

Fig. 1. Mobile check-out service

Thus, the omnichannel app with a mobile device is becoming an important platform which enables the digital transformation of major retail firms, connecting customers with their omnichannel services efficiently. There are numerous ways which retailers can apply the mobile app to the omnichannel service format. For example, the retailers can use a mobile app for a location-based services to offer consumers discounts or rewards opportunities when they physically enter offline stores or use their mobile cameras to scan the product's barcode. The omnichannel service app can also offer a shopping guide tool to assist their purchase decision, by connecting the mobile app with the consumers. Consumers are becoming sophisticated enough to optimize their shopping experience, with thorough consideration of all possible alternatives in all possible channels (Gao and Su 2017). Consumers use the in-store mobile apps to browse and look for products, deals, coupons, and other promotional offers as well as to purchase products after researching them in the store (Kang et al. 2015). The mobile retail apps can assist customers and significantly improve in-store conversions and keep consumers from being influenced by retail competitors (Siwicki 2014).

As consumers' omnichannel usage increases, the retailers need to know the underlying factors that affect consumers' use of omnichannel apps in order to enhance consumers' shopping experience, impact loyalty, and develop effective consumer-preferred apps and targeted marketing techniques. Perceived quality is an attribute of a product/service that indicates how well it makes consumer's needs (Nagel and Cilliers 1990). Perceived quality resembles attitudes (Zeithaml 1988) and affects purchases, as consumers reflect judgments and evaluations about the quality of products/services according to their needs. Consumers' perceived quality of the OC app may have significant effect on their future intention to use the omnichannel retail service (i.e. loyalty) which will translate to the customer retention rate.

This paper proposes to empirically test a research model that evaluate the importance of selected antecedents of consumers' omnichannel shopping loyalty. In particular, this paper examines the influence of two variables (i.e. compatibility, omnichannel app quality) that have been rarely studied in understanding consumers' response to omnichannel retail service. Social cognitive theory and technology task fit theory are applied as theoretical frameworks, and the Technology Acceptance Model (TAM) is applied as a reference framework (Fig. 2) for the empirical research model. The proposed model is assessed with the partial least squares structural equation modeling (PLS-SEM), and the empirical data is collected from the U.S. and Korea.

2 Literature Review and Model Development

2.1 Perceived Quality of Omnichannel (OC) App

The omnichannel (OC) app may play an important role in facilitating retailers' OC service to consumers. When consumers purchase a product in the OC platform, they are likely to compare the OC app or the site quality of alternative services. Therefore, how consumers perceive the app quality can play a key role in retaining consumers. Consumers may use the OC app to access product information and to make purchase process, and the quality of the OC app is closely connected to consumers' shopping experience. In other words, the OC app needs to fulfil two functional aspects of the OC service, providing information and assisting the purchase process.

Information is a fundamental part of the website and the quality of information is considered to be important part of a marketing tool that ensures smooth execution of transactions in online shopping (Xu and Koronios 2005). One of the biggest challenges in the OC environment is to effectively communicate information (Bell et al. 2014). Because consumers are actively looking for information about product value and inventory availability, retailers may need to manage their sources of information to influence their shopping paths (Gao and Su 2017). In addition, retailers need to provide consumers with consistent and integrated information to facilitate adoption and use of omnichannel (Park and Kim 2018). The information quality may play a similar role in the OC app as an important marketing tool for the OC retailers. Kim and Niehm (2009) found that perceived information quality was positively associated with loyalty intention, supporting findings of previous research (e.g., Parasuraman and Grewal 2000; Chiu et al. 2005). Lin and Lu (2000) found a positive link between the quality of information and the usefulness of a website. In this study, the perceived information quality refers to consumers' overall judgment and evaluation of the quality of information, which is assessed by the degree of accuracy, timeliness of the information which are provided by the OC app.

Li et al. (2018) conceptualized that consumers averseness toward risk or uncertainties as important determinants of consumer's shopping behaviour. Thus, the OC app also need to entail an efficient system quality, ensuring privacy and guarantee for the OC product/service. This feature of the OC app is a proxy for consumers' trust in the OC, which was found to be essential in successful acceptance of the OC by consumers regardless of their individual differences (Park and Kim 2019). In this study, the system quality refers to customer's perception of protection mechanisms, such as online credit card guarantees and privacy protection that exists to protect consumers against potential risks in the OC environment. Perceived quality of the OC app can be conceptualized as a composite of two dimensions such as the information quality and the system quality, having impact on consumers' perceived usefulness of the OC service and their loyalty toward a retailer.

H1. Perceived quality of the OC app has a positive effect on perceived usefulness of the OC retailers.
H2. Perceived quality of the OC app has a positive effect on consumer's loyalty towards the OC retailers.

2.2 Perceived Compatibility

Compatibility is the degree to which an innovation is perceived to be consistent with the potential users' existing values, previous experiences, and needs (Rogers 1995). In the literature on diffusion of innovation, compatibility has traditionally been regarded as a fundamental attribute of new behaviour or technology. According to the Technology Task Fit Theory, technology is important for users' compatibility with existing values and beliefs, previously introduced ideas and needs (Gillenson and Sherrell 2002; Ozturk et al. 2016). We define compatibility as the degree to which the OC technology fits the lifestyle and experiences of individuals. Compatibility is a key factor for consumers' attitude towards online shopping (Gillenson and Sherrell 2002), affecting consumers' behavioural intention for a mobile shopping, and has effects on both perceived usefulness, and actual use (Wu and Wang 2005). Compatibility is also considered to be important in users' mobile device activities (Koenig-Lewis et al. 2010). Ewe et al. (2015) states that in order to increase the usage of mobile banking, a mobile banking system needs to be easy to use and is compatible with users' lifestyles. According to Akturan and Tezcan (2012), compatibility is a key precursor of perceived ease of use.

Compatibility of mobile OC retail apps can be defined as the degree to which consumers view using apps as fitting in with their needs and preferences. Kim et al. (2009) demonstrated that value compatibility, such as the preferred lifestyle, had an impact on the intention to adopt a mobile service, and Meuter et al. (2005) found that compatibility was a determinant of consumer readiness and trial of self-service technologies (e.g., telephone banking, automated hotel checkout). Yang et al. (2016) has suggested that perceived compatibility of wearable devices should be one of the key determinants of perceived usefulness. Likewise, consumers may develop more positive perception (i.e. perceived usefulness and ease of use) toward the OC app, as they have higher levels of compatibility, which refers to the degree to which the OC app is perceived to be consistent with their beliefs, lifestyle, existing values, experience, and current needs

H3. Perceived compatibility has a positive effect on perceived usefulness of the OC retailers.
H4. Perceived compatibility has a positive effect on perceived ease of use with the OC retailers.
H5. Perceived compatibility has a positive effect on consumer's loyalty towards the OC retailers.

2.3 TAM Variables

Technology acceptance model (TAM) integrates various theoretical perspectives of social psychological research framework (i.e. theory of reasoned action (TRA) and theory of planned behaviour (TPB) with technical approaches. TAM is widely known for its simplicity and parsimony (Dutot et al. 2019), and has been applied and validated for a wide range of new technologies such as e-commerce, m-gaming, smartphones and mobile-based technology (Dutot et al. 2019). TAM (Davis 1989) proposes two main predictors (i.e. perceived usefulness and perceived ease of use) of the acceptance and use of a new information system or technology. Davis (1989) defined the 'ease of use' as the degree to which he believes the use of a particular system requires no effort. According to Ozturk et al. (2014), perceived ease of use has a positive impact on the intention to use smartphone apps.

Use of new technologies or devices typically requires consumers to have additional learning efforts, and this may increase if the new technology is difficult to use. When consumers perceive the OC app to be not easy to use, they are likely to be discouraged from adoption and continued usage. Consumers may expect an enhanced shopping experience if the OC app is perceived to be easy to use. In this study, we adopted Davis's (1989) definition and defined the perceived ease of use as the degree that individuals consider the OC apps to be easy to use. Particularly, the effect of perceived ease of use on perceived usefulness has been established in the initial TAM (Davis et al. 1989) and re-established in TAM2 (Venkatesh and Davis 2000). In addition, this link has been found to be important in several contexts, including m-commerce (Cyr et al. 2006) and mobile app adoption (Kumar et al. 2018). If a consumer perceives that an app is easier to use, it is more likely that he/she will consider it to be useful (Kumar et al. 2018).

Loyalty is conceptualized as customers' favourable attitude towards a brand (Keller 1993) or an intention for a repeat usage. Loyal customers show their attachment and commitment to a company and are not interested in competitors' offerings (So et al. 2013; Ozturk et al. 2016). Firms can develop a long-term and mutually beneficial relationships with their customers if they can create loyalty (Pan et al. 2012). The term e-loyalty is defined as consumer's intention to revisit a website or repurchase from an online vendor (Flavián et al. 2006). In the context of e-commerce, the mobile loyalty depends on consumers' intention to revisit a mobile website resulting in repeat purchasing behaviour (Cyr et al. 2006). Numerous previous studies have shown that positive perceived ease of use and usefulness can generate loyalty for particular websites in the context of online retailing (Gefen et al. 2003; Ribbink et al. 2004; Flavián et al. 2006; Kim and Niehm 2009; Ozturk et al. 2016). Consumers' assessment of the service usefulness is one of the main determinants for its future use (Venkatesh and Davis 2000). The perceived usefulness also positively influences loyalty for mobile commerce (Cyr et al. 2006). A similar relationship has been established between the perceived usefulness and the loyalty for a retailer in e-services context (Cyr et al. 2006). Hence, this study proposes the following hypotheses.

H6. Perceived ease of use has a positive effect on perceived usefulness of the OC app.
H7. Perceived usefulness has a positive effect on consumer's loyalty toward the OC retailers.
H8. Perceived ease of use has a positive effect on consumer's loyalty toward the OC retailers.

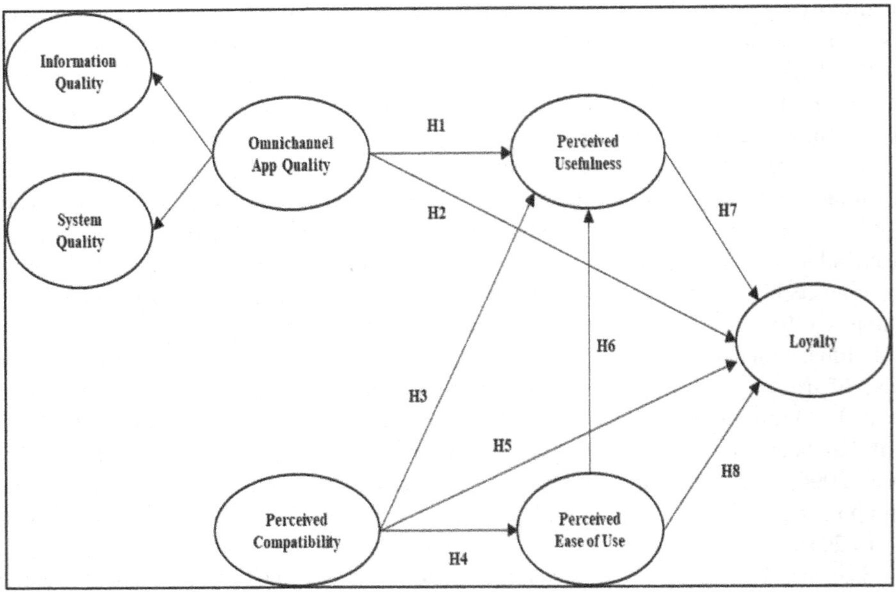

Fig. 2. Conceptual model.

3 Research Methodology

A web-based survey was developed to collect data from consumers who have experience using the OC apps. The questionnaire consisted of two parts. The first section includes sample demographics (gender, age, education, occupation and income) and the second section consists of 18 items to measure the selected variables, using a Likert-5 scale (strongly disagree to strongly agree). Appendix A offers a detailed list of the 18 items. The data collection was performed in the U.S. and South Korea by a third party that has a large number of panels on an online survey platform. After the survey link had been distributed to the panel members, data screening revealed that 143 responses from the U.S. and 139 from South Korea had been obtained. Thirteen responses from the U.S. and 16 responses from South Korea were excluded, and in total, 130 responses and 123 responses were used for further analysis from the U.S. and South Korea, respectively. The majority of the South Korea participants were in their twenties and thirties, and 35 percent of them were male and 80 percent were female. Among U.S. participants, the numbers of male and female respondents were almost equal, and the majority of U.S. participants were in their twenties and thirties. Table 1 provides more details on socio-demographic characteristics.

Table 1. Demographic characteristics

Variable	Group	U.S.		Korea	
		Frequency	Percent	Frequency	Percent
Age	10 s	12	9.2	29	23.6
	20 s	85	65.4	72	58.5
	30 s	26	20.0	17	13.8
	40 s	3	2.3	5	4.1
	50 s over	4	3.1	0	0
	Total	130	100.0	123	100.0
Gender	Male	67	51.5	121	50.6
	Female	63	48.5	118	49.4
	Total	130	100.0	239	100.0
Education	Less than 12th grade	2	1.5	3	2.4
	High school diploma	25	19.2	22	17.9
	Vocational degree	3	2.3	19	15.4
	Bachelor's degree	39	30.0	58	47.2
	Master's degree and above	61	46.9	21	17.1
	Total	130	100.0	123	100.0
Income	<$2,000	86	66.2	87	70.7
	$2,001–$3,5000	25	19.2	23	18.7
	$3,501–$5,000	4	3.1	5	4.1
	$5,001–$6,5000	3	2.3	1	0.8
	>$6,501	12	9.2	5.7	0
	Total	130	100.0	123	100.0
Occupation	Student	80	61.5	83	67.5
	Government official	3	2.3	4	3.3
	Professions	21	16.2	12	9.8
	Unemployed	1	0.8	0	0
	Office worker	13	10.0	9	7.3
	Self-employed	3	2.3	2	1.6
	Service workers	1	0.8	2	1.6
	Other	8	6.2	11	8.9
	Total	130	100.0	123	100.0

4 Data Analysis and Results

Partial least squares-Structural equation modelling (PLS-SEM) was used to test the proposed research model. PLS-SEM provides researchers with more flexibility in terms of data requirements, model complexity and relationship specification (Sarstedt et al. 2014). The statistical software used in this study is Smart-PLS (v 3.2.8).

4.1 Reliability and Validity of the Model

To assess construct reliability, Cronbach's alpha (Cronbach 1951) was computed. Nunnally (1994) suggested that a value of at least 0.70 indicates adequate reliability. Cronbach's α value of our finding showed a value between 0.749 and 0.900 (USA) and between 0.753 and 0.895 (Korea) in all items exceeding recommended thresholds.

If composite reliability (CR) is more than 0.7, internal consistency reliability is secured, and average variance extracted (AVE) is more than 0.5, the measurement model has convergent validity (Fornell and Larcker 1981). Findings show that the CR is greater than 0.7, the AVE is greater than 0.5, and the square root of AVE is greater than the correlation coefficient. Thus, construct validity is ensured, and the measurement model has convergent validity and discriminant validity (Tables 2 and 3). According to Hair et al. (2014), the cut-off value for VIF (collinearity) should be smaller than 0.5, and our VIF results were smaller than 0.5 (from 1.379 to 4.048) as shown in Table 4.

Table 2. Construct reliability and validity

Measures	USA			Korea		
	Cronbach's alpha	Composite reliability	Average Variance Extracted (AVE)	Cronbach's alpha	Composite reliability	Average Variance Extracted (AVE)
IQ	0.869	0.919	0.792	0.842	0.905	0.760
LY	0.844	0.906	0.763	0.866	0.918	0.789
PC	0.848	0.908	0.766	0.753	0.858	0.669
PE	0.872	0.921	0.796	0.853	0.911	0.773
OQ	0.853	0.892	0.584	0.860	0.896	0.591
PU	0.900	0.937	0.833	0.895	0.935	0.827
SQ	0.749	0.856	0.665	0.791	0.878	0.706

Information Quality: IQ, Perceived Compatibility: PC, Perceived Ease of Use: PE, Omnichannel App Quality: OQ, Perceived Usefulness: PU, System Quality: SQ, Loyalty: LY

Table 3. Discriminant validity

USA	IQ	LY	PC	PE	OQ	PU	SQ
IQ	0.89						
LY	0.746	0.874					
PC	0.684	0.766	0.875				
PE	0.254	0.309	0.383	0.892			
OQ	0.918	0.793	0.725	0.405	0.764		
PU	0.704	0.788	0.757	0.458	0.783	0.913	
SQ	0.605	0.668	0.607	0.495	0.871	0.697	0.815
Korea	IQ	LY	PC	PE	OQ	PU	SQ
IQ	0.872						
LY	0.677	0.888					
PC	0.678	0.761	0.818				
PE	0.396	0.381	0.301	0.879			
OQ	0.906	0.762	0.727	0.423	0.769		
PU	0.699	0.788	0.667	0.458	0.771	0.909	
SQ	0.613	0.691	0.626	0.361	0.889	0.683	0.84

Information Quality: IQ, Perceived Compatibility: PC, Perceived Ease of Use: PE, Omnichannel App Quality: OQ, Perceived Usefulness: PU, System Quality: SQ, Loyalty: LY

Table 4. Collinearity (VIF)

USA				Korea			
Items	VIF	Items	VIF	Items	VIF	Items	VIF
LY1	2.400	PE1	2.662	LY1	2.269	PE1	2.386
LY2	1.673	PE2	2.052	LY2	2.053	PE2	1.954
LY3	2.536	PE3	2.480	LY3	2.700	PE3	2.096
IQ1	2.368	PU1	4.085	IQ1	1.998	PU1	3.081
IQ1	2.451	PU2	2.076	IQ1	2.146	PU2	2.238
IQ2	2.089	PU3	4.551	IQ2	1.869	PU3	3.467
IQ2	2.657	SQ1	1.651	IQ2	2.239	SQ1	2.167
IQ3	2.462	SQ1	2.276	IQ3	2.589	SQ1	2.477
IQ3	2.508	SQ2	1.379	IQ3	2.787	SQ2	1.740
PC1	2.111	SQ2	1.445	PC1	1.446	SQ2	2.021
PC2	1.883	SQ3	1.562	PC2	1.583	SQ3	1.543
PC3	2.302	SQ3	1.652	PC3	1.526	SQ3	1.653

Information Quality: IQ, Perceived Compatibility: PC, Perceived Ease of Use: PE, Omnichannel App Quality: OQ, Perceived Usefulness: PU, System Quality: SQ, Loyalty: LY

4.2 Hypothesis Testing

To identify the direct and indirect relationships among the constructs, t-values and beta-coefficients have been calculated using Smart-PLS at 95% confidence interval level. These values are shown in Table 5. This study finds the significant direct relationship of the 5 predictors (perceived quality of the OC app, perceived compatibility, perceived ease of use, perceived usefulness) with the key construct – consumer loyalty. H5 (perceived ease of use) is the only hypothesis which is not supported in both country cases. The 'perceived quality of the OC app' construct had direct impact on two constructs (i.e. perceived usefulness and loyalty) in both countries. The 'perceived compatibility' construct has a significant direct relationship with three constructs - 'perceived usefulness', 'perceived ease of use' and 'loyalty' in both countries. Although 'perceived ease of use' shows an insignificant direct relationship with 'loyalty', it does impact 'perceived usefulness' significantly.

Table 5. PLS-SEM results

	Variables	Path coefficients	T statistics (|O/STDEV|)	P values	Remarks
USA					
H1	OQ->PU	0.459	5.75	0.000	Supported
H2	OQ->LY	0.369	4.472	0.000	Supported
H3	PC->PU	0.375	4.743	0.000	Supported
H4	PC->PE	0.383	5.178	0.000	Supported
H5	PC->LY	0.292	3.284	0.001	Supported
H6	PE->PU	0.128	2.161	0.031	Supported
H7	PU->LY	0.324	3.451	0.001	Supported
H8	PE->LY	−0.1	1.752	0.080	Not supported
	OQ->IQ	0.918	68.633	0.000	Second-order
	OQ->SQ	0.871	39.56	0.000	Second-order
Korea					
H1	OQ->PU	0.535	6.631	0.000	Supported
H2	OQ->LY	0.197	2.072	0.039	Supported
H3	PC->PU	0.229	2.637	0.009	Supported
H4	PC->PE	0.301	3.085	0.002	Supported
H5	PC->LY	0.348	4.168	0.000	Supported
H6	PE->PU	0.163	2.814	0.005	Supported
H7	PU->LY	0.401	4.921	0.000	Supported
H8	PE->LY	0.009	0.16	0.873	Not supported
	OQ->IQ	0.906	51.317	0.000	Second-order
	OQ->SQ	0.889	36.616	0.000	Second-order

Information Quality: IQ, Perceived Compatibility: PC, Perceived Ease of Use: PE, Omnichannel App Quality: OQ, Perceived Usefulness: PU, System Quality: SQ, Loyalty: LY

5 Discussion and Implications

This study identifies the key determinants of loyalty towards the OC retailers and explains the relationships among perceived quality of the OC app, perceived compatibility and perceived usefulness and perceived ease of use. The empirical results confirm most of the hypothesized relationships among the selected constructs. These results show that customers' loyalty to the OC retailers can be strengthened by effectively communicating usefulness and ease of use of the OC apps, and the marketing communication may need to emphasize the quality of the OC apps and compatibility of the OC apps with consumers. While, all hypothesized relationships were significantly positive both in the U.S. and Korea findings, but contrary to our predictions, the construct –'perceived ease of use' shows no significant effect on 'loyalty'. However, 'perceived ease of use' has a positive effect on 'perceived usefulness', suggesting an indirect effect on 'loyalty' through 'perceived usefulness'. Findings suggest that the path of 'perceived quality of the OC app' (OQ)-> 'perceived usefulness' (PU)-> 'loyalty' (LY) is the most influential in both countries. More specifically, 'perceived quality of the OC app' (OQ) and 'perceived compatibility' (PC) constructs show significant effects on 'loyalty' (LY) in the U.S. case. In the Korean case, 'perceived compatibility' (PC) has a relatively greater impact on 'loyalty' (LY).

5.1 Theoretical Implications

Recent research and reports have shown that it is important to understand the omnichannel business from the customer's viewpoint and it is becoming to pay more attention to consumers' perception of the OC usage and experience. This study contributes to a new research flow in the following aspects. First, the study identifies the key determinants of omnichannel loyalty, and meaningful secondary factors which affect the perceived quality of the OC app. In addition, we developed a an empirical research model of consumers' behavior toward the OC app from technology perspectives of the Technology Task Fit Theory and TAM, and future research may adopt this approach for further analysis of predecessors and results, in expanding the existing literature. Recent studies have shown that customers are increasingly looking for an integrated shopping that reflects a variety of channel choices, continuous touch-points, and lifestyles (Shi et al. 2020), which is considered as the driving force of the omnichannel development (Brynjolfsson et al. 2013). However, previous studies show little attention to the importance of compatibility and the omnichannel app quality, which can be considered as the main links between customers and the omnichannel retailers. This study enhances understanding of consumers in a technology-intensive and dynamic omnichannel environment by addressing the unique characteristics of evolving omnichannel retail platform and consumer needs.

5.2 Managerial Implications

This study provides insights to practitioners in the omnichannel business and provide insightful guidelines for successful OC strategies. Omnichannel retailers should strive to improve the quality of the OC app to strengthen customer loyalty. In doing so, the OC retailers may need to invest substantial resources in developing a reliable OC system which can build consumer trust, and strives to provide accurate and timely information through the OC app. In particular, integration and consistency among channels are important to improve information quality which are provided to consumers (Park and Kim 2019). This require the OC retailers to ensure that customers can access consistent information through apps and receive consistent responses across channels. The OC retailers need to ensure privacy and credit safety of the system, and may provide customized services such as personal recommendation and promotion by analyzing big-data about customer information, data and shopping records. These functional features of the OC app can effectively enhance consumers experience of the OC app, translating into their loyalty toward the OC retailer.

Concurrently, the OC retailers must recognize the importance of consumers' perceived compatibility. In other words, they need to effectively communicate how the OC service, including the OC app can facilitate consumers' needs and preferences. This may require the retailers to look at consumers in more holistic way, paying attention to changes in consumer shopping habits, lifestyles, and preferences to have better understanding of consumers' needs and preference. As customer expectation rapidly change with technology development (augmented reality, smart devices), retailers should continue to update consumer needs and preferences. Many OC retailers are also providing additional incentives to consumers who uses the OC apps in their purchasing process, in order to draw more consumers to their OC system.

6 Limitations and Future Research

There are some limitations to this study. the survey questionnaire may need to be expanded to explore the relationships among the constructs (i.e. loyalty, perceived ease of use, perceived usefulness, perceived compatibility and omnichannel app quality) more in-depth. This study did not assess the effects of the demographic backgrounds of the omnichannel consumers on the hypotheses, and further analysis may provide more detailed information on antecedents of the OC loyalty for different consumer segments. Future research may apply other theoretical frameworks, such as the Unified Acceptance and Technology Use (UTAUT) model, to investigate the antecedents of omnichannel loyalty.

Appendix A

Information Quality	Omnichannel app offers necessary information about products that I need	Gao and Su (2017); Beck and Rygl (2015); Shin et al. (2013)
	Omnichannel app offers variety of information in a useful format	
	Omnichannel app provides much information that helps me with purchasing decision	
System Quality	I think omnichannel app provides very reliable service	Fang et al. (2014); Gao and Su (2017); Shin et al. (2013)
	I think that omnichannel app is secure to use	
	I think that omnichannel app provides fast responses to my inquiries	
Perceived Compatibility	I would appreciate using omnichannel app instead of alternative modes to find the information	Kapoor et al. (2015); Gillenson and Sherrell (2002); Ozturk et al. (2016); Sánchez-Prieto et al. (2019)
	Using omnichannel app is completely compatible with my current situation	
	Using omnichannel app fits my lifestyle	
Perceived Ease of Use	It would be easy for me to become skillful at using omnichannel app	Davis (1989); Kumar et al. (2018); Cyr et al. (2006)
	I would find omnichannel app easy to use	
	Learning to use omnichannel app would be easy for me	
Perceived Usefulness	I evaluate omnichannel app as useful	Davis (1989); Kumar et al. (2018); Cyr et al. (2006)
	I evaluate omnichannel app as functional	
	I evaluate omnichannel app as effective	
Loyalty	Using omnichannel app is a good idea	Cyr et al. (2006); Kumar et al. (2018); Floh and Treiblmaier (2006); Zhang et al. (2011)
	I think omnichannel app would make my life more interesting	
	I intend to recommend others use omnichannel app	

References

Akturan, U., Tezcan, N.: Mobile banking adoption of the youth market: perceptions and intentions. Mark. Intell. Plan. **30**(4), 444–459 (2012)

Beck, N., Rygl, D.: Categorization of multiple channel retailing in Multi-, Cross-, and omni-channel retailing for retailers and retailing. J. Retail. Consum. Serv. **27**, 170–178 (2015)

Bell, D.R., Gallino, S., Moreno, A.: How to win in an omnichannel world. MIT Sloan Manag. Rev. **56**(1), 45 (2014)

Brynjolfsson, E., Hu, Y.J., Rahman, M.S.: Competing in the Age of Omnichannel Retailing, pp. 1–7. MIT, Cambridge (2013)

Chiu, H.C., Hsieh, Y.C., Kao, C.Y.: Website quality and customer's behavioural intention: an exploratory study of the role of information asymmetry. Total Qual. Manag. Bus. Excell. **16** (2), 185–197 (2005)

Cronbach, L.J.: Coefficient alpha and the internal structure of tests. Psychometrika **16**(3), 297–334 (1951)

Cyr, D., Head, M., Ivanov, A.: Design aesthetics leading to m-loyalty in mobile commerce. Inf. Manag. **43**(8), 950–963 (2006)

Davis, F.D.: Perceived usefulness, perceived ease of use, and user acceptance of information technology. MIS Q. **13**, 319–340 (1989)

Davis, F.D., Bagozzi, R.P., Warshaw, P.R.: User acceptance of computer technology: a comparison of two theoretical models. Manag. Sci. **35**(8), 982–1003 (1989)

Dutot, V., Bhatiasevi, V., Bellallahom, N.: Applying the technology acceptance model in a three-countries study of smartwatch adoption. J. High Technol. Manag. Res. **30**(1), 1–14 (2019)

Ewe, S.Y., Yap, S.F., Lee, C.K.C.: Network externalities and the perception of innovation characteristics: mobile banking. Mark. Intell. Plan. **33**(4), 592–611 (2015)

Fang, Y., Qureshi, I., Sun, H., McCole, P., Ramsey, E., Lim, K.H.: Trust, satisfaction, and online repurchase intention. MIS Q. **38**(2), 407–427 (2014)

Flavián, C., Guinalíu, M., Gurrea, R.: The role played by perceived usability, satisfaction and consumer trust on website loyalty. Inf. Manag. **43**(1), 1–14 (2006)

Floh, A., Treiblmaier, H.: What keeps the e-banking customer loyal? A multigroup analysis of the moderating role of consumer characteristics on e-loyalty in the financial service industry. In: A Multigroup Analysis of the Moderating Role of Consumer Characteristics on E-Loyalty in the Financial Service Industry (2006)

Fornell, C., Larcker, D.F.: Evaluating structural equation models with unobservable variables and measurement error. J. Mark. Res. **18**(1), 39–50 (1981)

Gao, F., Su, X.: Online and offline information for omnichannel retailing. Manuf. Serv. Oper. Manag. **19**(1), 84–98 (2017)

Gefen, D., Karahanna, E., Straub, D.W.: Trust and TAM in online shopping: an integrated model. MIS Q. **27**(1), 51–90 (2003)

Gillenson, M.L., Sherrell, D.L.: Enticing online consumers: an extended technology acceptance perspective. Inf. Manag. **39**(8), 705–719 (2002)

Hair Jr., J.F., Sarstedt, M., Hopkins, L., Kuppelwieser, V.G.: Partial least squares structural equation modeling (PLS-SEM). Eur. Bus. Rev. **26**, 106–121 (2014)

Kang, J.Y.M., Mun, J.M., Johnson, K.K.: In-store mobile usage: downloading and usage intention toward mobile location-based retail apps. Comput. Hum. Behav. **46**, 210–217 (2015)

Kapoor, K.K., Dwivedi, Y.K., Williams, M.D.: Examining the role of three sets of innovation attributes for determining adoption of the interbank mobile payment service. Inf. Syst. Front. **17**(5), 1039–1056 (2015)

Keller, K.L.: Conceptualizing, measuring, and managing customer-based brand equity. J. Mark. **57**(1), 1–22 (1993)
Kim, H., Niehm, L.S.: The impact of website quality on information quality, value, and loyalty intentions in apparel retailing. J. Interact. Mark. **23**(3), 221–233 (2009)
Kim, K., Kim, G.M., Kil, E.S.: Measuring the compatibility factors in mobile entertainment service adoption. J. Comput. Inf. Syst. **50**(1), 141–148 (2009)
Koenig-Lewis, N., Palmer, A., Moll, A.: Predicting young consumers' take up of mobile banking services. Int. J. Bank Mark. **28**(5), 410–432 (2010)
Kumar, D.S., Purani, K., Viswanathan, S.A.: Influences of 'appscape' on mobile app adoption and m-loyalty. J. Retail. Consum. Serv. **45**, 132–141 (2018)
Li, Y., Liu, H., Lim, E.T., Goh, J.M., Yang, F., Lee, M.K.: Customer's reaction to cross-channel integration in omnichannel retailing: the mediating roles of retailer uncertainty, identity attractiveness, and switching costs. Decis. Support Syst. **109**, 50–60 (2018)
Lin, J.C.C., Lu, H.: Towards an understanding of the behavioural intention to use a web site. Int. J. Inf. Manag. **20**(3), 197–208 (2000)
McDonald, T., Siegall, M.: The effects of technological self-efficacy and job focus on job performance, attitudes, and withdrawal behaviors. J. Psychol. **126**(5), 465–475 (1992)
Meuter, M.L., Bitner, M.J., Ostrom, A.L., Brown, S.W.: Choosing among alternative service delivery modes: an investigation of customer trial of self-service technologies. J. Mark. **69**(2), 61–83 (2005)
Nagel, P.J., Cilliers, W.W.: Customer satisfaction: a comprehensive approach. Int. J. Phys. Distrib. Logist. Manag. 2–46 (1990)
Nunnally, J.C.: Psychometric Theory 3E. Tata McGraw-Hill Education, New York (1994)
Ozturk, A.B., Bilgihan, A., Nusair, K., Okumus, F.: What keeps the mobile hotel booking users loyal? Investigating the roles of self-efficacy, compatibility, perceived ease of use, and perceived convenience. Int. J. Inf. Manag. **36**(6), 1350–1359 (2016)
Pan, Y., Sheng, S., Xie, F.T.: Antecedents of customer loyalty: an empirical synthesis and reexamination. J. Retail. Consum. Serv. **19**(1), 150–158 (2012)
Parasuraman, A., Grewal, D.: The impact of technology on the quality-value-loyalty chain: a research agenda. J. Acad. Mark. Sci. **28**(1), 168–174 (2000)
Park, J., Kim, R.B.: A new approach to segmenting multichannel shoppers in Korea and the US. J. Retail. Consum. Serv. **45**, 163–178 (2018)
Park, J., Kim, R.B.: The effects of integrated information & service, institutional mechanism and need for cognition (NFC) on consumer omnichannel adoption behavior. Asia Pac. J. Mark. Logist. (2019)
Ribbink, D., Van Riel, A.C., Liljander, V., Streukens, S.: Comfort your online customer: quality, trust and loyalty on the internet. Manag. Serv. Qual.: Int. J. 446–456 (2004)
Rogers Everett, M.: Diffusion of innovations. New York, p. 12 (1995)
Sánchez-Prieto, J.C., Hernández-García, Á., García-Peñalvo, F.J., Chaparro-Peláez, J., Olmos-Migueláñez, S.: Break the walls! Second-Order barriers and the acceptance of mLearning by first-year pre-service teachers. Comput. Hum. Behav. **95**, 158–167 (2019)
Sarstedt, M., Ringle, C.M., Smith, D., Reams, R., Hair Jr., J.F.: Partial least squares structural equation modeling (PLS-SEM): a useful tool for family business researchers. J. Family Bus. Strategy **5**(1), 105–115 (2014)
Shi, S., Wang, Y., Chen, X., Zhang, Q.: Conceptualization of omnichannel customer experience and its impact on shopping intention: a mixed-method approach. Int. J. Inf. Manag. **50**, 325–336 (2020)
Shin, J.I., Chung, K.H., Oh, J.S., Lee, C.W.: The effect of site quality on repurchase intention in internet shopping through mediating variables: the case of university students in South Korea. Int. J. Inf. Manag. **33**(3), 453–463 (2013)

Siwicki, B.: The best and worst mobile commerce apps, according to consumers (2014). http://www.internetretailer.com/2014/05/20/best-and-worst-mobile-commerce-apps-according-consumers

So, K.K.F., King, C., Sparks, B.A., Wang, Y.: The influence of customer brand identification on hotel brand evaluation and loyalty development. Int. J. Hosp. Manag. **34**, 31–41 (2013)

Venkatesh, V., Davis, F.D.: A theoretical extension of the technology acceptance model: four longitudinal field studies. Manag. Sci. **46**(2), 186–204 (2000)

Wu, J.H., Wang, S.C.: What drives mobile commerce?: An empirical evaluation of the revised technology acceptance model. Inf. Manag. **42**(5), 719–729 (2005)

Xu, H., Koronios, A.: Understanding information quality in e-business. J. Comput. Inf. Syst. **45** (2), 73–82 (2005)

Yang, H., Yu, J., Zo, H., Choi, M.: User acceptance of wearable devices: An extended perspective of perceived value. Telematics Inform. **33**(2), 256–269 (2016)

Zeithaml, V.A.: Consumer perceptions of price, quality, and value: a means-end model and synthesis of evidence. J. Mark. **52**(3), 2–22 (1988)

Zhang, Y., Fang, Y., Wei, K.K., Ramsey, E., McCole, P., Chen, H.: Repurchase intention in B2C e-commerce—A relationship quality perspective. Inf. Manag. **48**(6), 192–200 (2011)

Optimising Customer Engagement Through Digital Intelligence

Normada Devi Bheekharry(✉)

Marketing and Management, Université des Mascareignes,
Beau Bassin-Rose Hill, Mauritius
nbheekharry@udm.ac.mu

Abstract. Understanding customer online behaviour is critical for strategic marketing decision making and organisation survival and success. The internet has dramatically changed the key concept of marketing. Customers use different digital interface to communicate and share valuable information about their lifestyles, likes and dislikes, experiences, expectations, opinions and behaviours. Customers digital interactions have given rise to a huge amount of information contributing to digital marketing intelligence (DMI). Gathering and analysing customers' online information from a variety of online platform can give marketing practitioners and researchers new opportunities to better understand customers' online behaviour.

Digital marketing intelligence is a new and emerging science in the digital marketing analytics arena. The purpose of this paper is to present the role of digital data analytics as an enabler of marketing decision making. The paper argues that digital intelligence represents an important tool for prospecting, acquiring and holding on customers.

Keywords: Online customer · Digital marketing intelligence · Customer engagement · Knowledge management

1 Introduction

Over the past few decades intensive innovation in technology has altered the marketing landscape, creating new opportunities and challenges for companies. The proliferation of the internet and the constant growth of internet users have made the internet a vital and attractive platform for organisations to interact. One feature of the marketplace is its increasing digitization. Woon et al. (2010) outline that technological changes have made traditional marketing more efficient and effective in reaching and selling to markets. Web 2.0 is a powerful marketing tool and is pivotal to share ideas and create customer values. The notion of value and value proposition is central to marketing. Kotler (2000) defines value from perspective of the customer and he posits that customer value is the result of customer's assessment in weighing the bundle of benefits against the bundle of cost they expect to incur in evaluating, obtaining and using the product or service. One of the main role of marketing is to understand and explain the value an intended consumer derives from the product or service. Digital media has

F. J. Martínez-López and S. D'Alessandro (Eds.): *Advances in Digital Marketing and eCommerce*, SPBE, pp. 179–187, 2020.
https://doi.org/10.1007/978-3-030-47595-6_22

created over recent years an unprecedented capacity to generate and capture customer demand through a variety of forms and through different channels.

Web 2.0 technologies have three distinctive characteristics: collaboration, participation and communication and they are being used by customers and firms for different purposes, such as: information gathering and sharing. Some authors mention that organizations are using Web 2.0 technologies to improve decision cycle times, organizational effectiveness and innovation. Sharma and Baoku (2013) states that "Web 2.0 provides benefits by delivering access to collaboration and allows information to be spread more efficiently". Palacios-Marques (2013) relates that Web2.0 adoption might help organisation to generate and disseminate market intelligence and at the same time they have the potential to increase firm's innovativeness by fostering knowledge creation and sharing. Evans (2008), defines Web2.0 as web pages that use a two way streams of communication between users allowing them to socialize online and to share their own user generator content. Examples of popular Web 2.0 applications which allow for online user generated content sharing or social media interactions include, but are not limited to: file-sharing sites (Flickr for photo sharing), blogs (e.g. Blogger.com), wikis (e.g. Wikipedia), and social networking sites (e.g. Facebook, Twitter). Since Web 2.0 technologies are easy to use, customers and employees are using them for different purposes. We believe that thanks to these characteristics customers are sharing on the web a lot of information about their experiences with products and services. Therefore, firms would tend to acquire that market intelligence using Web 2.0 technologies. Additionally, it has been argued that internet blog narratives can be used to determine one firm's competitive position (Crotts et al. 2009). Finally, Web 2.0 has the potential to ease the dissemination of market intelligence within the firm. In recent years, innovation in internet technology can be summed up by the evolution of Web 1.0 into Web 2.0 and the emergence of the semantic web technologies and their integration into Web 3.0. The research conducted by Garrigos-Simmon et al. 2012, demonstrates the effectiveness of social networks and how Web 3.0 are changing firm structures and value network or value chain and organisation decision making process.

2 Digital Marketing Intelligence (DMI)

The role of analytics and knowledge management has been researched by many practitioners and academicians, over the past two decades. However little research has been conducted in the field of digital marketing intelligence (DMI) as a main topic comprising of competitor intelligence (CI), business intelligence (BI), customer intelligence (CI)and market intelligence. Digital Marketing Intelligence provided through the study of consumer analytics reinforced the understanding of consumer online behaviour. This has been brought forward through a study conducted by Erevelles et al. in 2014. Data from different online sources provide behavioural insight about consumers. Analysing and interpreting data from these different digital sources provide marketers excellent choice in decision making and improving many business functions

(Khan and Vorley 2017). IBM attested that as much as 80% of data available are unstructured (George et al. 2014) and so a latent opportunity to leverage. The main challenge remains in unlocking this potential knowledge and how to apply analytics to extract meaningful information to reinforce competitive advantage and form sound proactive strategic decisions (Rajaraman and Ullman 2011). In a research paper conducted in 2007, by Davenport et al., it was outlined and deeply discussed how Amazon, ebay, Walmart, Proctor & Gamble, Google, Facebook, Marriott, Fedex, Astra Zeneca have survived during information technology breakout are. According to the authors, Davenport and Harris, these companies go beyond using analytics as a mere support function but as a mean to gain competitive edge. Managing vast amount of data, communicating with customers and enhancing operations are the main attributes of successful organisation competing in the twenty first century.

Customers are essentially changing the aspects of the marketplace. The digital market has become a medium in which both the consumer and customer play an active and decisive part in creating and competing for value (Prahalad and Ramasawmy 2000). The changing feature of the customer: that of an eager willingness to participate, engage in active dialogue, learn and experiment has become a new source of competence for organisation to exploit and investigate. Microsoft has used digital intelligence to acquire customers' feedback on a beta version of Microsoft's Windows 2000. Customers were allowed to test the product in their environment instead of it being tested in laboratories. Participating and collaborating in this test helped many customers in the creation of their own value. Harnessing the competencies of customers build on customer intelligence (CI). However, dealing actively with diversified customers is quite challenging. Examining ongoing active dialogues among digital active customers and engaging customers for feedback, contribute to new knowledge which is important to enhance and enable knowledge management (KM) by using digital analytics. The aim of this paper is to show the importance of analytics in interpreting digital intelligence. The paper demonstrates the use of analytics as research method of discovering hidden and unexplored data for marketing practices.

3 Knowledge Management (KM)

Summarising the general views and research carried by different academician it is found that knowledge management (KM) deals with the creation, acquisition, capturing and sharing of data from processes and practices (Khan and Vorley 2017; Cockrell and Stone 2010; Scarbrough and Swan 2001). KM has also been defined as set of justified which can be managed to enhance the organisation's capability for effective action (Alavi and Leidner 2001). The three core processes of KM are namely, acquisition, conversion and application of knowledge. Developing on the above criteria, knowledge acquisition can be viewed as developing new idea and/or knowledge from data knowledge conversion, that is transforming the gathered information useful for the organisation and knowledge application is using knowledge to perform task (Magnier-Watanabe and Seenoo 2010; Orzano et al. 2008; Sabherwal and Sabherwal 2005). Other authors contributed to the understand of KM, namely Grant (1996) and Magnier-Watanabe and Seenoo (2010) and came to the common decision that KM facilitates organisation to capture, store and transfer knowledge efficiently and effectively. The need to transform data and information into practical knowledge for decision making remains the critical factor for business success.

After reviewing several research articles, the more concise definition of analytics can be best summarised as engaging in use of data-structured or unstructured, with formal analysis tools either statistical or machine learning to provide insights in making better organisation decision for the benefits all key stakeholders. Analytics in business existed at the very start of business itself. It has been said that the big paradigm shift, happened with the introduction of Internet and e-marketing, which was around 1995.

4 Customer Online Behaviour

One of the main impacts of the Internet, e-marketing and innovation in information technology is the vast amount of data that is now accessible to be analysed. Everything that the user do on any digital platform-including uploading or downloading music, clips, videos, visiting and browsing websites, clicking, navigating, selling or buying, chatting and sharing of views via blogs, Facebook or forum among can be easily captured and analysed. Resulting from internet/e-marketing revolution, was mobile devices revolution and another field of study that of mobile marketing and App marketing. Mobile devices generate huge streams of analysable data. Marketers are using mobile devices as a promotional device for a more one to one communication tool compared to advertising through television, media or any other promotional channel. These new sources of data accentuated the paradigm shifts is different fields: knowledge management, business intelligence, customer intelligence and analytics. The evolution of data from traditional data sources has been revolutionised to digital marketing intelligence (DMI), whereby the main concept of interest of this paper. Marketing is an ongoing process where changes from the environment: which can be from decrease/increase of sales, change in customer demand, entrance of a new competitor, new product development, developing new product or new markets, change in political, social, technological, legal elements. Marketers should always keep tract of marketing information (MI) and act accordingly. The integration and combination of MI, information technology and organisational mindfulness for time and cost management has given much importance to dynamic system known as marketing information system (MKIS) was brought forward by Chandra et al. (1995) and Schmidt (1993). MI has a huge potential to harness useful information, actionable knowledge and critical insights for marketing managers to enhance competitiveness, customer demand and solve business processes for more effective and cost related operations (Amidon et al. 2005; He et al. 2015). The explosive increase in digital marketing: TV, media, mobile, social media and other platforms have created a major opportunity for companies to leverage data analytics solutions to harness customer opinions; device new ways to better understand their perception, motivation prior to brand choice, product and/or service or a company (Stieglitz and Dang-Xuan 2013). Digital marketing analytics platforms as outlined by Suneel Grover, Advisory Solutions Architect at SAS, are technology applications used by customer intelligence ninjas to understand and improve consumer experiences. Marketers need to understand how customer behave on different digital platforms deriving prospective insight for marketing optimization strategies. Powerful digital intelligence uses timely delivery of prescriptive insights to positively influence customers experience.

5 Customer Engagement

Social media platforms provide customers with an ideal environment to interact and in accordance to the Econsultancy State of Customer Engagement Report, which states that companies throughout the world consider the importance of customer engagement. Organisations are encouraging and increasingly seeking for customer commitment and participation, providing a total set of predictive behavioural activities. The engagement concept, according to Hollebeek et al. (2014), determines the motivational factor which stimulates an individual to interact which may be a brand, offerings, organisation products and or service, organisational activities beyond purchase. Individuals are no longer passive but without any reserve share their views with the company or among themselves- they have become a proactive ambassador in the co-creation of value through enhanced experience sharing, customer feedback, referrals, commitment, satisfaction and loyalty.

6 Managerial Implication

The application of information technology to traditional marketing results in E-marketing and Strauss defines e-marketing as:

"the use of information technology in the processes of creating, communicating, and delivering value to customers, and for managing customer relationships in ways that benefit the organization and its stakeholders".

The constant optimization of a firm's business activities through digital or information technology is known as E-business and it involves attracting and retaining the right customers and business partners. Under this practice we have digital communication, e-commerce, and online research, and it is used by every business discipline. Organisation needs to maintain a proper fit between their main objectives, skills and expertise, resources and the continuous changing market opportunities for growth, competitive position and geographic scope. The fundamental changes that the internet has brought to traditional marketing have changed the effectiveness and efficiency of marketing functions.

Decision making is central to what managers do and is integrated into all kinds of management functions. Studies conducted by Day 2011 outlines that mangers have often struggled to keep pace with the impact of technological change. Decision making is synonymous to the entire process of management and making effective strategic decisions is one of the critical abilities that managers are required to have and develop to lead their organisation in the increasingly volatile and competitive business world. Consumers have become an "incessant generator" of data which are structured, transactional as well as contemporary unstructured behavioural data.

The digital environment produces a vast array of data ranging from clickstream data, customer reviews and ratings, blogs, tags and social interaction data to customer responses to marketing actions and information on collaborators and competitors. New sources and types of data sets available to marketers as there are increasingly more interactions with customers taking place in social media, online and on mobile devices. This data generated is very informative for a company first to understand and analyse online customer behaviour, develop effective and efficient marketing strategies and ultimately to measure the effectiveness of its actions and tactics on marketing outcomes. The success or failure of firm relies mainly on the manager's ability to make strategic decisions. Because of the extensive uncertainty ambiguity and risk associated with strategic decisions, gathering, analyzing and considering reliable data and information are critically important in strategic decision making.

7 Conclusion

According to Brian Hopkins, a Forrester analyst, firms that excel at using data and analytics to optimize their digital businesses will together generate $1.2 trillion per annum in revenue by 2020. And digital intelligence—the practice of continuously optimizing customer experiences with online and offline data, advanced analytics and prescriptive insights—supports every insights-driven business. Digital intelligence is the solution to the weaknesses of analytically immature platforms. Digital marketing must be organised around customer data, technology and content. As data keep on growing and changing it should be continuous updated and marketing analytics which is made up of an integrated platform of digital technologies should be used to better understand customer needs and interests.

- Meeting the expectations of today's ever demanding multi-channel customers is very challenging.
- It is important for marketers to use analytics to continuously expand their understanding of customers and build customer relationship to extend the customer life cycle.
- Customer are proactive buyers.
- Customers' experience counts and marketers should find solution to optimise their experience.
- Managers should be more focus on platform management instead of product development.
- Managers should keep up with customers through machine learning, data science and advanced learning.

Many researchers and practitioners are concentrating on big data and big data analytics. However, looking at the characteristics of big data in terms of volume it is applicable to many countries throughout the world. In addition to that big data analytics is costly and need expert in data science. This paper is a conceptual one however both quantitative and qualitative research can be conducted to analyse whether organisation understand the notion of digital marketing intelligence and how they management their digital data.

7.1 Further Research

This paper presents the role of digital data analytics as an enabler of marketing decision making and the effective management of digital intelligence to acquire and retain customers. However much research needs to conducted to better understand which aspect of consumer behaviour whether conative, cognitive or affective promotes online purchase behaviour. Importance is put on customer engagement but how organisation should be re engineered towards this new management practice is undetermined.

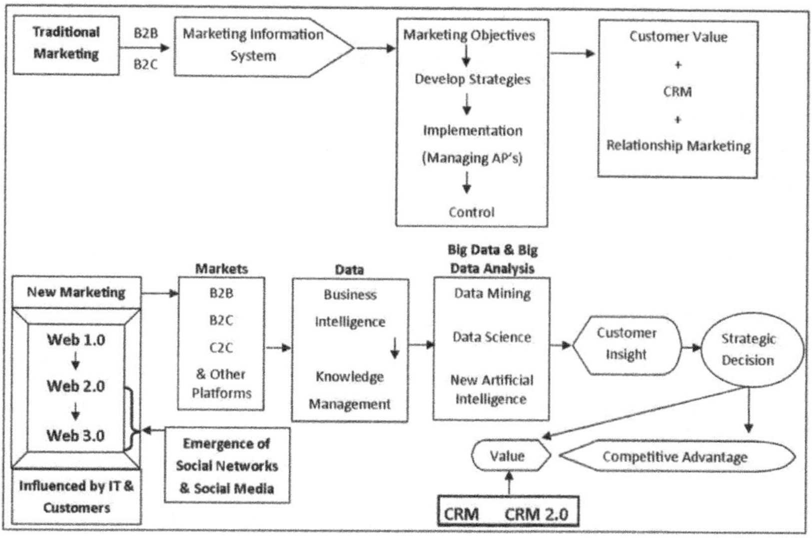

Source: Own elaboration based on literature review

References

Agrawal, D.: Analytics based decision making. J. Indian Bus. Res. **6**(4), 332–340 (2014)

Alavi, M., Leidner, D.E.: Review: knowledge management and knowledge management systems. Concept. Found. Res. Issues **25**(1), 107–136 (2001)

Amidon, D.M., Formica, P., Mercier-Laurent, E.: Knowledge Economics: Emerging Principles, Practices and Policies. Faculty of Economics and Business Administration, University of Tartu, Tartu (2005)

Amaravadi, C.S., Samaddar, S., Dutta, S.: Intelligent marketing information systems: computerized intelligence for marketing decision making. Mark. Intell. Plan. **13**(2), 4–13 (1995)

Chen, H., Chiang, R.H., Storey, V.C.: Business intelligence and analytics: from Big Data to big impact (2012)

Chern, C.C., Lei, W.U., Chen, S.Y.: A decision-tree-based classifier for credit assessment problems under a big data environment. In: Proceedings of the 2015 Decision Sciences Institute Annual Meeting, Seattle, WA, 21–24 November 2015 (2015)

Cockrell, R.C., Stone, D.N.: Industry culture influences pseudo-knowledge sharing: a multiple mediation analysis. J. Knowl. Manag. **14**(6), 841–857 (2010)

Constantinides (ed.) Consumer Information Systems and Relationship Management: Design, Implementation, and Use, pp. 51–73. IGI Global, Hershey (2013)

Crotts, J.C., Mason, P.R., Davis, B.: Measuring guest satisfaction and competitive position in the hospitality and tourism industry: an application of stance-shift analysis to travel blog narratives. J. Travel Res. **48**(2), 139–151 (2009)

Davenport, T.H.: Analytics 3.0. Harvard Bus. Rev. **91**(12), 64–72 (2013)

Davenport, T.H.: Big Data at Work: Dispelling the Myth, Uncovering the Opportunities. Harvard Business Review Press, Boston (2014)

Erevelles, S., Fukawa, N., Swayne, L.: Big Data consumer analytics and the transformation of marketing. J. Bus. Res. **69**(2), 897–904 (2016)

George, G., Haas, M.R., Pentland, A.: Big data and management. Acad. Manag. J. **57**(2), 321–326 (2014)

Gold, A.H., Malhotra, A., Segars, A.H.: Knowledge management: an organizational capabilities perspective. J. Manag. Inf. Syst. **18**(1), 185–214 (2001)

Grant, R.M.: Toward a knowledge-based theory of the firm. Strateg. Manag. J. **17**(10), 109–122 (1996)

He, W., Shen, J., Tian, X., Li, Y., Akula, V., Yan, G., Tao, R.: Gaining competitive intelligence from social media data: evidence from two largest retail chains in the world. Ind. Manag. Data Syst. **115**(9), 1622–1636 (2015)

Kannan, P.K., Hongshuang, A.: Digital marketing: a framework, review and research agenda (2017)

Khan, Z., Vorley, T.: Big data text analytics: an enabler of knowledge management. J. Knowl. Manag. **21**(1), 18–34 (2017). https://doi.org/10.1108/JKM-06-2015-0238

Kulkarni, U.R., Ravindran, S., Freeze, R.: A knowledge management success model: theoretical development and empirical validation. J. Manag. Inf. Syst. **23**(3), 309–347 (2007)

Magnier-Watanabe, R., Senoo, D.: Shaping knowledge management: organization and national culture. J. Knowl. Manag. **14**(2), 214–227 (2010)

Nonaka, I.: A dynamic theory of organizational knowledge creation. Organ. Sci. **5**(1), 14–37 (1994)

Orzano, A.J., Mcinerney, C.R., Scharf, D., Tallia, A.F., Crabtree, B.F.: A knowledge management model: implications for enhancing quality in health care. J. Am. Soc. Inform. Sci. Technol. **59**(3), 489–505 (2008)

Prahalad, C.K, Ramasawmy, V.: Co-opting Customer Competence, HBR January–February Issue (2000)

Rajaraman, A., Ullman, J.D.: Mining of Massive Datasets. Cambridge University Press, Cambridge (2011)

Sabherwal, R., Sabherwal, S.: Knowledge management using information technology: determinants of short-term impact on firm value. Decis. Sci. **36**(4), 531–567 (2005)

Scarbrough, H., Swan, J.: Explaining the diffusion of knowledge management: the role of fashion. Br. J. Manag. **12**(1), 3–12 (2001)

Schmidt, D.: Automated production planning: a new solution to the old problem of promotion cost-effectiveness. J. Advert. Res. 4–8 (1993)
Stieglitz, S., Dang-Xuan, L.: Social media and political communication: a social media analytics framework. Soc. Netw. Anal. Min. **3**(4), 1277–1291 (2013)

Amazon Effect? An Analysis of User-Generated Content on Consumer Electronics Retailers' Facebook Pages

Agostino Vollero(✉), Alfonso Siano, and Domenico Sardanelli

Department of Political and Communication Sciences (POLICOM),
University of Salerno, Salerno, Italy
{avollero, sianoalf, dsardanelli}@unisa.it

Abstract. This working paper aims at exploring the so-called "Amazon effect" in consumer electronics retail industry, and specifically the impact Amazon has generated in terms of consumers' expectations when consumers buy (or willing to buy) these type of products. The paper reviews the meaning of Amazon effect (or Amazonification) in different fields of study, and then focuses on the escalation of customer expectations towards retailers. A content analysis of users' comments drawn from Facebook pages of three leading consumer electronics retailers in Italy across a two-year span (2016–2018) serves to evaluate the relevance of different customer expectations. The preliminary findings show that consumers' conversations related to "Amazon effect" seem widely diffused on consumer electronics retailers, especially regarding effectiveness of customer service, online purchasing experience, and fast delivery times. The paper argues the need for further research to better disentangle the Amazonification concept in terms of customer impatience, also going beyond price and logistics issues, usually considered as the main constitutive factors.

Keywords: Amazon effect · Consumer expectations · E-commerce · User-generated content · Customer impatience · Consumer electronics

1 Introduction

Digital revolution has progressively changed ways firms operate, thus transforming significantly both manufacturing, with flexible and personalized forms of production (Mourtzis and Doukas 2014) and service industries, by dematerializing all the stages of consumer buying process (Nylén and Holmström 2015).

The most significant impact however is likely to affect the different models and formats of retail industry (Hagberg et al. 2016). "Death by Amazon" (Solon and Wong 2018) is the most common expression to identify the progressive decline of sales in (or even closing of) physical stores affected directly or indirectly by the e-commerce leader. This effect is usually explained by the perceived customer benefits recognized to Amazon (low pricing, huge product selection, excellent customer service, efficient shipping and return policy) combined with the company's "customer obsession" based on the analysis of customer-based metrics (Denning 2019). This makes Amazon (and

F. J. Martínez-López and S. D'Alessandro (Eds.): *Advances in Digital Marketing and eCommerce*, SPBE, pp. 188–193, 2020.
https://doi.org/10.1007/978-3-030-47595-6_23

similar e-commerce big players) able to anticipate customer needs and fulfil them better than any competitor in almost all industries.

Although this so-called "Amazon effect" has been (and continued to be) in the spotlight, research related to consumers are almost non-existent. As far as we know, no study has tried to identify analytically on which specific aspects Amazonification acts in concrete terms. The present working paper aims at filling to some extent this gap by analyzing consumers' conversations on three Facebook pages of retailers in consumer electronics retail industry in Italy.

2 What Is Amazonification?

In retail industry, Amazonification (or "Amazon effect") has been generally used to identify progressive transformation of e-commerce websites and physical retailers to be "more like Amazon" but, by extension, it also denotes massive change in consumers' expectations and habits (Jelodari Mamaghani and Davari 2020), especially in a customer-centric perspective of supply chain (Melnyk and Stanton 2017).

"Amazon effect" has in fact generally associated to logistics issues, where implementation of same day delivery services (like Prime Now) and (almost unconditioned) 30-day return policy have increased "customer impatience" (Daugherty et al. 2019). Customers have become more and more difficult to satisfy as evidenced by the decision of some of the biggest US retailers (i.e. Macy's and Office Depot) to integrate their delivery system, with parameters including population density and proximity of goods to customers to offer same day delivery from the nearest point when customer places her/his order.

Other evidences of consumers' shifting behaviours are represented by showrooming (Basak et al. 2017), the practice in which consumers are increasingly browsing and purchasing online while in-store, especially for price reasons. Amazon usually varies product prices by leveraging dynamic pricing algorithms (Chen et al. 2016), thus adapting them in real time on the basis of demand, competitors, time of the day, and customer buying patterns. In macroeconomic terms, such pricing strategies have been studied to analyze potential pressure on price discounts of retailers and on inflation rate (Charbonneau et al. 2017).

In cultural studies, Amazon effect has been linked to "filter bubble" (Pariser 2011). Filter bubble indicates a state of intellectual isolation, in which information and content (e.g. recommendations on e-commerce websites) are showed on the basis of search history and past online behaviours, being for example the result of a collaborative filtering algorithm as in the case of Amazon (Linden et al. 2003). This process makes user searches and queries more personalized and effective but at the same time tends to make people unaware of conflicting or different viewpoints, products, etc., thus isolating them in their own "cultural bubbles". Similar considerations have been also developed in design studies to indicate a progressive homogenization towards Amazon website features (Porter 2008).

In this paper, Amazon effect has been analyzed in terms of consumers' expectations (price, customer service, sales personnel, shipping, etc.) towards specialized click-and-mortar retailers of consumer electronics whose business models are still focused on physical stores.

3 Methodology

Researchers posit the content analysis of spontaneous "conversations" on social media in retailing industry a proper method to disclose Amazon-related themes. Content analysis is a research method that uses a series of systematic procedures to draw significant and replicable inferences from texts (Krippendorf 2004). This method tends to reduce textual, verbal or multimedia communication to data that can be also treated from a quantitative point of view (Riffe et al. 2014). Analysis of UGCs on Facebook pages of three retailers operating in Italy have been carried out to have a first "proof" of the phenomenon and to perform an exploration of its constitutive aspects.

The units of analysis are the UGCs on the official Fb pages of Trony, Mediaworld and Unieuro (2016–2018), three large and specialized groups in consumer electronics retail industry in Italy. Following procedures in computational linguistics/Natural Language Processing (Jackson and Moulinier 2007; Bhogal et al. 2007) UGCs have been grouped around similar topics through a two-step process:

1. Extraction of conversations with specific reference to Amazon (n = 471) and tagging of topics in each message. 21 topics have been identified with at least one tag (n = 403, in the remaining 68 no tagging have been made due to ambiguity or irrelevance of comments);
2. for each topic relevant keywords have been identified and queries have been made on the whole corpus (92861 messages) excluding explicit mentions to Amazon, thus generating a second dataset made up of 3044 comments. This step has allowed to verify similarities in the two corpus to discover an "indirect" Amazon effect and its distinctive features.

4 Preliminary Findings

According to the above-mentioned procedure, specific queries have been defined from extracted conversations in the first step of analysis (see Table 1).

Boolean queries[1] were used to develop ontologies[2] of the topics on the total corpus of 92861 messages, excluding explicit mentions to Amazon. A manual ontology-based query expansion techniques has been used to iterate queries and refine the results (Bhogal et al. 2007). This procedure allowed to identify similar topics beyond specific mention to the e-commerce website. In this second step, topics have been further aggregated due to noticeable similarities and to have a minimum number of comments for each topic (11 topics with minimum of 40 comments).

[1] Ex. Query for "Product availability": (((product OR products OR goods) AND ("unavailable" OR out of stock OR sold out OR urgent)) ~ 5) OR ("limited availability" OR "urgent purchase").

[2] An ontology is intended hereby as specification of the conceptualization and corresponding vocabulary used to describe a domain/specific theme.

Table 1. Topic related to "Amazon effect", number of conversations, excerpts Note: only 9 categories with frequencies >10 are reported.

Topic	N# of comments	Examples of excerpts
Price	74	You can get it one week ago on Amazon for 50€ ✌
Customer service	50	Ahahahah I can't help laughing …they don't know Amazon customer service... let it go...
Shipping	42	Get better with shipping …otherwise Amazon beats you 1-0
Sales personnel (assistance)	19	I'll buy it on Amazon so I don't waste 10 hours to find one of your sales assistant
Product availability	14	I don't have this problem, if I have wanted the game at Day One, I would have bought it on Amazon (always infallible). If you wish to get the game at Day One, you should get it elsewhere, not on Mediaworld website
Return	13	With Amazon's return service I don't even bother going to see the products in person
Warranty	11	Buy from Amazon. 2 year full guarantee. If you don't want it anymore they will refund you
Refund	11	Amazon would have already credited you with the total order amount
Online customer experience	8	The most frozen website in the world! Amazon light years ahead

The three main categories in which Amazon-related effect seem relevant are:

- customer service (1207 comments), considered as ineffective and slow implicitly compared to Amazon standards;
- online customer experience (443 comments) in which consumers identified low usability of electronic retailers' e-commerce platforms, obstacles in completing their purchases, missing information (or confirmation) about their orders, etc., as elements of dissatisfaction;
- shipping/delivery (229 comments), in which consumers complained shipping times over two days when Amazon is able to deliver in 24 h or less.

Further confirmation related to Amazon effect can be found also in other topics, i.e. consumers' expectations involving sales personnel assistance, product availability, price, return & refund, etc.

5 Future Research

The results of this study seem to confirm the broad impact of Amazon effect on consumers' expectations in consumer electronics retailing industry. Considering the wide range of topics in which Amazon has been mentioned, it is interesting to note that Seattle-based company seems to act as "global private consumer protection regulator" (Winn 2016).

Further studies are however needed to confirm and disentangle Amazon effect in all its facets. Equally interesting would be to analyze dynamics of proximity of different topics to shed light on the interplay of the different factors. This would be also desirable to explore possible countermeasures for traditional and online retailers. Lastly, Amazon's strategies in traditional retailing (e.g. Amazon Go stores; acquisition of the 450 stores of the Whole Foods chain) are likely to show that Amazonification is only at the beginning and its effects still have to unfold.

Acknowledgements. The authors gratefully acknowledge Emilia Nunzia Maria Gaudio (The Fool srl) for useful insights and for helping with collection of data.

References

Basak, S., Basu, P., Avittathur, B., Sikdar, S.: A game theoretic analysis of multichannel retail in the context of showrooming. Decis. Support Syst. **103**, 34–45 (2017)

Bhogal, J., MacFarlane, A., Smith, P.: A review of ontology based query expansion. Inf. Process. Manag. **43**(4), 866–886 (2007)

Charbonneau, K., Evans, A., Sarker, S., Suchanek, L.: Digitalization and inflation: a review of the literature, Bank of Canada (2017). https://www.banqueducanada.ca/wp-content/uploads/2017/11/san2017-20.pdf

Chen, L., Mislove, A., Wilson, C.: An empirical analysis of algorithmic pricing on Amazon marketplace. In: Proceedings of the 25th International Conference on World Wide Web, pp. 1339–1349 (2016)

Daugherty, P.J., Bolumole, Y., Grawe, S.J.: The new age of customer impatience: an agenda for reawakening logistics customer service research. Int. J. Phys. Distrib. Logist. Manag. **49**(1), 4–32 (2019)

Denning, S.: How Amazon uses metrics to drive success. Strategy Leadersh. **47**(6), 9–14 (2019)

Hagberg, J., Sundstrom, M., Egels-Zandén, N.: The digitalization of retailing: an exploratory framework. Int. J. Retail Distrib. Manag. **44**(7), 694–712 (2016)

Jackson, P., Moulinier, I.: Natural Language Processing for Online Applications: Text Retrieval, Extraction and Categorization, vol. 5. John Benjamins Publishing, Amsterdam (2007)

Jelodari Mamaghani, E., Davari, S.: The bi-objective periodic closed loop network design problem. Expert Syst. Appl. **144**, 113068 (2020)

Krippendorff, K.: Content Analysis: An Introduction to its Methodology, 2nd edn. Sage, Thousand Oaks (2004)

Linden, G., Smith, B., York, J.: Amazon.com recommendations: item-to-item collaborative filtering. IEEE Internet Comput. **1**, 76–80 (2003)

Melnyk, S.A., Stanton, D.J.: The customer-centric supply chain. Supply Chain Manag. Rev. **20** (12), 28–39 (2017)

Mourtzis, D., Doukas, M.: Design and planning of manufacturing networks for mass customisation and personalisation: challenges and outlook. Procedia CIRP **19**, 1–13 (2014)
Nylén, D., Holmström, J.: Digital innovation strategy: a framework for diagnosing and improving digital product and service innovation. Bus. Horiz. **58**(1), 57–67 (2015)
Pariser, E.: The Filter Bubble: What the Internet is Hiding From You. Penguin, UK (2011)
Porter, J.: Designing for the Social Web. New Riders, Berkeley (2008)
Solon, O., Wong, J.C.: Jeff Bezos vs the world: why all companies fear 'death by Amazon'. The Guardian (2018). Accessed 24 Apr 2018
Riffe, D., Lacy, S., Fico, F.: Analyzing media Messages: Using Quantitative Content Analysis in Research. Routledge, London (2014)
Winn, J.K.: The secession of the successful: The rise of Amazon as private global consumer protection regulator. Arizona Law Rev. **58**(1), 193–212 (2016)

Daily Active Users of Social Network Sites: Facebook, Twitter, and Instagram-Use Compared to General Social Network Site Use

Johan Hellemans(✉), Kim Willems, and Malaika Brengman

Vrije Universiteit Brussel, Brussels, Belgium
Johan.hellemans@vub.be

Abstract. Most research on Social Network Sites (SNS) has focused on Facebook. Some scholars have argued to abandon the focus on a single platform in favor of studying SNS in general (GSNS). Others call for more comparative research of different SNS. With this study, we contribute to both approaches by taking a multi-cross platform approach comparing specific SNS as well as GSNS and their underlying user-profile. We obtained cross-sectional data from 5500 Belgians between 18–64 that answered a self-completed survey via quota-sampling, administered via an online panel. Logistic regression analyses on the number of daily active users (DAU) show individual differences in sociodemographic background per specific SNS use by Facebook, Twitter, Instagram, as well as GSNS, confirming the concern that the focus on Facebook is a justified critique, and that insight derived from Facebook cannot necessarily be generalized to other SNS. Additionally, our results indicate that the overall indicated usage frequency by GSNS is lower than when incidence is reported for an additive measure of specific SNS as well as Facebook. Consequently, research with a focus on GSNS tends to report lower usage frequency and heavy usage incidence rates and, therefore, possibly also lower problematic usage. This suggests that users might activate an averaging response model besides an additive model when answering GSNS.

Keywords: Social Network Sites · Facebook · Twitter · Instagram

1 Introduction

With the growth of SNS and the large part it plays in people's daily lives, research investigating SNS use has increased rapidly over the years (Liu et al. 2017; Sa'ed et al. 2018). With its success, SNS has also altered the way that business in general and marketing is conducted (Xu et al. 2012). The field of SNS itself remains eclectic, given new SNS emerge and existing SNS change their modalities while other SNS loose popularity or get suspended (Boyd and Ellison 2007; Rains and Brunner 2015).

This poses a challenge to a researcher interested in investigated SNS phenomena in selecting the right social network platform(s) for their research purposes. To deal with the extensive scope of SNS, academic researchers of SNS have relied mainly on three strategies; (1) singling out a specific SNS, (2) a cross-platform approach comparing different SNS, and (3) to study SNS more generally, detaching it from a specific

F. J. Martínez-López and S. D'Alessandro (Eds.): *Advances in Digital Marketing and eCommerce*, SPBE, pp. 194–202, 2020.
https://doi.org/10.1007/978-3-030-47595-6_24

platform. The central aim of this paper is to contribute to the further understanding of SNS use and its determinants by addressing some shortcomings of each of these strategies indicated by previous research. These are discussed next.

The first strategy is to focus solely on a single SNS. Given Facebook remains by far the most used SNS within this changing landscape, most research so far has selected Facebook, indicating low to no research interest in other SNS like Twitter and Instagram (Rains and Brunner 2015; Stoycheff et al. 2017). Some recent meta-analyses on the determinants and consequences of SNS use (Huang 2017, 2019) as well as problematic use (Marino et al. 2018) come to similar conclusions. A recent shifting trend has been noted towards Twitter with a focus on sentiment analysis and microblogging within specific fields like health, politics, and journalism (Liu et al. 2017). Also, Blank and Lutz (2017) report an increase in studies on Facebook and Twitter but recognize that while research on Facebook has investigated adoption, usage, and user characteristics that such a focus received limited attention for Twitter and even more so for other SNS like Instagram.

Second, researchers also have started to take a cross-platform approach comparing individual SNS mainly on motivations (Alhabash and Ma 2017; Barker 2009; Davenport et al. 2014; Oh and Syn 2015; Phua et al. 2017; Primack et al. 2017) and personality (Hughes et al. 2012; Kim et al. 2017; Panek et al. 2013). Five studies related to demographic comparisons were identified (Hargittai 2007; Archambault and Grudin (2012); Mellon and Prosser 2017; Blank and Lutz 2017; Gazit et al. 2019). The main point of all seem to suggest that behavior, motivations and user profile differ across specific SNS, confirming the overarching concern that the predominant focus on Facebook is a justified critique, and that insight derived from such perspective cannot necessarily be generalized to other SNS.

The third strategy suggests that research on SNS should be detached from a specific platform like Facebook (Griffiths 2012). As Griffiths (2012) states, researchers need to remember that Facebook is just one of many websites where social networking can take place and so should not be regarded as being synonymous with social networking, nor should findings applicable to Facebook be generalized to other SNS. Consequently, a call was made to study SNS more generally, in addition to specific SNS like Facebook (Griffiths et al. 2014). Following up on this critique researchers modified measurement instruments that were initially developed to operationalize mainly Facebook use, -engagement and- addiction, to apply (more broadly) to social media in general by merely altering "Facebook" with the words' social media', with social media defined as "Facebook, Twitter, Instagram and the like" in the instructions (Andreassen et al. 2017; Kircaburun et al. 2018; Lee 2019; Sigerson and Cheng 2018). A generalized approach on SNS was also used in the field of the digital divide, investigating the impact of demographic factors and which groups in society have access to SNS or not (Haight et al. 2014; Yu et al. 2016).

Given the dominant focus of researchers on Facebook, research concerning the antecedents of other SNS use has been limited. Even for Facebook, research considering other demographic variables besides gender and age has been scarce, and more research is warranted for other SNS as well as Facebook. Even fewer studies have begun to take a multi-cross platform approach comparing SNS and the underlying sociodemographic profile. There is still a lack of differentiated statistical evidence of the sociodemographic characteristics of users of distinct SNS or in comparison with GSNS. Furthermore, the question remains to which degree an approach using a self-reported measure of GSNS frequency captures actual use across several SNS overall and how it relates to self-reported measures of specific SNS frequency. So far, no study to our knowledge has contrasted how specific SNS frequency and GSNS frequency are related. Moreover, little is known about how users respond to such a question when probing for a user's GSNS frequency or how responses might vary across different types of users. Our study moreover contributes to the few studies on SNS user characteristics by investigating such determinants of three dominant SNS in Belgium; Facebook, Twitter, and Instagram, as well as GSNS.

2 Research Questions

This research aims to contribute to two main goals. First, the current paper contributes on how SNS users report on GSNS usage versus specific SNS use, in terms of daily active usage (DAU), providing an answer on (1) the relationship between self-reported specific SNS use and GSNS use, (2) the kind of response model that is activated with GSNS use, and (3) how this might differ between individuals (RQ1).

In response to the self-reported measure of frequency of GSNS, SNS users might activate two different response models in similar vein as self-report measures (individual's item response) to represent an underlying latent trait by averaging or summing items (Fraley et al. 2000); (1) In an additive model, a user will report a higher rate when the frequency of usage is high of at least one SNS or when several SNS in use are added up to a level the SNS user assumes to be high. (2) When the user activates an average model and averages out across SNS, this might not be the case even when SNS use of one SNS is high while the frequency of use of other SNS is deemed lower. This has significant consequences for research activating GSNS measures. If respondents average out, such an approach might underestimate SNS usage frequency and heavy usage incidence rates and, therefore, possibly also lower problematic usage.

We, as such, hypothesize that the self-reported GSNS DAU frequency is lower compared to the specific usage DAU of Facebook; still, the most used SNS, given that we expect a certain number of users to activate an averaging response model. Further, we hypothesize that GSNS DAU frequency is also lower compared to an additive measure (ASNS) for a similar reason. It is further expected that the response model enabled might also vary across different types of users.

Second, this paper contributes to the recent stream of research that takes a cross-SNS approach by (1) comparing Facebook, Twitter and Instagram use in terms of daily active usage (DAU) and (2) the underlying individual differences in terms of specific socio-demographics: age, gender, student, education, relationship status, working, and income (RQ2). Based on previous research, we hypothesize on underlying individual differences per SNS. Particularly, we expect more female users on Instagram and Facebook and more males on Twitter, more students, and younger ages on all three SNS and even younger ages on Instagram. The limited research on relationship status seems to suggest that singles, not currently in a committed relationship, are more on SNS. With regard to the economic factors, the previous findings remain inconclusive, showing mixed results in general and per specific SNS on education, working status, and income. Specific research on Twitter indicates that we can expect more Twitter adoption for higher social class, so we expect it to be positively related to working, higher education, and income.

These questions are not only important from a sociological or psychological point of view but also from a marketing point of view. The selection of media budget to advertise on SNS or digital strategies overall might depend on many factors like penetration in the market, brand equity achieved, communication goals, the importance of promotion in the marketing mix, and the size and characteristics of the audience group that can be reached and targeted (Bolotaeva and Cata 2010). The number of users that can be reached overall and per specific SNS is one of the critical parameters to assess the latter. Companies and brands also conduct market research to develop digital strategies often with filter questions to determine a relevant sample of SNS-users. The decisions are taken, or outcomes might differ when brands or companies rely on SNS-information in general or on SNS-information per specific SNS. Marketers should also be aware that a specific SNS user profile by no means suggests being a representation of the general population or even their customer base.

3 Methodology

3.1 Sampling

Cross-sectional data were obtained from a nationally representative Belgian online panel that on a regular frequency probes for SNS usage by a self-completed survey amongst a quota selection of its panelists. Data from the years 2017 (N = 1500), 2018 (N = 2000) to 2019 (N = 2000) were selected, resulting in a sample of N = 5500 respondents, of which 50.9% being female. The average age reported is 43.7 years (SD = 13.7). Besides age, other sociodemographic variables included as binary dummy variables are: (1) female, (2) graduate degree, (3) student, (4) single, (5) working, and (6) higher income.

3.2 Usage Measure

Scholars have operationalized regular SNS usage by a myriad of user-related actions. In practice, the popularity and growth of specific SNS that companies and industry press report on, relies on the number of active users defined as the number of daily or monthly users that logs in to an SNS. Facebook, for example, revealed it now has more than 1.62 billion daily active users (DAU) on average (Facebook, 2020). Far less is known about how many DAU there are across different SNS. Such information is not available at a single company, and the industry and academics are as such to rely on survey information.

In this study, participants rated how frequently they consulted different SNS on a 7-point frequency scale designed to obtain the number of DAU users per SNS platform going from "not at all" (i.e., score 1) to "daily-to several times a day" (i.e., score 7). DAU users are defined as users that go on their profile at least once a day (Score 7).

This scoring was obtained for Facebook, Twitter, Instagram, and Social Network Sites in general (GSNS). Also, research on SNS adoption makes use of a dichotomized measure or dichotomize their measure during the analytical stage (Haight et al. 2014; Yu et al. 2016).

4 Results

4.1 GSNS Versus Specific SNS

Given the non-normal distribution of the user frequencies, and the obtained DAU measure is usually presented as binary data, the results will be further analyzed with non-parametric statistical testing. Table 1 shows the obtained DAU users for each specific SNS and GSNS as well as the frequency of DAU users by a calculated additive answering model (ASNS) (At least daily usage of one of the SNS under investigation deduplicated; Facebook, Twitter, Instagram; user of multiple SNS counts once) on the total sample. The R Hetcor package available in SPSS was run to estimate the polychoric correlation between our DAU-measures presented in Table 2. Facebook remains by far still the most frequently used site with DAU reaching 61.4% in 2019 up again after a decline from 2017 to 2018. Instagram further attains up to 24.3% DAU users. As can be seen from Table 1, the frequency of DAU, when probed for in general (53,6%) is lower than for Facebook (60.4%) as well as lower than the obtained frequency of ASNS (63%). A McNemar test of SNS generic DAU with Facebook DAU (Chi-square = 154.6, $p = 0.00$) and the additive DAU (Chi-square = 301.1, $p = 0.00$) indicates a significant difference.

Table 1. DAU frequency per specific SNS and SNS in general and year

Year	2017	2018	2019	Total
TOTAL N	1500	2000	2000	5500
FACEBOOK	60.9%	59.1%	61.4%	60.4%
TWITTER	7.8%	10.2%	9.5%	9.3%
INSTAGRAM	11.8%	18.1%	24.3%	20.2%
GSNS	50.5%	53.2%	56.4%	53.6%
ASNS	62.3%	62.1%	64.4%	63.0%

Table 2. Polychoric correlations DAU frequency scores

Year	FACEBOOK	TWITTER	INSTAGRAM	GSNS
TWITTER	0.51			
INSTAGRAM	0.60	0.71		
GSNS	0.90	0.51	0.60	
ASNS	0.86	0.84	0.87	0.83

Comparing the difference between GSNS and ASNS, three situations can occur. (1) No difference between both measures. Overall, 50.3% of users are considered DAU, and 33.8% are not in both measures. (2) a minority of users indicate (3.3%) to be daily active when asked for generically while they do not indicate to be daily active on a specific SNS. The difference is positive. In both these situations, users apply an additive response model. (3) Further, we find that 12.6% is considered a daily user using ASNS, while they do not indicate themselves as such when GSNS applied. This indicates that they applied an averaging strategy when answering GSNS use. Hence while the majority do seem to apply an additive response model, several SNS-users do not apply an additive model but rather activate an averaging model when responding to SNS-frequency in general versus SNS-specifically and that SNS-frequency might underscore heavy SNS use as measured by DAU relative to SNS-specifically. On the other hand, the strong significant positive correlations between GSNS, with each specific SNS DAU as well as with the ASNS in Table 2, show that SNS-users reporting on SNS, in general, are consistent.

4.2 Individual Differences in SNS Usage

To contribute to understanding individual differences, logistic regressions were run on the proportion of those applying an average response model (12.6%) (ARM), as dependent (averaging = 1, not averaging = 0) as well as each DAU measure of Facebook (FB), Twitter (TWT), Instagram (INSTA), SNS generic (GSNS), and SNS additive (ASNS) as dependent (DAU = 1, Non-DAU = 0 per measure) and the available sociodemographic variables as determinants.

In Table 3, the results on ARM show that not all SNS-users use the same response model to a similar degree. Users that are in a working status ($b = -0.30$, $p < 0.05$), those having a higher degree ($b = -0.20$, $p < 0.05$) or those with higher income ($B = -0.36$, $p < 0.05$) average out less and use an additive method more. Age has a marginal positive significant effect with an older age averaging out more ($b = 0.01$, $p < 0.10$). This also results in other individual differences in GSNS compared to ASNS. Higher-income ($b = 0.19$, $p < 0.05$) and working users ($b = 0.17$, $p < 0.05$) show a significant positive effect on GSNS while this is not the case for ASNS. Further, it can be noticed that applying the general SNS approach levels out certain individual differences between SNS. TWT shows significantly more male DAU-users ($b = -0.48$, $p < 0.05$) while Instagram ($b = 0.43$, $p < 0.05$) and FB ($b = 0.45$, $p < 0.05$) show more female DAU-users. The negative effect of a graduate degree observed both for GSNS ($b = -0.19$, $p < 0.05$) and ASNS ($b = -0.36$, $p < 0.05$) only applies to FB ($b = -0.35$, $p < 0.05$). The effect of working is most observable for INSTA ($b = 0.25$, $p < 0.05$). The higher income effect only is applicable for TWT ($b = 0.24$, $p < 0.05$). The negative effect of age and the positive effect of being a student seem to be the only demographics effects being consistent across each DAU-measure. The effects of gender, age, and being a student for each measure is in line with previous findings. Also, the income effect for Twitter has been supported before, while the hypothesized relationship with working and graduate degree are not confirmed but are in line with the mixed results so far found.

Table 3. B-coefficients logistic regressions on DAU per specific/general SNS

	ARM	ASNS	GSNS	FB	TWT	INSTA
Female	0.08	**0.45***	**0.37***	**0.45***	**−0.48***	**0.43***
Age	*0.01***	**−0.02***	**−0.03***	**−0.02***	**−0.03***	**−0.07***
Single	−0.12	0.06	*0.11***	0.09	−0.12	0.10
Graduate degree	**−0.30***	**−0.36***	**−0.19***	**−0.35***	−0.09	−0.03
Working	**−0.20***	0.09	**0.17***	*0.11***	−0.02	**0.25***
Student	0.11	**0.71***	**0.45***	**0.48***	**0.69***	**0.87***
Higher income	**−0.36***	0.04	**0.19***	0.00	**0.24***	0.12
Constant	**−1.99***	**0.97***	**0.63***	**0.58***	−0.38	−0.06
χ^2	**55***	**345***	**344***	**258***	**187***	**853***
Nagelkerke R^2	**0.02**	**0.08**	**0.08**	**0.06**	**0.07**	**0.24**

*$p < 0.05$ **$p < 0.10$

5 Discussion, Implications, and Limitations

The landscape of SNS is continuously changing. Scholars in this field have primarily investigated Facebook, which is still the dominant SNS platform in terms of users. This remains by far the case in Belgium as well. Our results looking into the sociodemographic differences of different SNS confirms the view that Facebook should not be equated with SNS in general, and findings applicable to Facebook might not be generalized to other SNS. SNS not only have different specific features, but they also attract different types of users. Our findings seem to imply that deploying a generic usage measure like GSNS to overcome this specificity should be used with caution and gives different results in terms of incidence and profile of SNS usage compared to specific SNS. The difference seems to be the outcome of an averaging response model, which results in a lower incidence of SNS use when an overall generic SNS cue is applied. GSNS incidences are impacted by age, with older people averaging out more and higher sociographic profiles in terms of education, work, and salary, averaging out less compared to lower social status groups.

Future research can look at other related measures of SNS usage in which measures developed for specific sites like Facebook are adapted to a GSNS measure. All our usage measures are self-reported, so we cannot state whether a specific versus general approach is better in terms of reflecting actual usage and has better criterion validity. This can be assessed by future research by taking actual usage into account by tracking login and time spent on specific SNS electronically. Given the differences between each of the specific SNS and given the discrepancy between specific SNS use and GSNS use, it could be more beneficial to focus on specific SNS use and adopt a cross SNS approach. Nonetheless, the correlations between the GSNS measure and each of the specific SNS measures suggest that a generic measure is useful in reflecting SNS usage where a cross SNS approach cannot be applied, due to time or budget restrictions.

Marketers involved in developing digital strategies relying on SNS-usage should be cautious when they estimate the size and profile based on SNS in general. Indeed, to define reach and for targeting purposes, it is advisable to stick to measures per specific

SNS given the differences in profile it can generate. Also, market researchers devising survey-instruments to support such strategies should be aware that if they select participation based on GSNS use, it might lead to fewer respondents fitting this criterion. Researchers are advised to create survey questions that are specific as possible to the SNS of interest. Finally, especially consumer research into problematic SNS usage should be cautious, given they might underestimate SNS-usage and problematic usage like an addiction if they apply GSNS measures.

References

Alhabash, S., Ma, M.: A tale of four platforms: motivations and uses of Facebook, Twitter, Instagram, and Snapchat among college students? Soc. Media+ Soc. **3**(1), 2056305117691544 (2017)

Andreassen, C.S., Pallesen, S., Griffiths, M.D.: The relationship between addictive use of social media, narcissism, and self-esteem: findings from a large national survey. Addict. Behav. **64**, 287–293 (2017)

Archambault, A., Grudin, J.: A longitudinal study of Facebook, Linkedin, & Twitter use. In: Proceedings of the SIGCHI Conference on Human Factors in Computing Systems, pp. 2741–2750, May 2012

Barker, V.: Older adolescents' motivations for social network site use: the influence of gender, group identity, and collective self-esteem. Cyberpsychol. Behav. **12**(2), 209–213 (2009)

Blank, G., Lutz, C.: Representativeness of social media in great Britain: investigating Facebook, Linkedin, Twitter, Pinterest, Google+, and Instagram. Am. Behav. Sci. **61**(7), 741–756 (2017)

Bolotaeva, V., Cata, T.: Marketing opportunities with social networks. J. Internet Soc. Netw. Virtual Commun. **2010**, 1–8 (2010)

Boyd, D.M., Ellison, N.B.: Social network sites: definition, history, and scholarship. J. Comput.-Mediat. Commun. **13**(1), 210–230 (2007)

Davenport, S.W., Bergman, S.M., Bergman, J.Z., Fearrington, M.E.: Twitter versus Facebook: exploring the role of narcissism in the motives and usage of different social media platforms. Comput. Hum. Behav. **32**, 212–220 (2014)

Fraley, R.C., Waller, N.G., Brennan, K.A.: An item response theory analysis of self-report measures of adult attachment. J. Pers. Soc. Psychol. **78**(2), 350 (2000)

Gazit, T., Aharony, N., Amichai-Hamburger, Y.: Tell me who you are, and I will tell you which SNS you use: SNSs participation. Online Inf. Rev. (2019)

Griffiths, M.D.: Facebook addiction: concerns, criticism, and recommendations—a response to Andreassen and colleagues. Psychol. Rep. **110**(2), 518–520 (2012)

Griffiths, M.D., Kuss, D.J., Demetrovics, Z.: Social networking addiction: an overview of preliminary findings. In: Behavioral Addictions, pp. 119–141 (2014)

Haight, M., Quan-Haase, A., Corbett, B.A.: Revisiting the digital divide in Canada: the impact of demographic factors on access to the internet, level of online activity, and social networking site usage. Inf. Commun. Soc. **17**(4), 503–519 (2014)

Hargittai, E.: Whose space? Differences among users and non-users of social network sites. J. Comput.-Mediat. Commun. **13**(1), 276–297 (2007)

Huang, C.: Time spent on social network sites and psychological well-being: a meta-analysis. Cyberpsychol. Behav. Soc. Netw. **20**(6), 346–354 (2017)

Huang, C.: Social network site use and Big Five personality traits: a meta-analysis. Comput. Hum. Behav. **97**, 280–290 (2019)

Hughes, D.J., Rowe, M., Batey, M., Lee, A.: A tale of two sites: Twitter vs. Facebook and the personality predictors of social media usage. Comput. Hum. Behav. **28**(2), 561–569 (2012)

Kim, D.H., Seely, N.K., Jung, J.H.: Do you prefer, Pinterest or Instagram? The role of image-sharing SNSs and self-monitoring in enhancing ad effectiveness. Comput. Hum. Behav. **70**, 535–543 (2017)

Kircaburun, K., Alhabash, S., Tosuntaş, Ş.B., Griffiths, M.D.: Uses and gratifications of problematic social media use among university students: a simultaneous examination of the Big Five of personality traits, social media platforms, and social media use motives. Int. J. Mental Health Addict. 1–23 (2018)

Lee, S.L.: Predicting SNS addiction with the Big Five and the Dark Triad. Cyberpsychol.: J. Psychosoc. Res. Cyberspace **13**(1) (2019)

Liu, J.S., Ho, M.H.C., Lu, L.Y.: Recent themes in social networking service research. PLoS ONE **12**(1) (2017)

Marino, C., Gini, G., Vieno, A., Spada, M.M.: A comprehensive meta-analysis on problematic Facebook use. Comput. Hum. Behav. **83**, 262–277 (2018)

Mellon, J., Prosser, C.: Twitter and Facebook are not representative of the general population: political attitudes and demographics of British social media users. Res. Polit. **4**(3), 2053168017720008 (2017)

Oh, S., Syn, S.Y.: Motivations for sharing information and social support in social media: a comparative analysis of Facebook, Twitter, Delicious, YouTube, and Flickr. J. Assoc. Inf. Sci. Technol. **66**(10), 2045–2060 (2015)

Panek, E.T., Nardis, Y., Konrath, S.: Defining social networking sites and measuring their use: how narcissists differ in their use of Facebook and Twitter. Comput. Hum. Behav. **29**(5), 2004–2012 (2013)

Phua, J., Jin, S.V., Kim, J.J.: Uses and gratifications of social networking sites for bridging and bonding social capital: a comparison of Facebook, Twitter, Instagram, and Snapchat. Comput. Hum. Behav. **72**, 115–122 (2017)

Primack, B.A., Shensa, A., Escobar-Viera, C.G., Barrett, E.L., Sidani, J.E., Colditz, J.B., James, A.E.: Use of multiple social media platforms and symptoms of depression and anxiety: a nationally-representative study among US young adults. Comput. Hum. Behav. **69**, 1–9 (2017)

Rains, S.A., Brunner, S.R.: What can we learn about social network sites by studying Facebook? A call and recommendations for research on social network sites. New Media Soc. **17**(1), 114–131 (2015)

Sa'ed, H.Z., Sweileh, W.M., Awang, R., Al-Jabi, S.W.: Global trends in research related to social media in psychology: mapping and bibliometric analysis. Int. J. Mental Health Syst. **12**(1), 4 (2018)

Sigerson, L., Cheng, C.: Scales for measuring user engagement with social network sites: a systematic review of psychometric properties. Comput. Hum. Behav. **83**, 87–105 (2018)

Stoycheff, E., Liu, J., Wibowo, K.A., Nanni, D.P.: What have we learned about social media by studying Facebook? A decade in review. New Media Soc. **19**(6), 968–980 (2017)

Xu, C., Ryan, S., Prybutok, V., Wen, C.: It is not for fun: an examination of social network site usage. Inf. Manag. **49**(5), 210–217 (2012)

Yu, R.P., Ellison, N.B., McCammon, R.J., Langa, K.M.: Mapping the two levels of digital divide: internet access and social network site adoption among older adults in the USA. Inf. Commun. Soc. **19**(10), 1445–1464 (2016)

Surfing the Waves of New Marketing in Luxury Fashion: The Case of Online Multi-brand Retailers

Simone Guercini[1](✉), Matilde Milanesi[1], Pedro Mir-Bernal[2], and Andrea Runfola[3]

[1] Department of Economics and Management, University of Florence, Via delle Pandette 9, 50127 Florence, Italy
{simone.guercini,matilde.milanesi}@unifi.it

[2] ISEM, Fashion Business School, University of Navarre, Marquesado de Santa Marta 3, 28027 Madrid, Spain
pmir@unav.es

[3] Department of Economics, University of Perugia, Via Pascoli 20, 06123 Perugia, Italy
andrea.runfola@unipg.it

Abstract. The digital environment as a context and set of tools for marketers' actions is the subject of considerable and growing interest in literature. The phenomenon is significant in many industries, with specificity within particular sectors in which, as in luxury fashion, the development of the online market has been particularly significant over the years. This article explores the case of online multi-brand retailers in the luxury fashion and the new marketing that characterizes their business model. Online technologies are general purposes, but the fields of application and the use of tools can have different effects in particular contexts, where companies that form a specific type of player operate. The paper presents the case of an online multi-brand retailer operating in the luxury fashion sector, a strategic group consisting of a few dozen players globally. The case of one of these companies, based in Italy, is then examined as a success story and shows new marketing strategies and specific capabilities as key aspects of the business model.

Keywords: Digital marketing · Luxury fashion · Multi-brand retailers · Business model · E-commerce

1 Introduction

This article explores the case of online multi-brand retailers in the luxury fashion and the new marketing that characterizes their business model. Luxury fashion has undergone a profound change in recent decades (Chandon et al. 2016), especially considering the impact of the Internet. The online sphere was interpreted at the dawn of its development as inconsistent with the strategies of the companies operating in the luxury sector (Kapferer 2014). However, over the years the technological evolution and the changes in consumption patterns towards omnichannel logics (Verhoef et al. 2015),

F. J. Martínez-López and S. D'Alessandro (Eds.): *Advances in Digital Marketing and eCommerce*, SPBE, pp. 203–210, 2020.
https://doi.org/10.1007/978-3-030-47595-6_25

as well as the rising of new customers in emerging markets (Li et al. 2012), have led to the need to rethink the adoption of new marketing practices. Among the actors that have had a development, there is the online multi-brand retailer. In fact, previous literature has emphasized the birth and development of luxury fashion marketplaces that have acquired a major role within the luxury sector's key business stakeholders, such as global Griffes or fashion bloggers, and among consumers, due to their ability to develop digital skills as well as logistic and distribution processes on a global scale (Guecini and Runfola 2015).

Marketing literature seems to have understudied the digital marketing dimensions of multi-brand retailers. Thus, this article emphasizes the ability of online multi-brand retailer to offer a digital experience (Morgan-Thomas and Veloutsou 2013) by building a brand reputation (De Chernatony 1999) capable of maintaining a sustainable business model, in light of the evolution of online luxury that could represent a threat as well as an opportunity. In particular, the present article investigates the following research question: RQ1) What are the features of the digital reputation of online multi-brand retailers in luxury fashion? RQ2) How does marketing help in developing opportunities for these players?

The answer to these research questions lies in the ability of multi-brand retailers to build an online reputation for their brand that allows keeping strong links with both luxury fashion companies (multi-brand retailers' suppliers) and consumers. In particular, the paper discusses the digital marketing of luxury multi-brand retailers, considering two key concepts of their activity: the "surfing" and the "influence" capabilities. From a methodological point of view, the paper presents an emblematic case study (Eisenhardt 1989). The company under analysis is LVR (acronym of Luisa Via Roma), an Italian multi-brand luxury fashion retailer operating on a global scale. The company experienced significant development over time in the online world; starting from a physical boutique, it has become a leading company in the online luxury fashion.

Consequently, the article is structured as follows. The theoretical background is presented in the next paragraph. After a methodological section, the case is presented. Finally, the article discusses the theoretical and managerial implications of the study.

2 Digitalization and Luxury Fashion: Key Players in Retailing

In recent years, the rapid digitalization process has exerted a strong influence on various business activities and, at the same time, has put pressure on companies, sometimes forcing them to rethink their current and future strategies, to evaluate new opportunities deriving from the digital world and, not least, to change their business model (Rachinger et al. 2019). The movement into the digital age has a major impact on the luxury segment, which is facing tremendous changes and challenges that require new marketing strategies and entirely new business models (Heine and Berghaus 2014). Digitalization goes hand in hand with an evolution on the consumer side. On the one hand, luxury consumers are increasingly expressing a growing desire for authentic products with artisanship roots that are also sustainable (Kapferer and Michaut-Denizeau 2014). On the other hand, there is a shift from "owing" to "sharing and experiencing" (Atwal and Willaims 2017).

In this evolution, digital is having an even greater impact on how luxury consumers choose the brands and goods to buy. Luxury sales are "digitally influenced" in the sense that, in their luxury shopping journey, consumers hit several digital touchpoints, seek advice of peers on social media, look for suggestions from trusted bloggers and "influencers", before entering a store or buying online, and then they post about their purchase afterward (Dauriz et al. 2014; Liu et al. 2019). Luxury companies cannot ignore these developments on the consumer side.

In terms of the way in which luxury companies build their business model, to be understood as the value proposition (i.e., the offer and the target customer segment), the value creation and delivery system, and the value capture system (Richardson 2008), digital represents a critical source of growth that enables companies to reimagine key processes, both front-end, and back-of-house. Achille et al. (2018) discuss the "age of digital Darwinism" in which a "Luxury 4.0" model is emerging that allows capturing emerging customer preferences and enhancing customer relationships and experiences with luxury brands.

This appears particularly true for luxury fashion brands. The development of digitalization within the fashion business has been particularly relevant and has been accompanied by the emergence of new online business forms of marketing related to the growth of online markets and e-commerce businesses (Guercini et al. 2018). Thus, luxury fashion companies are experiencing major changes in their business models. The first key element is internationalization that is a constitutive element of the luxury fashion business model (Guercini and Milanesi 2017) and becomes evident in e-commerce, which may have different degrees of internationalization (Mir-Bernal et al. 2018; Guercini and Runfola 2015). Other key elements, especially for online retailers in luxury fashion, are the new digital technologies and the use of digital marketing tools to take customer knowledge, relationships, and experiences to another level.

In a report developed by Microsoft in 2018, it is discussed that a possible new business model for luxury fashion retail is the "luxury-as-a-service model". For example, rental companies in luxury fashion, like Rent the Runway and Girl Meets Dress, have developed a business model by providing digital platforms for consumers to rent high-end clothes and accessories for a period of time, giving consumers on a budget the opportunity to wear luxury fashion. Another example is Opulent Box that has adopted a subscription model and offers a collection of jewelry from top designers in a subscription box, sent quarterly to its members. Thus, consumers benefit from personalized service and explore new experiences, and brands reap the benefits of predictable revenue.

When it comes to digital marketing tools, social media are in the spotlight as they allow interaction with – and between – consumers and lead to the generation of big data that can be analyzed and used to create relevant information for the fashion industry (Acharya et al. 2018). On the one hand, social media are increasingly become essential part of the business model (Iankova et al. 2019) of luxury fashion companies that exploit them to build their brands, value proposition, and digital brand reputation, and to communicate with consumers and other relevant actors of the online markets, such as blogger and influencers (Jin 2012). In fact, fashion bloggers and influencers play a central role on social media and become strategic actors for luxury fashion companies, which try to identify the most influential ones who can bring their brand closer to consumers (SanMiguel and Sádaba 2018). On the other hand, the increased popularity of social media, such as Facebook and Instagram, has opened opportunities for new business models for e-commerce, referred to as social commerce, namely the possibility to buy directly on social platforms, with the help of social interaction and user contributions to assist online buying and selling of products and services (Liang and Turban 2011).

Moreover, considering the changes in consumer behavior as well as the importance of new sustainability issues, the luxury fashion retail is also providing platforms for second-hand products (D'Arpizio and Levato 2018). Hence, the universe of luxury fashion retail is extremely varied and dynamic and includes both multi-brand retailers, luxury companies competing with their online stores, and players of different types that are able to integrate and capture new trends (such as social commerce sites, luxury renting website or second-hand luxury platforms, as mentioned above). Altagamma-BCG (2019), however, highlights three main types of players that dominate the online luxury retailing, with roughly 85% of the total sales, namely multi-brand luxury fashion retailers, mono-brand stores of luxury companies and global online retailers not specialized in the fashion luxury.

3 Methodology

The paper presents the results of the case study (Eisenhardt 1989; Eisenhardt and Graebner 2007) of a multi-brand retailer in the fashion luxury. The case study is exploratory in nature and shows the development of the company focusing on the main features of the digital marketing implemented over the years. Data gathered for the case study refers to secondary materials collected by the authors such as company's reports, articles published on national and international specialized journals, video interviews by founders and managers of the company. Then, data have been supplemented by direct observation of the company. In fact, some of the authors of this paper had the occasion to directly contact the company, having informal meetings and company visits in the last years.

4 New Marketing of Online Multi-brand Retail: The LVR Case

Luisa Via Roma (LVR) and its online store (www.luisaviaroma.com) represents a successful case of the multi-brand online retailer in luxury fashion. Operating for decades as an offline fashion store, LVR opens its website in the '90s. In 2000, LVR started to sell many luxury fashion brands in its e-commerce that has grown rapidly in recent years, reaching about € 165 million of online sales in 2019. The evolution of the company's turnover from 2007 to 2019 is shown in Table 1. The company originated in 1929 in Florence, Italy, where it is still based today. The nephew of the founder is now the owner and the company's CEO. LVR has been for decades an offline fashion store, located in the prestigious via Roma (the flagship store is still there today), in the historic center of Florence. LVR is a case that does not reach the turnover of other realities of e-commerce (e.g., Yoox-Net-à-Porter), but it shows a particular position in the luxury segment. The case is interesting not only for its economic and financial results but also for the specific characteristics. It has been defined as "heaven for directional fashion" (Financial Times), a "champion of emerging and avant-garde designers" (The Independent), "the story that continues to surprise the entire market" (Corriere Economia).

Table 1. LVR's turnover evolution (2007/2019) (million €)

Year	Sales (mln €)	Online sales (%)	Extra EU sales (%)
2007	11.4	20%	10%
2013	87.9	82%	49%
2019	165.0	>90%	Not available

Source: company's annual reports (2019 anticipated on newspapers)

LuisaViaRoma.com (www.luisaviaroma.com) is the core of the company's business model; it's an important online luxury fashion virtual destination with about 9 million visitors per month (in 2019) and worldwide delivery. The site offers clothing, shoes, and accessories for men, women, and children, created by designers of prestigious and renowned fashion "Griffes" and emerging designers/creatives (around 600 in total). The online store has the ambition to offer young talents alongside some of the most famous and consolidated brands in the fashion industry. These collaborations consist essentially of designing special items offered exclusively for LVR. These collaborations help to build an LVR's image as an actor a step forward in the continuously evolving world of fashion, creating value for consumers.

Today, more than 230 people from many different countries are employed. In fact, the native language is needed to manage website pages and customer care in the eight different languages of LuisaViaRoma.com online store, and this helps to create a multicultural environment, as well as a creative one, due to the average age of employees. The online store is entirely created in-house through the graphic design team of the company and its own IT department. This element allows going much further in the customization of the website. Within the same logic of customization, it is possible to make purchases in different currencies. The shipping of products is also managed directly by the company. Many of the LVR competitors, especially the online stores of American department stores, recur to external suppliers for shipping services or for customer care, which implies a less direct relationship with the final customer. LVR manages customer services directly, with the intent to give highly customized service to its customers.

Consistent with these choices, the online store has a special and creative approach that is specific to each country. In this sense, it represents not only a reality capable of creating a customized offer, but it is also a multicultural organization, which is able to keep in touch with different cultural contexts, thanks to the people from different countries who work there. Thus, in addition to IT, other key features of the company's business model are related to the logistics and customer service, as well as to the marketing and the buying team. The three teams (IT, Marketing, and Buying) work closely. A well-defined organizational choice in the company is to work in a single open space, with the intent to produce integration and interaction conditions that are not always possible at other companies.

LVR online store could count on 4.5 million visitors (unique visitors) in 2008, up to 8 times more in 2013 when they became 36 million, and 70 million in 2019 (unique visitors). There is also an intense use of social media. Social key performance indicators include followers (end 2019) on Instagram (866k), Facebook (1,9 million), Twitter (125k), Weibo (480k). The company, in addition to the online store (90% of the total turnover) and the flagship store in Via Roma, can count on a third store, in the city of Florence, where they sell products with a discount outlet logic (along with the flagship store, the remaining 10% of the turnover). The flagship store in via Roma, Florence, which also generates revenues, presents itself primarily as a platform for the marketing activities of the company, including some of the events that are an important component for the process of establishing a brand reputation in the digital environment. In the near future, the LVR sign will be used by a physical store opened by commercial promoters in Riyadh, Saudi Arabia.

The new marketing of an actor like LVR projects itself on a global perspective but feeds on resources linked to its history and roots. Cultural heritage is proposed as a fundamental lever for the brand reputation, in a mix that includes links to some of the most influential fashion icons worldwide. To access this heritage, the interaction with local institutional actors is very important. LVR also synthesizes these assets through the creation of unique events that have proved successful over time. In this context, it was developed the event Firenze4Ever, which has been the first party for global fashion bloggers and influencers ever organized by online fashion retailers. For some years (from 2010 to 2017), Firenze4Ever has been widely recognized as a permanent event in the fashion calendar, the starting point of each new fashion season, just prior to the Florence's Pitti Immagine (an important fashion exhibition) and the international fashion weeks. Firenze4Ever proposed not only a mix of fashion and technology but also connected these with music and visual arts. The event raised a lot of visual materials (photos, video) that were posted on social media, thanks to fashion bloggers and influencers. Begun in June 2010 to celebrate the 10th anniversary of the LVR online store, together with the eighty years from the foundation of the company, Firenze4Ever has put together trendsetters and influential people in fashion and online technologies for 14 editions. In particular, the event promoted and encouraged interaction between brands and bloggers, providing both the opportunity for creativity and learning in a face-to-face meeting.

However, the approach to events is never static and celebratory, and it evolves with the company and the new technologies in a logic of continuous dynamism. For this reason, when bloggers and fashion influencers of fashion and luxury ceased to be a novelty and establish themselves as one of the recognized players, LVR ceased the series of events and started looking for new initiatives and new themes. From

Firenze4Ever to LuisaViaRoma 90th Anniversary, defined in the company reports as "the first multi-brand show ever done", with 10,9 million media impact value, 5,7 from Instagram; Unicef Summer Gala 2019, a charity event in Porto Cervo; a partnership with Extreme E, the new off-road car race with electric SUVs for sustainability.

5 Conclusions

The paper has shown the case of an online multi-brand luxury fashion retailer and the new marketing that characterizes its business model. The new marketing, in the case study discussed, is oriented to establishing and preserving the brand image and digital reputation in the digital context where the e-commerce business is based, through the use of new strategies, new technologies, and digital marketing tools for approaching the global market. The case shows that the company is placed in a "surfer" position compared to new marketing trends. A key aspect of the business model is the integration of the online and offline worlds that allows building the brand reputation. In event communication, the management of the company emphasizes that LVR believes that customers seek experiences, not only products. Events are created to develop communication through word of mouth and to enhance brand reputation, often in partnership with other companies involved in the process, applying new experimental marketing techniques. Two key aspects emerge. First, the "surfing" capability, which implies the ability to stay on the technological frontier as well as the capacity of capturing new trends within the market at the dawn of their development (such as the role of fashion blogs in the last decade and more recently the topic of sustainability). Second, their influence capability, namely the actor's capability to influence luxury market trends, in particular through the definition of innovative, fashionable, and attractive assortments of luxury. From a managerial standpoint, this paper emphasizes the need to consider a complementarity between offline and online initiatives for building an online brand reputation. This seems to suggest the importance of considering the interplay between online and offline for branding strategies even for pure online players.

References

Acharya, A., Singh, S.K., Pereira, V., Singh, P.: Big data, knowledge co-creation and decision making in fashion industry. Int. J. Inf. Manag. **42**, 90–101 (2018)

Achille, A., Marchessou, S., Remy, N.: Luxury in the Age of Digital Darwinism. McKinsey (2018)

B.C.G. Altagamma: The true-luxury global consumer insight (2019). www.altagamma.it

Atwal, G., Williams, A.: Luxury brand marketing–the experience is everything! In: Advances in Luxury Brand Management, pp. 43–57. Palgrave Macmillan, Cham (2017)

Chandon, J.L., Laurent, G., Valette-Florence, P.: Pursuing the concept of luxury: introduction to the JBR special issue on "luxury marketing from tradition to innovation". J. Bus. Res. **69**(1), 299–303 (2016)

D'Arpizio, C., Levato, F.: Altagamma 2018. Market Monitor Worldwide Luxury. Bain & Company (2018)

Dauriz, L., Remy, N., Sandri, N.: Luxury shopping in the digital age. Perspectives on retail and Consumers Goods. McKinsey (2014)
De Chernatony, L.: Brand management through narrowing the gap between brand identity and brand reputation. J. Mark. Manag. **15**(1–3), 157–179 (1999)
Eisenhardt, K.M.: Building theories from case study research. Acad. Manag. Rev. **14**(4), 532–550 (1989)
Eisenhardt, K.M., Graebner, M.E.: Theory building from cases: opportunities and challenges. Acad. Manag. J. **50**(1), 25–32 (2007)
Guercini, S., Milanesi, M.: Extreme luxury fashion: business model and internationalization process. Int. Mark. Rev. **34**(3), 403–424 (2017)
Guercini, S., Runfola, A.: Internationalization through e-commerce. The case of multi-brand luxury retailers in the fashion industry. Adv. Int. Mark. **26**, 15–31 (2015)
Guercini, S., Mir-Bernal, P., Prentice, C.: New marketing in fashion e-commerce. J. Glob. Fashion Mark. **9**(1), 1–8 (2018)
Heine, K., Berghaus, B.: Luxury goes digital: how to tackle the digital luxury brand–consumer touchpoints. J. Glob. Fashion Mark. **5**(3), 223–234 (2014)
Iankova, S., Davies, I., Archer-Brown, C., Marder, B., Yau, A.: A comparison of social media marketing between B2B, B2C and mixed business models. Ind. Mark. Manag. **81**, 169–179 (2019)
Jin, S.A.A.: The potential of social media for luxury brand management. Mark. Intell. Plan. **30**(7), 687–699 (2012)
Kapferer, J.N.: The future of luxury: challenges and opportunities. J. Brand Manag. **21**(9), 716–726 (2014)
Kapferer, J.N., Michaut-Denizeau, A.: Is luxury compatible with sustainability? Luxury consumers' viewpoint. J. Brand Manag. **21**(1), 1–22 (2014)
Li, G., Li, G., Kambele, Z.: Luxury fashion brand consumers in China: perceived value, fashion lifestyle, and willingness to pay. J. Bus. Res. **65**(10), 1516–1522 (2012)
Liang, T.P., Turban, E.: Introduction to the special issue social commerce: a research framework for social commerce. Int. J. Electron. Commer. **16**(2), 5–14 (2011)
Liu, S., Perry, P., Gadzinski, G.: The implications of digital marketing on WeChat for luxury fashion brands in China. J. Brand Manag. **26**(4), 395–409 (2019)
Microsoft: The digital opportunity for luxury retail (2018)
Mir-Bernal, P., Guercini, S., Sádaba, T.: The role of e-commerce in the internationalization of Spanish luxury fashion multi-brand retailers. J. Glob. Fashion Mark. **9**(1), 59–72 (2018)
Morgan-Thomas, A., Veloutsou, C.: Beyond technology acceptance: brand relationships and online brand experience. J. Bus. Res. **66**(1), 21–27 (2013)
Rachinger, M., Rauter, R., Müller, C., Vorraber, W., Schirgi, E.: Digitalization and its influence on business model innovation. J. Manuf. Technol. Manag. **30**(8), 1143–1160 (2019)
Richardson, J.: The business model: an integrative framework for strategy execution. Strategic Change **17**(5–6), 133–144 (2008)
SanMiguel, P., Sádaba, T.: Nice to be a fashion blogger, hard to be influential: an analysis based on personal characteristics, knowledge criteria, and social factors. J. Glob. Fashion Mark. **9**(1), 40–58 (2018)
Verhoef, P.C., Kannan, P.K., Inman, J.J.: From multi-channel retailing to omni-channel retailing: introduction to the special issue on multi-channel retailing. J. Retail. **91**(2), 174–181 (2015)

Sales Model Based on the Behavior on Facebook

Mabela Atanasovska Penić and Smilka Janeska Sarkanjac(✉)

Faculty of Computer Science and Engineering, Ss Cyril and Methodius University in Skopje, Skopje, Republic of Macedonia
mabela@grow-up.me,
smilka.janeska.sarkanjac@finki.ukim.mk

Abstract. This study investigated the steps for the successful implementation of Facebook marketing by enterprises, and offers a sales model segmenting the users by their behavior on Facebook. The model uses the marketing communication model developed by Hoffman and Novak (1996), and its further development by Yang (2012) that tested the impact of the transferring messages through media on the message receiver's decision-making behavior.

The model emerged from discussions led and Facebook campaigns conducted for the focus group of 150 small business entrepreneurs in the last two years. The finding shows that the model can indeed be applied in strategic use of social media for marketing purposes.

The proposed model serves as a guideline for small business entrepreneurs on how to strategically use social media for marketing, on ways to enhance customer acquisition, loyalty and retention. In addition, the study found that using social media is the most cost-effective way for marketing and is thus suitable for small business.

Keywords: Digital marketing · Facebook advertising · Online sales · Facebook audiences · Behavioral marketing

1 Introduction

Facebook continues to play an increasingly important role in the marketing endeavors, especially in the small and medium business companies. Unlike traditional channels of corporate communication, Facebook allows for uncensored, unpredictable, two-way conversations. Currently, lots of enterprises widely use social network site for marketing campaigns. Due to its increasing popularity and rising number of its users, the phenomenon of Facebook has aroused academic interest as well.

This study investigated the approach of a company in the Facebook communications with its clients, and offers a sales model based on Facebook. The model uses the marketing communication model developed by Hoffman and Novak (1996), and its further development by Yang (2012) that tested the impact of the transferring messages through media on the message receiver's decision-making behavior. The communication approach is based on the Attention, Interest, Desire, and Action (AIDA) model, developed by Lewis in 1898 (Hassan et al. 2015).

F. J. Martínez-López and S. D'Alessandro (Eds.): *Advances in Digital Marketing and eCommerce*, SPBE, pp. 211–218, 2020.
https://doi.org/10.1007/978-3-030-47595-6_26

Hoffman and Novak in 1996 propose a new communication model, fundamentally different from the model in the era of mass media, a process model of network navigation in a hypermedia computer-mediated environment, which sure is Facebook today. They examine the flow, consumer heterogeneity, consumer behavior and the consequences.

Yang (2012) develops this model, by researching the determinant factors for the successful implementation of Facebook marketing by enterprises. The findings are that advertising messages provided by close friends only affect consumer brand attitudes, but advertising messages provided by commercial sources affect both consumer brand attitudes and purchasing intentions. Utilitarian and recreational advertising messages affect consumer advertising attitude, brand attitudes, purchasing intentions and involvement. Lastly, consumer involvement partially mediates the effects of utilitarian advertising and recreational advertising on advertising attitude, brand attitudes and purchasing intentions.

In recent years, scholars have been researching the relationship between marketing communication efforts and consumer behavior, i.e. popularity of a Facebook post as a function of the post's type (videos, images, questions, or links); characteristics, content; placement on the site (Hodge et al. 2015; de Vries et al. 2012; Sabate et al. 2014). There are papers on optimization of Facebook use as a marketing channel (Hansson et al. 2013), on analysis of existing Facebook marketing practices and tools, their benefits, and concerns associated with this type of social media marketing (Ramsaran-Fowdar and Fowdar 2013), on uses of Facebook in the different industries: library services (Xia 2009), hotel industry (Leung et al. 2015), food and beverage (Freeman et al. 2014), and many others, but there is a shortage of models that examine the whole process of segmenting, targeting and communicating with the company's Facebook page audience, in order to sell the product or the service of the company. This paper tries to fill this gap.

The sales model presented in this paper is also based on discussions led, survey and Facebook campaigns conducted for the focus group of 150 small business entrepreneurs in the last two years. The respondents were small companies from Macedonia, Serbia, Croatia, Montenegro and Slovenia. In a series of specific questions and comments, the respondents were asked to follow the seven-step sales model, rate the actions taken in each step, and analyze the Facebook metrics following each step. The results gave companies a clear idea of how to effectively use Facebook in their marketing efforts.

The finding shows that the model can indeed be applied in strategic use of social media for marketing purposes. The proposed model serves as a guideline for small business entrepreneurs on how to strategically use social media for marketing.

2 Facebook Audiences - Whom, When and What to Show?

First step in design of a marketing strategy, both for offline and online approach is segmenting the market. Facebook offers powerful segmenting tools, because of its precise and detailed data on its users – their characteristics, behavior, interests, their social network.

We are going to examine and explain 5 types of audiences that can be created and approached in different ways on Facebook.

- Visitors to the Facebook page (Page visits) - These are the people who at some point came to a Facebook page, no matter what the reason for their visit was, and whether or not they had an interaction. This audience shows interest in the topic or problem the Facebook page is talking about, but isn't quite sure about what it is selling. Therefore, it is important that they see fun, useful and interesting content constantly (our experience with the focus group suggests this should be done at least 3 times a day). For this audience it is ideal to promote the content through the Boost option. It is likely that these individuals, as well as their friends, have not yet clicked "Like" on the page. By boosting posts as well as "Promote my page option", they can be invited to follow the page and click the "Like" button.
- Those who responded to a post or an ad (Post Engagement) - This category includes all those who have responded to a post or ad, no matter whether they have clicked "Like", "Share", "Comment" or clicked on a link, i.e. engaged in a sense of Javornik and Mandelli (2012) state. It is again likely that these people and their friends, have not yet clicked "Like" on the Page. They can be invited to do so via the "Promote my page option". Also, there is a better, more direct, and cheaper option: the "Invite" option for each post. It is recommended to boost the posts to this audience with the "Get More Engagement" option.
- Pixel Audience - The Facebook pixel installed on a web or landing page says a lot about the interests and needs of the audience. The marketing strategy is created depending on the previous steps of the potential buyers. Facebook pixel tracks the audience previous activities (and demographics) and this information is used to offer similar content or personalized offer (like in Booking.com case, where they track their customers' activities and then in another ad show the room or hotel they have chosen previously).
- People who have already bought something (Email list or database) - a list of customers or potential buyers, whether it's a mailing list or a phone number list, can be uploaded to Facebook and show them an ad. The same goes for the "Linked In" contacts. They can be exported and added to Facebook and thus, show them an ad without bothering them with messages. If a new Facebook page is opened and the company has a customer list from before, it can invite them to follow the Facebook page. If it's a list of existing buyers, a promotion or special offer can be communicated. If the company has lists of products or service categories that people have already purchased, then it can show them more information, offer them free tips and get them interested in what they have already bought, or a new, similar, product or service.

3 Seven Phases of Sales on Facebook

In the digital world, marketing communications stress three important steps which are creating awareness of a product or service, building relationships, and creating mutual value with customers (Rowley 2002).

After we have examined five types of Facebook audience, we will propose a seven-phase sales model. How do the company move its potential customers in the buyer decision process on Facebook, i.e. from liking to buying? (Pöyry et al. 2013).

The seven phases we propose in this model are following:

Phase 1: Facebook campaign, towards a previously segmented audience;
Phase 2: Quality content keeps the audience that comes through ads;
Phase 3: Precise audience segmentation into three categories;
Phase 4: Audience qualification based on their behavior in the campaign and communication focus;
Phase 5: Creating interest by showing the value and the positive effects;
Phase 6: Selling to a qualified buyer;
Phase 7: Sharing of the content easily and with a proper reward.

Phase 1. Facebook campaign

The process of Internet sales starts with an ad, targeting a segment of the audience and getting their attention. Often, reduced sales are very likely a result of an insufficient traffic. Facebook offers quick, and relatively cheap way to provide more traffic to the company's web site. In the Balkans, the Facebook price in 2020 is 700–1000 views per euro, depending on the target audience and the content.

After segmenting the market, the target groups may consist of 15,000–20,000 people, that means that for 15–20 euros all the segments can be tested, with the graphics and tone of communication to each segment individually (Hodge et al. 2015), and found out which one is the best message for each audience for the product or service.

Phase 2. Creating a relationship with the customer community

Facebook page of the company has become a part of the "social proof". Our experience with companies (from the focus group) and their customers, shows that customers, even if they truly want or need the product or service, over 85% of them will click on the Facebook page to check who the seller is. If the Facebook page is empty, or there are only a few ads and a few hundred followers, the likelihood of buying is much smaller than if they have come across a page full of fans and action, useful content, comments, and interaction.

Phase 3. Market segmentation

Audience segmentation in this model consists of three large segments: well-known audience, look alike audience based on the well-known one and unknown audience.

- Well-known audience is a list of existing or potential customers, with their email addresses or phone numbers. A Facebook ad will be served to them first.
- Lookalike audience from the well-known – this expanded audience is based on the first segment and the audience registered by Facebook pixel. Facebook can find up to 10% of the total number of Facebook users in a particular country, but we don't recommend looking for more than 3%. These users are recognized by Facebook that have behavior, habits, or interests most similar to the company's base or those who have shown interest for the particular offer, that leads to a better reach, and thus a better chance of conversion.

- The unknown - These are the so-called general campaigns, which produce the worst results compared to the previous two. There are two reasons for these bad results – insufficient budget to reach large number of unknown people, and a direct sale message for people that are contacted for the first time.

Phase 4. Qualifications
Behavioral targeting to push promotional offers to members of a social network is the way to qualify best potential clients (Phelps et al. 2004). The selection and redemption of promotional offers can increase by providing members of a social network with relevant and high value offers. In addition, marketing campaigns can increase their effectiveness with knowledge and identification of members having a high degree of influence on other members. As Yang (2012) states, advertising messages provided by commercial sources affect both consumer brand attitudes and purchasing intentions.

After figuring out which segment of the market would first respond to the ads, and showed them an ad, now it is time to offer a useful and interesting content, in order to present the company or the product in the right way (Kizilcec et al. 2018). In Yang's (2012) findings, utilitarian and recreational advertising messages affect consumer advertising attitude, brand attitudes, purchasing intentions and involvement.

The best example of presentation, for now, is an e-book. That means a free PDF guide on "How to…". Offering advice on how to do something or solve a problem, for an audience that may benefit from that advice, will not only attract attention but also position the company as a field expert in the eyes of the Facebook users.

Additionally, by using an automated e-mail marketing series, it can be tracked who of the potential customers downloaded the e-book, really "consumes" the shared content.

This way, the prospective clients will self-qualify themselves. Those who open the e-mail, click on some of the links offered, review the content or fill out the surveys, are likely to be potential customers who are worthy of spending additional resources, in order to be moved one step further in the sales process.

Talking about qualifications, the data from Facebook campaign analytics can be used. Some of those who saw the Facebook ad clicked on it, were redirected to an external landing/web page. Part of them left their data so they can download free content, but most of them didn't.

After leaving their data, the automated marketing e-mail series was sent. Some of the potential buyers open the e-mail, but some of them don't.

Some of those who have opened the e-mail have clicked on the link that leads to the offer and landed to the sales page.

It is recommended that the sales page contains a call for action. Some potential customers will click to see the offer, but most of them will not. In the end, some people will complete the purchase, and some will not.

Usually, the majority will not take action or click. Therefore, it is important to track each of these conversions so the audience can be qualified and "qualified buyers" are found: people or businesses that need, want, know how to use it, can afford and are willing to pay for the product or service the company sells.

Our experience with the focus group says that a maximum of 2–3% of the audience will click on the ad and make an action. That means, if a post is viewed by 1000 people, 20 of them will respond. If the advertising budget is bigger and the ad is viewed by 10,000 people, that means that about 200 Facebook users will make an action.

Phase 5. Creating an interest in buying

In the first four steps we have attracted the potential customers, some of whom we have established a communication with and gained their trust, some of them consider us experts in the field, and some of them are there solely to view and consume a free content. If the company treats everyone the same throughout the campaign, it will probably annoy most of the followers. For this reason, in the fifth phase, the focus is only on those potential customers who have taken the steps to reach this stage.

This is an example of one of the companies in the focus group. Of the 1,200 prospective customers who have registered on the landing page, only half of them opened the sent e-mail (600). Only half of them clicked on the link where the offer was presented (300). At this point, it's enough to just focus on these 25% and keep communicating further with them only.

Usually, the other 75% are redirected to the previous step, on a web, blog or landing page, where every 15 days, useful information is displayed. Although they are probably qualified buyers, they must not be attacked with sales offers. Getting them to the next stage, in which they believe the buying decision is their idea, takes 3 more steps:

- An evidence that the solution works - in the first part of the campaign the focus is on the problem. In this part of the campaign it has to be demonstrated that the solution works and it can have a positive effect on one's work, career or life.
- Proof that the company is worth the client's money - This part is especially important if the offering is a service on the market. Clients will primarily attach themselves to *the company* and *its story*, and then to the service offered.
- A story about the transformation - This is a kind of conclusion to the whole story. The company has to show the problem and its negative effects, and *what* is the cause of the problem. A story has to be told, and how the company came up with a solution, before presenting the product or service and the positive effects of using it.

Phase 6. Sales

If the previous steps are well presented, the potential customer has a clear picture: problem - solution - the positive effect of the solution. It means that they identify with the story of transformation. They believe that they can do what is expected of them to get the results they want.

If so, then this is a qualified buyer: someone who would like, need, know how to use it, can and want to pay for the solution.

Phase 7. Recommendations

In traditional sales, a good recommendation costs 10 times less than a new potential customer. For every euro the company spends for selling to a prospective client that is recommended, it must spend 10 euros to find a new client from scratch. On Facebook, these figures are on a similar scale, although advertising prices are much lower than those in traditional sales.

The social aspect of the Facebook is one of the most powerful tools in the sales process (Parsons 2002). The actions of the users are visible for their friends. If the company attracts fans, makes them engage with its content, their likes, comments and shares will generate additional engagement from their friends, free of charge, because people trust their friends more than advertisers (Pöyry et al. 2013). In Yang (2012), consumer involvement partially mediates the effects of utilitarian advertising and recreational advertising on advertising attitude, brand attitudes and purchasing intentions.

4 Conclusion

Small businesses face a number of challenges, and one of the biggest is how to attract customers through marketing endeavors. One of the potential solutions to these challenges is the use of social media. Social media allows small businesses to conduct marketing activities effectively, despite limited financial resources, lack of expertise, and competition with large business organizations (Hassan et al. 2015).

Despite its limitations, the seven-phase sales model proposed in this paper offers valuable theoretical and managerial insights. Firstly, it serves as a guideline for small business entrepreneurs on how to strategically use social media for marketing, on ways to enhance customer acquisition, loyalty and retention. Secondly, it successfully examines the need of segmenting, targeting and conveying appropriate message to different segments of audience, and qualifying the audience according to their behavior on Facebook. Furthermore, it proposes problem - solution - the positive effect of the solution approach of the company's communication.

In addition, the study found that using social media is the most cost-effective way for marketing and is thus suitable for small business.

References

de Vries, L., Gensler, S., Leeflang, P.S.: Popularity of brand posts on brand fan pages: an investigation of the effects of social media marketing. J. Interact. Mark. **26**(2), 83–91 (2012). https://doi.org/10.1016/j.intmar.2012.01.003

Freeman, B., Kelly, B., Baur, L., Chapman, K., Chapman, S., Gill, T., King, L.: Digital junk: food and beverage marketing on Facebook. Am. J. Publ. Health **104**(12), e56–e64 (2014)

Hassan, S., Nadzim, S.Z.A., Shiratuddin, N.: Strategic use of social media for small business based on the AIDA model. Proc.-Soc. Behav. Sci. **172**, 262–269 (2015)

Hansson, L., Wrangmo, A., Søilen, K.S.: Optimal ways for companies to use Facebook as a marketing channel. J. Inf. Commun. Ethics Soc. **11**(2), 112–126 (2013)

Hodge, C., Pederson, J.A., Walker, M.: How do you "Like" my style? Examining how communication style influences Facebook behaviors. Int. J. Sport Commun. **8**(3), 276–292 (2015)

Hoffman, D.L., Novak, T.P.: Marketing in hypermedia computer-mediated environments: conceptual foundations. J. Market. **60**(3), 50–68 (1996)

Javornik, A., Mandelli, A.: Behavioral perspectives of customer engagement: an exploratory study of customer engagement with three Swiss FMCG brands. J. Database Market. Cust. Strateg. Manage. **19**(4), 300–310 (2012)

Kizilcec, R.F., Bakshy, E., Eckles, D., Burke, M.: Social influence and reciprocity in online gift giving. In: Proceedings of the 2018 CHI Conference on Human Factors in Computing Systems, p. 126. ACM (2018)

Leung, X.Y., Bai, B., Stahura, K.A.: The marketing effectiveness of social media in the hotel industry: a comparison of Facebook and Twitter. J. Hospitality Tourism Res. **39**(2), 147–169 (2015)

Parsons, A.G.: Non-functional motives for online shoppers: why we click. J. Consum. Market. **19**(5), 380–392 (2002)

Phelps, J.E., Lewis, R., Mobilio, L., Perry, D., Raman, N.: Viral marketing or electronic word-of-mouth advertising: examining consumer responses and motivations to pass along email. J. Advertising Res. **44**(4), 333–348 (2004)

Pöyry, E., Parvinen, P., Malmivaara, T.: Can we get from liking to buying? Behavioral differences in hedonic and utilitarian Facebook usage. Electron. Commer. Res. Appl. **12**(4), 224–235 (2013)

Ramsaran-Fowdar, R.R., Fowdar, S.: The implications of Facebook marketing for organizations. Contemp. Manage. Res. **9**(1), 73–84 (2013)

Rowley, J.: Information marketing in a digital world. Libr. Hi Tech **20**(3), 352–358 (2002)

Sabate, F., Berbegal-Mirabent, J., Cañabate, A., Lebherz, P.R.: Factors influencing popularity of branded content in Facebook fan pages. Eur. Manage. J. **32**, 1001–1011 (2014). https://doi.org/10.1016/j.emj.2014.05.001

Xia, Z.D.: Marketing library services through Facebook groups. Libr. Manage. **30**(6/7), 469–478 (2009)

Yang, T.: The decision behavior of Facebook users. J. Comput. Inf. Syst. **52**(3), 50–59 (2012)

Author Index

F. J. Martínez-López and S. D'Alessandro (Eds.): *Advances in Digital Marketing and eCommerce*, SPBE, pp. 219–220, 2020.
https://doi.org/10.1007/978-3-030-47595-6

The manufacturer's authorised representative in the EU is Springer Nature Customer Service Centre GmbH, Europaplatz 3, 69115 Heidelberg, Germany. If you have any concerns regarding our products, please contact ProductSafety@springernature.com

Printed and bound by CPI Group (UK) Ltd, Croydon, CR0 4YY
30/09/2026
02225509-0005